simply
ancient grains

simply
ancient grains

FRESH AND FLAVORFUL WHOLE GRAIN RECIPES FOR LIVING WELL

Maria Speck

photography by Erin Kunkel

TEN SPEED PRESS
Berkeley

acknowledgments

Not too long ago, I was convinced that writing my first cookbook, *Ancient Grains for Modern Meals,* was the hardest thing I ever did. After all, I'm not a trained food professional but a news reporter and journalist with a one-dimensional and lifelong love for ancient grains. Little did I know that my second cookbook would be even more challenging. I assumed that knowing the whole arduous process of writing a cookbook would somehow free me from all the angst and trepidation I experienced the first time around. Instead, I found myself wanting to drop the proverbial pencil and call it quits just as often.

A little drama, of course, is in my Greek nature. My perfectionist German side doesn't help much either. Yet miraculously, after much struggle, they did unite to finish the job—but not without the help of an army of people.

Most important, I'm honored and thrilled beyond words that the terrific team at Ten Speed Press, headed by Aaron Wehner, took on my second cookbook as well. In today's cutthroat environment for hard copy books, it is beyond amazing how Ten Speed remains committed in its strong support for authors, guiding them with a gentle hand. And supported I felt, from the moment we started talking about this project to the very last edits.

I'm immensely thankful that my editor, Jenny Wapner, gave me the freedom to shape this book, and then skillfully contained my enthusiastic headnotes, untangled some of my writing, and patiently corrected my non-native's spelling mistakes. The designer, Ashley Lima, had me spellbound from the first drafts. I'm grateful to photographer Erin Kunkel and food stylists Valerie Aikman-Smith and George Dolese for their stunning presentation of my favorite food group. My gratitude extends to the copyeditor, Mikayla Butchart, and the proofreader, Jennifer McClain, for their diligence and dedication.

More than anything, I'm indebted to my whip-smart agent, Jenni Ferrari-Adler, who rescues her authors James Bond–style, from the driver's seat of her red Cabriolet—at least in my mind. Jenni is one of these people who somehow know when you are cracking and suddenly calls, seemingly out of the blue. And calls again, and again if needed, just to keep you going. Jenni understands my mad fastidiousness and has not let me down. Thank you!

This book could not have been written without the enthusiastic support of my number one recipe tester, Karen Levendusky, whose dedication is a cookbook author's dream. When she agreed to help again with this project, just like with the first one, I almost started dancing on my desk. Karen has cooked all the recipes at least once, sometimes more, including the many gluten-free options, and with lightning speed. She went out of her way to track down grains, she created tables, found spelling mistakes and other bloopers, and always kept on top of things. In the race to the end, she even came to my house to help with a task that seemed insurmountable. Her boundless energy and passion for grains and her kindness in all communications make her a role model. I'm also indebted to her husband, Joe, who seems to love grains as much as I do, and who never minds eating dessert.

I will be forever thankful to the vibrant Boston food community who helped in so many ways I can not describe. My gratitude goes to Ana Sortun of Oleana and Sofra Bakery, to Jason Bond of Bondir restaurant and Bondir Concord, and to Matthew Gaudet of West Bridge for serving grains on their menu the way I envision them. For their inspiration, I look to Chuck Draghi of Erbaluce for his exquisite style of cooking, purist and sensual all at once, as well as to Tony Maws of Craigie on Main and Kirkland Tap and Trotter and to Steve Johnson of the former Rendezvous. For support, I thank my amazing colleague Kathy Gunst of WBUR, and JJ Gonson, the most dedicated locavore I have ever met, Maggie Battista of the gorgeous Eat Boutique site, and the Chefs Collaborative who gave me the opportunity to introduce my passion to chefs.

Help came also from the endlessly curious folks at America's Test Kitchen, from Lori Galvin to Andrew Janjigian, who answered and even investigated science questions I had. And my friend Tzurit Or of *Tatte Bakery* fame, whose fast-growing and stylish venues have introduced some of the finest pastries to the United States. Tzurit sustained me on rare breaks with her amazing treats, and her undeterred drive and boundless energy are a constant inspiration.

I'm grateful to the enthusiastic team at *Fine Cooking* who first published my recipe for shortcut polenta and gave it the perfect name. And I cannot name all the countless colleagues and fellow authors from around the world who answered questions on cookie counts, slow cookers, dried fruits, and more. Among them are the bakers, par excellence, Peter Reinhart and Sam Fromartz, and fellow perfectionist Zoe Francois.

I owe a lot to blogging pioneer Heidi Swanson who kindly shared a recipe from my first book with her online community, to brilliant Sara Kate Gillingham, founder of Apartment Therapy's *The Kitchn* for inviting me to introduce ancient grains to readers, and to dynamo blogger Shauna Ahern of *gluten-free-girl* who changed the dialogue on celiac disease and who loves gluten-free whole grains. I will be forever thankful to Tim Mazurek of gorgeous *Lottie + Doof* who cooked millet when no one else thought it could taste good and to fellow Greek food lover Peter Minakis of the vibrant blog *Kalofagas*. Heartfelt thanks to Cheryl Sternman Rule, Domenica Marchetti, and Anne Bramley for their encouragement, last-minute help, and their friendship.

I will be forever grateful to the kind Anne Willan of the La Varenne cooking school, who provided most thoughtful advice and guidance when I was in dire need. When I despair in my quest for information, I look to food historian Rachel Laudan who always invites a dialogue on food and grains. Her book *Cuisine and Empire: Cooking in World History* is a must-read for grain lovers and anyone keen on better understanding our shared culinary history. And Deborah Madison who wrote lines that made me blush before we ever met. A very special thank-you goes to Suvir Saran, chef extraordinaire, who believed in my work from the moment he saw my first book, and whose unbridled enthusiasm for cooking brings joy to every visitor to his beautiful farm in upstate New York. And to Aglaia Kremezi and Harold McGee, who patiently answered questions that might seem trivial. Crucial research help came from the most knowledgeable Steven Jones of Washington State University, wheat expert par excellence, and from experts Glenn Roberts of Anson Mills and Abdullah Jaradat of the US Agricultural Research Service.

I would not be where I am today were it not for the inspiration of the pixilated world. My immensely gifted colleague, Aran Goyoaga of the blog *Cannelle et Vanille*, whose immaculate food styling and photography has forever changed the way I look at food in the digital age. My colleague Phyllis Grant, who curses like there is no tomorrow and who cooks, writes, blogs, and bakes as if her life depends on it—like a modern-day Scheherazade, my childhood hero. Thank you, Phyllis, for showing up on my Instagram feed somehow, and for keeping me going with your boundless embrace of life in all its mess. And my trilingual sibling of sorts, the brave Luisa Weiss of the *Wednesday Chef* blog and author of *Berlin Kitchen* for her moving, witty, and thoughtful book on living, loving, and eating between cultures and continents. And who reminded me that the struggle to put your dreams on paper is worth all the desperation and pain, and who gave me the confidence to do things my way when I needed it the most.

A long list of companies and dedicated farmers helped with this project by graciously sending their grains and flours for me to work with. I am especially thankful to the amazing people at Bob's Red Mill, who never abandoned the principle of offering true whole grains to customers. Locally, the lovely Liz L'Etoile of Four Star Farms in western Massachusetts has dropped off many packages of grains and freshly milled flours and even helped with recipe testing. Bluebird Grain Farms too sent their exquisite products, as did Community Grains, Baia Pasta, Lotus Foods, Sunnyland Mills, Sunrise Flour Mill, Maine Grains, and Tuscan Fields. Thank you also to Jovial, Attune Foods, Freekeh Foods, Roland Foods, and Goose Valley Wild Rice Company.

As a cookbook author who always battles an overflow of food to share with the world, I'm grateful for friends who drop by for meals, regardless if they include version 1 (pretty decent) or version 9 (almost there) of a recipe. First, our dear friends Julie Battilana and Romain Aubanel and their children Noé and Lou, who love sitting around a dinner table and eating together as much as I do. I'm especially grateful to Noé who has rated many of the dishes in this book on a scale from 1 to 10, making sure that I go back to the drawing board if needed so children enjoy them too. I'm thankful to our friend Lakshmi Ramarajan whose fine palate is always a sure measure of success, her husband, Nick, and their kids Meera and Aran. And our gracious neighbors Susie and Graham Taylor and their son James who accept treats whenever they come their way, and who even sent old-fashioned thank-you cards. My dearest friend, Alessandra Campana, who has helped in so many ways, and saved me in the rush to the deadline when she showed up in my kitchen with extra cup measures to spoon flour like a pro.

Last but not least I am thankful that my family still has the patience to listen to me rave about ancient grains as if I discovered my hunger for them yesterday. I'm especially grateful to my mother, an accomplished poet and translator, who cooks every day and who is my inspiration. Her passion for the purity of flavors is a constant reminder to let ingredients shine when my enthusiasm knows no bounds. And while she continues to be mystified by my strange profession as a food writer, she supplies me nonetheless with loads of material—news of chefs and culinary TV icons, food magazines and cookbooks, in both Greece and Germany.

Last, I have no words to describe the patience of my husband, Alnoor, who has to bear my endless wrestling and wailing over writing and recipe development. And who is a natural sous chef and the only one in the house with knife skills, and who keeps eating round after round of the same food without blinking an eye. Instead, he says with a smile whenever a recipe undergoes yet another test-run of a perfectionist: yes, please! And who is kind enough to acknowledge, while often in serious doubt, that indeed the results are worth the trouble. Thank you with all my heart for being the best eater I've ever met. And so much more.

More than anything I owe you, dear readers. I have heard from so many of you over the past few years—at events, in cooking classes, on my Facebook page, via Twitter, Instagram, and my website. Somehow your notes and messages always are perfectly timed to keep me going. Moreover, they are constant reminders why every minute of every challenge is worth it.

introduction

Since my first cookbook, *Ancient Grains for Modern Meals,* was published in 2011, we have seen a revival of traditional grains beyond my wildest dreams. Countless ancient grain products populate our supermarket shelves, and new items are added almost daily. Chefs across the country are experimenting with them, taking their subtle flavors and sublime textures to new levels. Schools, student dining halls, hospitals, and restaurants—including some of the biggest chains in America—are including whole grains on their menus. At the same time, interest in gluten-free food has exploded, from consumers with either celiac disease or gluten sensitivities. This has brought some of my favorite ancient grains such as millet, buckwheat, amaranth, and teff to our plates and palates. Because, in fact, *most* ancient grains are gluten-free.

Ancient Grains was an intensely personal panorama of the whole grains I love, from the first fistful of wheat berries I chewed as a six-year-old in a cemetery in Greece, to my mom's pillowy cornmeal polenta and my German dad's pitch-dark whole grain breads. I have been more than overwhelmed by the enthusiastic response to the book from readers, chefs, and colleagues—not only from the United States but also from Canada, the United Kingdom, Australia, France, Germany, Italy, and even India. For the good part of two years I have been writing, blogging, talking, texting, and tweeting about nothing but grains. Needless to say I've been in heaven, often sleepless and exhausted, but in heaven nonetheless.

Yet, despite all this fascination with humankind's oldest staple, I have learned that it is one thing to *want* to eat ancient grains but entirely another to actually *put them on the table* given our crazy busy lives. How do you incorporate something as delicious as whole wheat berries, spelt, or Kamut into your meals when, ideally, these grains should be soaked overnight and simmered for close to an hour? How do you cook up a pot of steel-cut oats for a warming breakfast when you'd like to be

out the door in 15 minutes? And how can you bring these supremely nourishing staples onto your plate every day without spending a good part of your day in the kitchen?

I can relate to these challenges, having worked as a journalist for the first half of my life, often with grueling work hours. Grains always were and, to this day, always are on my table. And I still frequently work late, and too much. Just ask my worried mother. With this book I invite you into my kitchen. I would like to share with you what I have learned and tried over the years to help you find ways to eat more ancient grains, and many different ones at that. I invite you to experience what has worked for me, what shortcuts I use, what tricks I have up my sleeve to enjoy ancient grains every day and all day. And it's not at all time-consuming. You will see.

With this book I would like to show how *easy* it is to cook up ancient grains in your busy life. I have experimented with countless methods and tested many different ways to help bring them to your table faster and to make cooking them more accessible. The results are essential home-cooked meals, elemental yet full of flavor to please your palate. Still, this is *not* a three- or five-ingredient cookbook that promises you dinner in 15 minutes. All too often, these promises don't hold up. And you won't need extra equipment; no rice cookers, pressure cookers, or slow cookers. Not even special knife skills.

I introduce a Two-Step Method (see "The Two-Step Philosophy," page 2) to help you along. It demonstrates that minimal changes in your home cooking can have a big impact on your breakfast, lunch, and dinner table. And even dessert. Yes, ancient grains make amazing desserts, in case you were wondering . . .

In addition, many of the recipes in this book are designed to create full meals for our fast-paced lives—they bring a protein to your table, a good amount of vegetables, and a grain to satisfy your hunger. Not only the main dishes but also the grain salads, the soups and stews, and many of the savory brunch dishes, which you can enjoy for dinner too. This is the beauty of using grains in your kitchen: if you combine them well, you have a full meal at the ready.

My own passion for cooking is rooted in bringing good food to the table. In my mind, a meal has to be thoroughly enjoyable and mightily delicious. That doesn't mean good food has to be complicated. Or time-consuming. On the contrary. Some of the best meals of my life were memorable in their simplicity, prepared with just a few ingredients. But at other times, I cherish a slower meal just as much, cooked up on a cold winter day, and scents wafting from the oven asking everyone to wait patiently for an enticing meal. None of my cooking is complicated—I'm a lazy cook at heart—but sometimes I don't mind that something simmers on the stove while I take a break and go about my life.

My passion extends to ingredients: I always choose products in their most natural state because this is, I believe, how they taste best and, I'm convinced, are also better for us. So many of the ingredients we have banned from our kitchens are having a comeback—it turns out, after all, they are actually good for us in moderation. This includes eggs, good fat, even butter, and extends to whole milk and even red meat when raised responsibly.

My own cooking has always been inspired by the two cultures I was raised in, my dad's Germany with its centuries-old grains traditions and an intense appreciation for purity, and my Greek mom's simple yet luscious Mediterranean cooking. There, traditionally, meat and fish portions were small, with lentils and beans, vegetables and greens, grains and nuts filling in. This is a supremely nourishing, delicious, and, as we are increasingly learning, healthful way to eat. What's not to like?

In this spirit, I hope you'll enjoy the process of experimenting with new ingredients and learn more about the pleasures of eating ancient grains, the foundation of our meals across cultures and for millennia. I invite you to try their immense range of subtle aromas and distinct textures, from soft and warming, to gently textured and plump, to supremely chewy. Because grains not only taste magnificent but also have staying power, and they will feed you well.

the two-step philosophy

Do you think you are too busy to cook ancient grains? To serve them on weeknights, let alone every day? You are not alone. Whenever I speak about eating more ancient grains, time or the lack of it seems to be the most pressing concern for everyone. How do you get a meal on the table at dinnertime when you are exhausted from work and your family needs your attention?

Helping with this conundrum has been on my mind almost continuously since my first cookbook came out. I have asked myself over and over, how do I cook grains every day, and how have I done it through my busy career, first as a journalist and now as a food writer? How has my mother done it? And before that, her mother? It is not that they had any fewer demands on their lives.

Then it occurred to me that many tasks in a well-run kitchen are accomplished by a two-step approach: marinating meats or fish ahead of time, soaking beans and grains overnight, creating the sponge for a bread, refreshing sourdough. I realized that all of these steps of kitchen wisdom not only take the stress out of everyday cooking but also often increase flavor. This is, of course, a win-win.

Naturally, experienced homemakers know this. They also know that such small steps don't take much time, just minutes. Thinking and working ahead bring big results but they do require a certain mind-set, a philosophy, and I hope you will become comfortable with it as you cook from this book.

First, to simplify your busy lives, I am introducing in this book the Two-Step Method for grains cooking. It expands on a technique I used in my first cookbook for speeding up the cooking of steel-cut oats with a simple 2-minute boil at night. This in turn reduces the cooking time to 5 minutes in the morning, which is all I can do before starting my workday.

I wanted to see if other grains could benefit from this method as well. The Two-Step Method brings you, for example, a whole grain polenta in minutes (see page 43). I love using this method on busy mornings for breakfast, with amaranth (see page 34), steel-cut oats (see page 44), and black rice (see page 38). Of course, I don't claim ownership of this idea. Ingenious grain cooks have always done this or similar things, but I have tested the method with certain grains—it doesn't work consistently for all of them—to help you succeed.

In addition, I apply this philosophy to meal planning and cooking more generally. I hope it will help you include more whole grains in your diet—from breakfast, lunch, and dinner to dessert. I also hope it will make your life easier, your diet better, and—most important—your meals more delicious.

BREAKFAST
You will discover that spending just a few minutes in the evening prepping grains will result in a quick, satisfying breakfast in the morning. Most of the time it requires nothing but pouring boiling water over a grain—as a result your grains cook up in minutes in the morning, not in the 20 to 40 minutes they normally would take.

LUNCH AND DINNER
The grains in my house are almost always cooked on the fly. I simply have learned over time to make grains part of my daily diet. During a busy workweek, I often use quick-cooking grains (see page 22), and on weekends I prepare slower-cooking grains. By making a larger amount of grains ahead of time, especially slower-cooking grains, you will get enough grains to cook up two or three meals later in the week (see the table "Pick Your Grains," page 24). Because your grains are already cooked, you are way ahead of the game.

SOAKING GRAINS
Slow-cooking chewy grains such as whole wheat, spelt, rye, and Kamut (see table page 23) benefit from soaking overnight, similar to dried beans. This not only helps them cook up faster and more evenly but also seems to make them easier to digest. This, of course, will make you more inclined to eat them again, right?

BAKING
Preparing batter or dough the day before using allows the bran in ancient grains to soften and creates more appealing baked goods. Not only do grain flours lose some of their "grittiness," but also the slow overnight rest in the refrigerator helps develop flavor. Again, I have invented nothing new here. But I recommend it now even for pancakes, waffles, muffins, and more because the outcome is so rewarding.

PICK YOUR GRAINS—
MENU INSPIRATIONS FOR THE WEEK AHEAD
Last but not least, I have created a table (see page 24) for weekly meal planning. This table is an invitation to get you excited. It allows you to choose a new or a familiar grain every week. Cook up a larger amount on the weekend and enjoy the grain in two or three meals during the following week. For example, if you cook 2 cups of raw farro, you can prepare the Tangy Farro with Honey-Roasted Kumquats, Feta, and Tomatoes (page 128) on one day and the Spring Salad with Asparagus Coins, Kamut, and Lemon Vinaigrette (page 103) on a different day. Or if you prepare wild rice ahead of time, you can use it in the Warm Wild Rice Salad with Herb-Roasted Mushrooms and Parmesan (page 112) or as a variation of the Chicken Stew with Honey-Balsamic Squash and Farro (page 154).

Look at the table as something similar to a restaurant menu for the next week. I want you to get enthusiastic about cooking and experimenting with ancient grains, all day, every day. Just like I do. I hope the table will help show you how versatile ancient grains can be, how easy it is to cook them and to cook with them, and how effortless it is to always have some on hand to use in whatever dish you fancy.

Most important, I hope all of this inspires you to learn to think ahead in your kitchen, just a few minutes, every day, or perhaps every few days. Don't forget to be kind to yourself as you learn more about cooking and enjoying grains. While I write this, I'm keenly aware that in my own kitchen I don't follow my own advice all of the time—on these superbusy days we simply eat pasta, made from a beautiful ancient grain, of course.

one good grain

In this book, I share a few distinctly pared-down grain recipes. I have developed them in the spirit of the introductory essay to this book, "One Pure Aroma" (page 28). Many of us still consider grains as a flavorless base to be rejected as plain or "blah," or consider them in need of a covering of sauce to make them appealing.

But to me, ancient grains have subtlety and nuance, and it is their fine unique character I passionately wish for us to rediscover. I call these recipes "One Good Grain." I hope they will make you pause and ponder ancient grains' bounty, their beautiful simplicity, and their boundless energy to nourish us.

about the recipes and how to use this book

You can approach this book in two ways:

- You can either look at the "Pick Your Grains" table at the start and get inspired (for more, see page 24). The table invites you to cook one or two types of grains ahead on the weekend so you have them at the ready to create several dishes during the week.

- Alternately, you can just open a page, get excited, and start cooking. All of the information you need, including the grain cooking instructions, are on the page.

In the recipes, you will find the following guidance:

VARIATIONS Here you will find suggestions on how to cook a meal with different ingredients if they are hard to find or seasonal so you can cook it up year-round.

GLUTEN-FREE Two thirds of the recipes in this book are gluten-free or have at least one, sometimes several, gluten-free options. All of these versions have been tested in my own kitchen and by my tireless and trusted recipe tester Karen Levendusky.

VEGETARIAN Most of the recipes in this book are vegetarian to begin with, with an emphasis on the use of vegetables, fruit, grains, dairy, and nuts. If meat or fish are used, I offer a meatless variation wherever possible.

MAKE AHEAD You will find countless tips to help you work ahead to de-stress your schedule. Many dishes can also be completely made ahead and later reheated. Either way, you will find detailed instructions along the way.

I have intensively tested and streamlined all of the recipes so that you can bring the dishes to your table as fast as possible without wasting any time. Please contact me with any questions, concerns, and thoughts: www.mariaspeck.com. And enjoy exploring ancient grains!

ancient grains 101

THE ANCIENT GRAINS AND FLOURS IN THIS BOOK

This section is an overview of the grains and flours used in this book. The selection I made here is personal but also, I hope, practical. Here I introduce you to the grains and flours I love with a special focus on availability.

Since *Ancient Grains for Modern Meals*, my first cookbook, was published in 2011, we have seen an explosion of previously obscure grains becoming mainstream and more widely available. The reason for this newfound popularity is twofold: There has been a huge increase in the number of people with celiac disease or gluten sensitivities who are looking for alternatives to gluten-containing grains such as wheat, rye, and barley. At the same time, an interest in healthier eating and home cooking has propelled whole grains front and center. Consumers are seeking out good carbohydrates to reduce the amount of "empty starches," such as those from refined grains and pasta, in their diets.

This has put many of my favorite ancient grains on store shelves across the country, including previously hard-to-find varieties such as freekeh and amaranth or almost unknown einkorn and teff.

Furthermore, we are in the midst of a grains revival in many parts of the United States (see "More Than One Good Wheat," page 182). Thanks to our passion for all things local, farmers have started to grow grains again and are quickly finding a market for their rye, wheat, and barley as well as their ancient wheat varieties and long-forgotten heirlooms (see sidebar "The Revival of Heirloom Wheat and Grains," page 15).

FAQS

Which grains are gluten-free?

Many grains are gluten-free—with the exception of wheat (including all of the members of its family; for more, see "Modern Wheats" and "Ancient Wheats," page 12), barley, and rye. Oats are gluten-free as well, but be sure to check that they have been processed in a gluten-free facility and are labeled as such. Otherwise, they might have been contaminated.

Are all grains "grains"?

Some grains such as amaranth, buckwheat, or quinoa are commonly referred to as pseudocereals or pseudograins because they are seeds, not grains. But they are included here because they have a similar nutritional profile and we eat them like grains.

Why did we start growing grains?

Early humans, the so-called hunter-gatherers, started cultivating grains around ten thousand years ago to help them through cold, lean winters. Unlike fresh meat, fruit, and leaves, grains could be collected and stored for later consumption—thus enabling humans to survive. In addition, unlike any other raw "material" grains were also extremely versatile and could be turned into many different and delicious ingredients such as bread, pasta, boiled dishes, and even drinks, as Rachel Laudan explains in her fascinating and well-researched book *Cuisine and Empire*. And, as humans started to settle, she writes, it was grain-based cuisines that supported cities starting around 1000 BC.

ancient grains a to z

AMARANTH (GLUTEN-FREE)

First cultivated in Central America about five thousand to eight thousand years ago, amaranth was a staple of the Aztecs. The tiny golden seeds, as small as poppy seeds, have a comforting risotto-style quality. This makes them well suited to soups, stews, and puddings. Please note that amaranth sometimes releases a strong grassy scent during cooking. This will not affect the final dish.

TEXTURE Delicate crunch
FLAVOR Subtle sweet grassiness
NUTRITION BONUS High in protein and the essential amino acid lysine
FLOUR Dense but intensely nutty-sweet—start by adding only up to 20 percent to a dough until you understand its character.

BARLEY (CONTAINS GLUTEN)

From the Chinese and the Egyptians to the Greeks and the Romans, barley was probably the most important grain of ancient civilizations. Highly adaptable to different climates, it was first cultivated in the Fertile Crescent about ten thousand years ago. Unlike any other grain, its fiber is not concentrated in the bran layer but throughout the grain; pearl barley thus has some nutritional benefits. Look for hulled (whole grain) barley for the best nutritional profile.

TEXTURE Nice supple chew; pearl barley has a comforting starchiness
FLAVOR Rich, earthy
NUTRITION BONUS Highest fiber content of all grains; low glycemic index
FLOUR Barley flour adds mild sweetness and rich character. But it is low in gluten, so don't replace more than about a third of your flour with it, otherwise your baked goods will not rise well.

BUCKWHEAT (GLUTEN-FREE)

Quick-cooking buckwheat is not related to wheat, despite its name, but part of the rhubarb and sorrel family. The flowering plant likely originated in China and Japan. Because it can grow in cold climates, it has been a staple in eastern Europe and Russia for centuries.

TEXTURE Pleasantly soft nibs
FLAVOR Mild and earthy for raw buckwheat kernels (also called groats); more assertive for roasted buckwheat (also called kasha)
NUTRITION BONUS High in the antioxidant rutin, which can improve blood circulation
FLOUR Best known for its use in pancakes, this gluten-free flour has an appealing aroma worth exploring in other baked goods, such as cakes and cookies.

BULGUR (CONTAINS GLUTEN)

Some refer to fast-cooking bulgur (also bulgar, burghul, or bulghur) as ancient fast food. Vital to the cuisines of the former Ottoman Empire, it is still widely used from Greece to Syria and Iraq. Bulgur is made by boiling whole wheat, then drying, cracking, and sorting it by size, a traditional technique going back centuries. Bulgur on store shelves is typically medium-coarse. In Middle Eastern stores, you can find a selection from fine (#1) to coarse (#4).

TEXTURE Appealing chewiness
FLAVOR Deep, nutty wheat flavor
NUTRITION BONUS Rich in fiber, more than quinoa, oats, and corn.

CORN, GRITS, POLENTA (GLUTEN-FREE)

A staple of the Aztec, Maya, and Native Americans, corn or maize is a type of grass native to the Americas. It spread rapidly around the globe after Columbus introduced it to the Old World. Supermarkets typically sell degerminated cornmeal, which means that the nutritionally valuable germ and bran have been removed. Always look for stone-ground whole grain cornmeal. Polenta and grits are typically refined, though more traditional whole grain grits, which often look speckled, have become available (see "Sources," page 251).

For the polenta recipes in this book, please use only grains labeled "polenta," preferably medium grind (do not use instant or quick-cooking polenta, which are precooked and lack texture and flavor). For consistency and flavor, I reach for Bob's Red Mill polenta, also known as corn grits. Stone-ground medium cornmeal can be used instead, but the outcome will be a softer, less textured polenta.

TEXTURE Richly textured, increasing from fine to coarse
FLAVOR Natural appealing sweetness
NUTRITION BONUS Whole grain cornmeal is rich in fiber as well as iron and zinc
FLOUR Cornmeal, be it fine, medium, or coarse, adds texture to baked goods. Corn flour is the finest, resulting in less crumbliness in baked goods.

COUSCOUS (CONTAINS GLUTEN)

Couscous is neither a grain nor a pasta but tiny flour pellets, traditionally made from coarsely ground durum wheat. In a labor-intensive process, the perishable germ and bran are coated with an envelope of starch, thus making the grain last. Couscous remains a staple across North Africa. Today's couscous is typically factory-made but valuable as a superfast, versatile staple.

TEXTURE Fluffy and light
FLAVOR Very mild with just a hint of nuttiness
NUTRITION BONUS Whole wheat couscous is more nutritious than refined.

EINKORN (ANCIENT WHEAT, SEE PAGE 13)

EMMER (ANCIENT WHEAT, SEE PAGE 13)

FARRO, FARRO PICCOLO, FARRO MEDIO, FARRO GRANDE (ANCIENT WHEAT, SEE PAGE 13)

FONIO (MILLET, SEE AT RIGHT)

FREEKEH (CONTAINS GLUTEN)

A staple in the Middle East, freekeh (or farik) is fast becoming a darling of chefs. It was probably discovered by accident when farmers had to harvest wheat early (in its green stage) during a rainy season. They then parched the grains to remove high moisture, which results in its rich, smoky aroma. Traditionally also cultivated in Germany as *Grünkern*, literally "green seed," it is often sold crushed. This helps it cook up quickly, great for our time-strapped lives.

TEXTURE Nice chewiness
FLAVOR Rich smokiness, especially when fresh
NUTRITION BONUS Fiber-rich with a low glycemic index.

KAMUT (ANCIENT WHEAT, SEE PAGE 13–14)

MILLET (GLUTEN-FREE)

Among the oldest staples of humankind, millet is quick-cooking and versatile, which makes it well suited for busy families and professionals. A staple in Africa, India, and northern China, it was first cultivated about ten thousand years ago. Fonio is the smallest of millets, cultivated in west Africa.

TEXTURE Fluffy, comforting
FLAVOR Appealing, mild
NUTRITION BONUS High in magnesium
FLOUR Golden millet flour has a natural subtle sweetness that makes it great for pancakes and muffins. Because it is gluten-free, use no more than 20 percent millet flour in bread so as not to lose elasticity.

OATS (GLUTEN-FREE)

Oats are a relative newcomer to our diet, first cultivated about 1000 BC in Europe. The germ and the bran are almost never removed during processing. Oats are gluten-free but can be contaminated in processing. You can choose between whole oat berries (or groats), steel-cut oats (groats, cut into pieces), and old-fashioned rolled oats (steamed and flattened whole oats). There are also quick-cooking oats (like rolled oats, but roughly cut beforehand), and instant oats (cut even finer, rolled thinner, and precooked).

TEXTURE Satisfying chewiness, especially in whole and steel-cut oats, but also in rolled oats
FLAVOR Toasty, deep natural sweetness
NUTRITION BONUS Eating oats helps lower LDL (low-density lipoprotein) "bad" cholesterol and may help lower blood pressure.

QUINOA (GLUTEN-FREE)

These trendy small seeds, popularized by gluten-free diets, were first cultivated about five thousand years ago. The Inca called quick-cooking quinoa (pronounced KEEN-wa) the mother of all grains. Banned by the Spanish explorers because of its ceremonial significance, it survived in the wild. Today much of our quinoa comes from Bolivia and Peru. The United Nations named the drought-resistant plant a "supercrop" for its potential to feed the poor. Most quinoa in the United States is prerinsed and does not need to be washed before cooking.

TEXTURE Crunchy, ranging from delicate in white quinoa to more pronounced in the stunning black seeds
FLAVOR Faint grassy sweetness
NUTRITION BONUS Quinoa contains all of the essential amino acids, making it the only plant food to provide a complete protein.

RICE: BROWN, RED, BLACK, AND MORE (GLUTEN-FREE)

Rice, a descendant of a wild grass, is a staple for half the world's population. In 2003, Korean archaeologists found a handful of burned rice kernels going back fifteen thousand years. Unlike in polished white rice, in brown rice the bran and the germ are intact. Today, many other fascinating whole grain rice varieties have become widely available, including stunning red rice and black rice (see "Sources," page 251). Some cook in just 20 minutes.

TEXTURE Delicate chewiness
FLAVOR Appealing mild nuttiness

NUTRITION BONUS Fiber and minerals such as magnesium, depending on the type
FLOUR Brown rice flour with its mild, nutty character is a good addition to pancakes or muffins, but since it has no gluten, adjustments need to be made.

RYE (CONTAINS GLUTEN)

First cultivated about 3000 BC, rye is a latecomer to the human diet. It can grow in cold, wet climates, which explains why it has been used for centuries in northern and eastern Europe as well as in Russia, especially for bread making. Dark dense German rye breads are legendary. The kernels have a beautiful grayish-green hue and may be used in salads and sides.

TEXTURE Supremely chewy
FLAVOR Subtle tanginess
NUTRITION BONUS Contains a type of fiber that makes you feel full fast
FLOUR Pumpernickel and dark rye flour are the whole grain flours milled from rye. Sourdough helps rye bread rise, as the flour doesn't contain much gluten and yeast alone doesn't produce desirable results.

SORGHUM (GLUTEN-FREE)

This nutrient-rich whole grain, cultivated for 10,000 years, arrived in the United States probably on slave ships. Today, most of it is grown for animal consumption but this is changing because of the growing interest in gluten-free grains. In the American South it has long been used to make sorghum syrup, a traditional sweetener. The plant is drought-resistant and still widely consumed in Africa and in parts of India. Its chewy grains are beautiful additions to salads and other meals, where its character is appreciated.

TEXTURE Rich chewiness
FLAVOR Mild, reminiscent of corn
NUTRITION BONUS Iron and B-vitamins
FLOUR Like for all gluten-free grains, adjustments need to be made in baking as to not create dense heavy baked goods.

SPELT (ANCIENT WHEAT, SEE PAGE 13)

TEFF (GLUTEN-FREE)

Traditionally cultivated in Ethiopia and Eritrea for at least three thousand years, probably longer, teff has gained popularity because it contains no gluten. It is best known for its use in naturally fermented *injera* flatbread, a staple in Ethiopian cuisine. Highly nutritious, teff is the smallest grain on the planet, which can be a challenge to harvest—its name means "lost" in Amharic. American farmers have started to grow the minuscule grains in Idaho and Kansas.

TEXTURE Creamy, with a delicate, comforting crunch
FLAVOR Deeply nutty with hints of cocoa, almost sweet
NUTRITION BONUS Its calcium content is superior, by a wide margin, to all grains
FLOUR Great for use in pancakes and muffins. It pairs well with nuts, oats, and chocolate, but it contains no gluten, so adjustments have to be made.

MODERN WHEATS (CONTAIN GLUTEN)

Wheat is among the oldest grains humans have domesticated, along with barley, millet, and rice. Today, two types of wheat are most commonly cultivated: durum wheat, a very hard grain that splinters when ground and is well suited for making pasta, and "hard" bread wheat. The term *hard* refers here to the protein content of the grain. Modern wheat is high in gluten, a protein that gives bread its elasticity, the desirable spring. Hard wheat is distinguished by its color, red or white, and—depending on when it was planted—by the growing season, spring or winter. In addition, there are a number of ancient wheat varieties that are having a huge comeback (see "Ancient Wheats," below).

Whole Wheat and Its Cousin, White Whole Wheat

Whole wheat berries bring a distinct chewiness and rich character to salads and stews. White whole wheat berries are a type of wheat with a lighter bran color and less tannins, which some people perceive as bitter. This makes white whole wheat berries especially attractive when ground into flour: "white" whole wheat flour has the same nutrients and fiber as regular whole wheat flour, but your family might not be able to tell the difference when you use it. Try it!

FLAVOR Regular whole wheat has a hearty aroma; white whole wheat is milder, with a tempting nuttiness
TEXTURE Supremely chewy
NUTRITION BONUS High in fiber and iron
FLOUR Both regular whole wheat and "white" whole wheat flour can be used interchangeably in recipes. I prefer the more pronounced flavor of regular whole wheat in bread and savory pizzas. White whole wheat flour, on the other hand, has an appealing golden color and a subtle sweetness that makes it well suited for more delicate baked goods such as muffins, pancakes, and cookies. But it's up to you. For the most interesting texture, always look for stone-ground whole wheat flour. You might even be able to locate freshly milled local flour in your area (see "The Revival of Heirloom Wheat and Grains," page 15).

Soft Whole Wheat

These wheat berries have a lower protein content than hard wheat. I prefer using them in salads or stews because they have a more appealing texture and cook a bit faster than hard wheat berries. While harder to find, they are worth seeking out.

FLAVOR Pleasing mildness
TEXTURE Less chewy than hard wheat berries
NUTRITION BONUS Fiber-rich, high in iron
FLOUR Called whole wheat pastry flour, it is great for pastries, cakes, muffins, and quick breads.

ANCIENT WHEATS (CONTAIN GLUTEN)

I'm a huge fan of the varied textures and aromas of ancient wheat varieties such as einkorn, emmer (often referred to as farro), spelt, and Kamut. All have rich character, with distinct subtle flavors and textures. They are, however, not easy to harvest and thus fell by the wayside when high-yielding modern wheat became dominant, starting in the early 1960s.

All ancient wheats have more nutrients than modern wheat because of their more extensive root system (see

"More Than One Good Wheat," page 182). In addition, they may be easier on the digestive system for people who experience discomfort or mild digestive issues when eating modern wheat. The research on this is fast evolving. Please do *not* eat any grain in the wheat family if you have been diagnosed with celiac disease or have a wheat allergy. Otherwise, I couldn't be happier if the recipes in this book make you curious to try all of them.

The Three Farros

Delectable farro has been a darling of chefs for many years, and home cooks have caught on as well. Still, there is a lot of confusion around the term *farro* because Italians use it to refer to not one, but three, ancient wheat varieties still cultivated in Italy: farro piccolo (also known by the German *einkorn*), farro medio (also known as *emmer*, which is the Hebrew word for "mother"), and farro grande (also known as spelt). Furthermore, you might also find American farmers selling their einkorn as *einka* to distinguish it from more commercial uses. It's a little complicated but in my opinion worth your time because the selection of amazing grains on your plate just grew so much bigger.

While the ancient wheats have a higher protein content but less gluten than hard modern wheat, they sometimes need less handling and kneading. Bakers across the country are now learning again how to use them. I find spelt, for example, beautifully suited to pasta, flatbreads, and pizza.

Einkorn (Farro Piccolo) Einkorn is the smallest of the ancient wheats and, together with emmer, the oldest. The whole grain largely survived in the wild and is getting a fair bit of attention as of late. Some call it the purest wheat because it has only two sets of chromosomes. There are two kinds of einkorn available. Einkorn from Italy is typically lighter in color, looks a bit more polished, and cooks up in about half the time. The einkorn grown by farmers in the United States and Canada is darker and takes up to 40 minutes to cook (see "Sources," page 251).

TEXTURE Mesmerizing starchiness, with a nice gentle chewiness
FLAVOR Alluring and mild
NUTRITION BONUS Rich in lutein, a powerful antioxidant, the B vitamin thiamin, and trace minerals
FLOUR See "The Three Farros," above.

Emmer (Farro Medio) The farro typically available in the United States is of the emmer variety and often comes from Italy. This charming, plump ancient wheat, with notes of cinnamon, is cultivated there to this day, especially in the Tuscany region. It is typically semipearled. Today, you can also find wonderful US-grown whole grain emmer farro, which is worth seeking out (see "Sources," page 251).

TEXTURE Tempting starchiness with a nice chew
FLAVOR Pleasantly nutty
NUTRITION BONUS Niacin, magnesium
FLOUR See "The Three Farros," above.

Spelt (Farro Grande) This ancient wheat with its distinct round kernel and reddish hue is experiencing a huge comeback in Europe as well as in the United States. A staple in German-speaking countries until the early twentieth century, and also in France and Spain, it lost ground because it is labor-intensive to grow and harvest. The German mystic Hildegard von Bingen (1098–1179) touted its healing properties and called it the best of all grains. Spelt is also the basis for *Grünkern* in Germany, better known as freekeh (see "Freekeh," page 9).

TEXTURE Appealing chewiness
FLAVOR Pleasantly mild
NUTRITION BONUS Magnesium and iron
FLOUR See "The Three Farros," above.

Kamut (Contains Gluten)

The stunning, bronze-colored kernels of Kamut are of the ancient Khorasan wheat variety, named after a historical region in today's Iran. Still grown in parts of Egypt and Turkey, the grain has been grown in Montana for over sixty years but has only more recently gained popularity.

If you buy Khorasan wheat under the trademark Kamut, you are assured that the grain has never been hybridized and that it is organically grown. On store shelves you might also see Turanicum, which is a Khorasan wheat as well but has not been certified.

TEXTURE Supremely chewy
FLAVOR Rich, buttery aroma
NUTRITION BONUS More protein than modern wheat and high in selenium
FLOUR An enticing golden color, it is fabulous in cakes, cookies, and crackers, and also makes a great addition to whole grain breads.

WILD RICE (GLUTEN-FREE)

Wild rice, revered by Native Americans, is not a grain but the seed of an aquatic grass native to North America. Much of the wild rice in stores today is cultivated in California and Minnesota, recognizable by its shiny pitch-black seeds. If you can locate "wild" wild rice, give it a try. Its seeds have a mottled brown look and an intense smoky aroma from parching over an open fire (see "Sources," page 251).

TEXTURE Nice chew
FLAVOR Intensely aromatic with a rich nuttiness
NUTRITION BONUS Wild rice has double the fiber and more protein than brown rice.

the revival of heirloom wheat and grains

The past decade has seen a revival of the local grains economy in the United States outside the Midwestern farm belt. Farmers have started to grow wheat, barley, rye, and triticale in areas where it had been long abandoned, such as in Maine, Massachusetts, Vermont, upstate New York, South Carolina, Arizona, and California. You can now find American-grown emmer, einkorn, spelt, and more. (For more, see "More Than One Good Wheat," page 182.)

Heirloom varieties that had fallen by the wayside as a result of high-efficiency modern agriculture are being replanted. They are often better suited to individual growing areas. In wheat, for example, you can now find Red Fife, Turkey Red, White Sonora wheat, Warthog, Glenn, and Arapahoe at farmers' markets or online (for sources, see page 252). In corn, old varieties such as Antebellum and Floriani Red Flint are being grown again. You will be surprised how many local grains are already out there, and every day there seem to be more.

Furthermore, you can find more and more farmers and local bakers who are milling fresh grain again. You might want to seek them out, especially when you learn that your typical supermarket bag of "whole wheat" flour might not necessarily contain what you think. Here's why: In traditional stone mills, whole grain kernels are simply added to a funnel to be ground into real whole wheat flour, with all its parts. In modern hammer mills, however, the bran and the germ are first separated to get the more desirable refined white flour, still the market leader. For whole wheat flour, companies later "recombine" the flour from different heaps of bran, starch, and germ. Bob Klein of Community Grains in Oakland, California, is working hard to change all of this with a quality standard for whole grains and flours (see "One Serious Passion for Pasta," page 162).

To connect readers and grain lovers with local farmers and millers across the country, I have started listing them on my blog. Please drop by and do let me know if you know grains farmers I haven't yet included: www.mariaspeck.com/blog

I believe we are at the start of a new revolution—following on the heels of local fruits, vegetables, bread, beer, and cheese. It is bringing us locally grown grains and freshly milled flours. And you, dear readers, are at the forefront of it. Ask for it, buy it, and eat it. That's the best way to create demand and secure its survival. Discover the new grains in your area and the nuances in flavor they bring to your plate—there is nothing like it.

how to cook ancient grains

Cooking a pot of grains is as easy as boiling a pot of pasta. There are two basic cooking methods, and which one you choose is a matter of preference. Try them for yourself and decide.

ABSORPTION METHOD

Bring the water with the grain to a boil in a heavy pot. Adjust the heat to maintain a simmer, cover, and cook until the grains are tender with a slight chew. Remove from the heat and allow to sit, covered, for 10 minutes, which typically absorbs any remaining liquid and nicely plumps up your grains. For the fluffiest grains, place a dish cloth between the lid and the pot to absorb moisture during the steaming. Drain if needed.

This is my go-to method for which a heavy saucepan with a tight-fitting lid is essential. Some prefer this method because they believe it retains more nutrients, as you don't toss out the cooking liquid.

PASTA METHOD

Bring a large pot of water to a boil, add salt to taste, and toss in your grains (the water should cover the grains by at least 3 inches). Cook, uncovered, at a rapid simmer. Taste for doneness toward the end of the suggested cooking time, then drain the grains in a fine-mesh sieve. Return them to the pot to steam, covered, for 10 minutes if you have time. This step nicely plumps up the grain.

This method appeals to some because it does not require you to measure the amount of liquid. It works for most grains such as millet, quinoa, and brown rice, and slower-cooking grains such as whole wheat berries, but less so for amaranth or teff—they are so small that you might lose them when draining in a fine-mesh sieve. These minuscule grains are best cooked like a porridge (see individual recipes).

OTHER METHODS

I learned to cook growing up in Europe, where kitchens are often very small and any extra equipment takes up precious counter space. Hence I simply use a good-quality set of pots for grain cooking (see "Equipment," page 20). However, grains can be cooked in a pressure cooker; rice cookers and slow cookers can be used as well.

RICE COOKER If you already own a rice cooker and enjoy using it, I suggest following the advice of blogger Jeanette Chen of *Jeanette's Healthy Living* (jeanetteshealthyliving.com), who has explained how to adjust for different grains in a post for the Williams-Sonoma blog: www.blog.williams-sonoma.com/how-to-cook-whole-grains-in-a-rice-cooker/

PRESSURE COOKER If you want to use a pressure cooker, I found Laura Pazzaglia's table at her site *Hip Pressure Cooking* very helpful: www.hippressurecooking.com/p/cooking-times.html

SLOW COOKER Many readers have told me that they simply add slower-cooking whole wheat, rye, or whole spelt berries to casserole-type dishes in their slow cooker. They will need 6 to 8 hours on low heat.

DONENESS

Typically you are looking for a tender kernel with just a slight bit of chewiness left. So take a spoon and taste a kernel. Doneness is also a matter of preference, similar to a steak or pasta. I, for example, prefer my grains well cooked and not overly chewy.

Not all batches of the same grain cook up in the same amount of time. One batch of fresh millet might be done in 15 minutes; another batch might need 25 minutes. I have cooked brown rice for 30 minutes and some batches for 50 to 60 minutes. No need to despair. Drain if there is too much water left or add a bit more water as needed.

I certainly don't mind if some of my grains burst (the starchy center shows) during cooking. On the contrary, I believe well-cooked grains are easier on your digestive system. I also find it makes for a more pleasing eating experience if my grains are not overly chewy.

RINSING

Most grains you buy in stores today are very clean. Unless you have a batch of dusty grains in front of you with lots of chaff, I consider rinsing unnecessary. But if you feel better, go ahead and give them a rinse.

In the rare case of a dirty batch, add the grains to a bowl of cold water and swish them around with your hands so any chaff and broken pieces can float to the top. Carefully pour out the water with any floating residue, repeat if needed, then drain the grains in a sieve.

SOAKING

I strongly recommend an overnight soaking in water for chewy slow-cooking grains such as whole wheat, spelt, or rye berries, similar to dried beans. These grains will cook not only a bit faster but also more evenly, and I find them easier to digest. Fast-cooking grains such as millet, quinoa, and buckwheat don't need to be soaked (see the tables, pages 22–23).

Cook in fresh or in soaking water?
Some people prefer to cook their grains in the soaking water to preserve nutrients. Others drain the soaked grains and use fresh water to cook them in. I often cook my grains in the soaking liquid out of convenience. Either works fine, and I have no preference.

Forgot to soak?
Use the quick-soak method: Cover the grains with at least 2 inches of water, bring to a boil, and cook for 2 minutes. Remove from the heat, cover, and allow to sit for 1 hour. Drain and cook as directed.

No time to cook your soaked grains?
Just put them in the fridge for the day, or until you can cook them (but no longer than 24 hours, as they might start to sprout).

TOASTING

Toasting small grains such as millet, quinoa, couscous, or buckwheat before cooking brings out their characteristic nutty aroma. Toasting also allows grains to cook up more distinctly. In certain meals I find this desirable but not always. I sometimes enjoy the unadorned character of plain ancient grains just as much. Try it and see what you prefer.

HOW TO Add the grains to a dry heavy saucepan over medium to medium-low heat and toast until they crackle and become aromatic. Carefully add water (it will splatter!) and cook as directed.

COOKING AHEAD

The easiest way to incorporate more ancient grains into your busy life is by cooking a large amount of grains ahead on the weekend. Use the "Pick Your Grains" table (page 24) to help you with meal planning. Cooked grains can be kept, covered, in the fridge for 5 to 7 days or frozen (see page 18).

MY TRICK I often simmer a pot of grains on a back burner, to have on hand for later, while preparing other food. And what I don't end up using within a few days—life happens—I just place in the freezer for another day. No waste!

REHEATING

Grains reheat very well. While chilling can harden the starch in grains, reheating will nicely soften them again. Be sure to separate any grains that have clumped together before cooking.

STOVE TOP Reheat grains over medium to medium-low heat, with about ¼ inch of water, cover, and cook until warmed through.

MICROWAVE Add the grains to a microwave-safe bowl. Cook each cup of grain on high until steaming hot, 1 to 2 minutes, stirring once.

FREEZING
Almost all grains freeze very well for at least 3 months. Many grains will be good for much longer. So go ahead and make more and freeze grains in portion-size containers or ziplock bags. Food writer Lorna Sass calls the grain supplies in her freezer a "grain bank" in her award-winning book *Whole Grains Every Day, Every Way*.

DEFROSTING You can use grains straight from the freezer. No need to defrost them. Simply add the frozen grains to a microwave-safe bowl or plate and heat in the microwave on high until hot, about 1 to 2 minutes per cup. Alternately, defrost grains overnight in the fridge and reheat as described above.

STORING GRAINS
I recommend storing grains in a cool, dark place in individual Ball or Mason jars with tight-fitting lids. Don't leave them in their packages or bags! Placing grains in glass jars further enables you to see at a glance which grains you have on hand, making it more likely that you will actually use them. These grain-filled jars also look beautiful.

SMALL AMOUNTS I keep small amounts of quick-cooking grains on a shelf in my kitchen, which helps me select one for dinner quickly.

LARGE AMOUNTS I suggest you store backup supplies of whole grains in a cool, dark pantry, basement, or other such place in the home. They will last many months.

REFRIGERATION
It is not necessary to store whole grains in the fridge. Whole grains will last many months (see above).

Personally, I find it impractical to look for them behind egg cartons, condiments, and packages of fish or meat—especially when you have more than one or two types of grains. In addition, I have little space to spare in my fridge. Of course, if it is convenient for you, grains may be stored in the fridge.

SHOPPING
In the past five years, good-quality grains have become widely available across the country.

FARMS AND FARMERS' MARKETS Local farmers have started to grow and sell their own fresh grains. This is my first choice, as you are most likely to get a premium grain, fresh from the last season. Eating fresh grains is a revelation just as fresh flour is (see "How to Bake with Ancient Grain Flours," at right). The grains cook up much faster and have a vivid flavor that is worth seeking out.

HEALTH FOOD STORES AND SPECIALTY MARKETS I like to buy my grains from a bulk bin with high turnover, which ensures freshness. Try several stores and take a whiff if you are not sure: there should be no off or bitter scent.

SUPERMARKETS The grains selection in supermarkets has exploded as well. Many good grains are now also found in gluten-free sections.

ONLINE Some of the less common grains such as einkorn or emmer are available online and will ship to your door quickly. Don't hesitate to use this option when you discover a grain you love.

ORGANIC OR NOT?
I personally always opt for organic. Whole ancient grains—with their outer skin or bran—are an important staple for me. And while pesticide residues might be negligible, my diet is built on grains. In addition, I like to support farmers who try to keep the soil healthy.

SPROUTED GRAINS—YES OR NO?
Sprouting grains by soaking them and waiting for small sprouts to appear creates a more nutritious grain.

According to some sources sprouted grains may be easier to digest and might have less allergens. There is no regulated definition of sprouted grain at the moment. However, baker extraordinaire Peter Reinhart explains that he likes working with sprouted whole grain flour because the sprouting activates enzymes that in turn give you a naturally sweeter baked good.

how to bake with ancient grain flours

Breads, rolls, cakes, and cookies are enhanced by the use of ancient grain flours. For one, their nutritional profile is improved. More important, the flours add rich character to your baking, with their varied textures and subtle flavors. It's a fascinating universe, and more and more passionate home cooks and bakers are exploring it.

THREE STEPS TO SUCCESS

MORE LIQUID Generally, a dough or batter with whole grain flours needs more liquid such as water, milk, or buttermilk.

RESTING TIME A period of resting the batter, at least 30 minutes and up to overnight, improves many baked goods with ancient grain flours.

Why? The rest allows the bran in the flour to soften by absorbing the extra liquid. This makes for more pleasing texture and deeper aroma and often also improves the overall outcome. Either clean up your kitchen in the meantime or work ahead. I often assemble muffin or pancake batter the night before and place it in the fridge overnight. This in turn takes the stress out of morning baking.

MEASURING MATTERS I strongly recommend using a digital scale (see page 21) for all your baking, even more so for whole grain baking. You will get much more consistent results if you measure your ingredients by weight instead of by volume.

WHY A SCALE MATTERS

Depending on how and by whom a measuring cup is filled, the weight can vary by 20 percent or more, which is significant if a recipe calls for 4 cups of flour or if you are baking a delicate cake. Weight is even more important when using delicious freshly milled local grains. These flours are generally fluffier—which means less flour per volume in your cup—than the whole grain flours you buy bagged in the store or in bulk bins where they will settle over time. A scale, however, will still give you the same results. In addition, humidity affects flour. A scale helps reduce all these inconsistencies.

GRAMS OVER OUNCES After much deliberation, I decided to use grams and *not* ounces in all the recipes where the weight of flours matters. Bakers the world over use grams to scale recipes because it simply is the easiest way to do so. Any inexpensive digital scale today can measure both in ounces and in grams at the push of a button.

---

measuring flour without a scale

Here is how to come closest to the weight measurements for flour used in this book. Please note that the cup measure is an estimate and corresponds only to the first flour listed in the ingredient list. If you want to use any of the listed alternatives, especially freshly milled flour, please use a scale (see page 21).

- Fluff or stir the flour in your container to aerate it (I do this with a fork).
- Spoon flour into your measuring cup until it is overflowing. Do not pat down, shake, or bang your measuring cup on the counter, as this will compress the flour.
- Using the thin blade of a knife or a slim metal spatula, sweep across the top to level the cup.

STORING FLOUR

Unless you live in a very humid area with no air conditioning, I find it practical to store my whole grain flour as I store my grains: in glass jars with tight-fitting lids and in a cool, dark place (see "Storing Grains," page 18). While these flours can go rancid (because of the natural oils in the germ), they don't go bad overnight.

Some bakers prefer to refrigerate or freeze all their whole grain flour because its composition starts to change after milling when it comes in contact with air, so if you wish and have the space, store your flours in the fridge or freezer. However, as a home cook, I find that I don't use products that I stash away in the freezer or in the fridge. When, on the other hand, I see my jars of whole grain flour, I get inspired to use them, which in turn increases the turnover of these ingredients in my kitchen.

TIP Be sure to smell your flour before using it. It should have no rancid, musty, or off scent. If it does, toss it.

GRAIN MILL

If you bake a lot and enjoy the use of whole grain flours, a countertop grain mill might be a great addition to your kitchen (for sources, see page 252). The fresh flavor of the flour is unsurpassed. Furthermore, you can grind only the grains you need.

equipment

FOR GRAIN COOKING

To successfully cook grains on a daily basis, you need two pieces of equipment: a heavy saucepan and a fine-mesh sieve. Done! Everything else is icing on the cake, or a birthday present down the line . . .

Heavy Saucepan
BASICS To cook grains of all kinds, you need at least one high-quality saucepan with a heavy bottom and a tight-fitting lid.

MORE For a small household, even a single 2-quart pot will do. If you like to cook, a good set of three pots (a 1-quart, 2-quart, and 4-quart pot) should last a lifetime. This is all I own to this day, and it is sufficient for everything I do in my kitchen.

Fine-Mesh Sieve or Strainer
Just try rinsing quinoa in a regular sieve and you'll know what I'm talking about. While a salad strainer might work for wheat berries or other larger kernels, many grains are small, and you'll make good use of a fine-mesh tool.

BASICS For rinsing and draining grains, this is an indispensable tool.

MORE I also use my strainer, placed on top of a bowl, to drain yogurt. This gives me delicious homemade Greek yogurt, also known as *labneh*.

FOR EVERYDAY COOKING

Cast-Iron Skillet
Over the years, I have become a huge fan of the humble cast-iron skillet. It started with a basic 10-inch Lodge skillet and now I have them in half a dozen sizes. Once you understand that the handle gets really hot (!), and that wasn't easy for me, they are amazing. Their heavy bottoms heat up slowly but evenly, and they can't be beat for searing steaks and fish, as well as panfrying vegetables, giving you the best browning for flavor. They can go from stove top to oven at any temperature, and their nonstick surface gets better with use. I find they excel even for making finicky omelets! Cast-iron skillets have replaced all of my nonstick pans, which, even with the best of care, eventually scratched up and lost their protection.

You can now buy preseasoned cast-iron if you like. I find them easy to care for. On a daily basis, I just use a vegetable brush to scrub off any residue under hot water (don't use soap). Then I place the skillet back on the burner until dry. Off the heat, I spritz on a bit of vegetable oil, just enough for a thin layer, and rub it in with paper towels (don't burn yourself!). When it's not necessary, I don't clean my skillet at all under running water but just wipe out any excess oil. That's what people used to do—my dad showed me that—and it works beautifully.

Digital Scale

If you love to bake, you should own a digital scale.

WHY? Place a bowl on the scale and add your ingredients by weight—and you are ready to go! No more messy cleanup of your kitchen counters from filling measuring cups and spilling flour, nuts, and sugar everywhere. In addition, you will be more accurate, and thus successful, in your baking because there are many variables in filling a measuring cup, especially with flour (see "How to Bake with Ancient Grain Flours," page 19).

But even in my busy everyday cooking, I find a scale helpful. For example, in the rush to dinner it is one easy step to weigh 1 pound of mushrooms compared to patiently filling and measuring several cups.

Dough Whisk

An ingenious tool, invented in Denmark, a dough whisk is for mixing dough and batter. Its design couldn't be more simple—two thick stainless steel wire loops on a plain wooden handle—yet it helps combine ingredients more efficiently than a wooden spoon or a spatula. This in turn results in less gluten development, which makes for more tender muffins, cakes, or pancakes.

Dutch Oven

Nothing beats a one-pot meal where your meat or fish simmers together with vegetables and grains. For slow-cooking stews and braises, a large Dutch oven of 5 or 6 quarts is a good investment. And stews get better overnight, so you can cook ahead for busy weeknights. There are many affordable models on the market.

Electric Kettle

I enjoy brewing tea and coffee at home, so I bought an electric kettle a few years ago—it has become indispensable. For one, it brings water to a boil almost in an instant, and it is energy efficient to boot.

Zester

Citrus—lemons, limes, and oranges—is a key ingredient in my Mediterranean-inspired cooking. I thus consider a good zester an invaluable tool. Having tried many different zesters over the years, nothing beats the ease of use of a handheld Microplane zester.

grain cooking table

QUICK-COOKING WHOLE GRAINS

GRAIN	AMOUNT (CUPS)	WATER/LIQUID (CUPS)	COOKING TIME (MINUTES)	APPROXIMATE YIELD (CUPS)
amaranth	1	3	20–25	3
buckwheat groats (not kasha)	1	1¾	15	3
bulgur, fine	1	1	10, steaming time	3
bulgur, medium and coarse	1	1¾	10–20	3
cornmeal, coarse	1	3½	30	4
couscous, whole wheat	1	1¼	5–10, steaming time	3
einkorn (farro piccolo), light	1	1¾	20–25	3
emmer (farro medio), semipearled	1	2	20–25	3
freekeh, cracked	1	2½	15–20	3
millet	1	1¾	15–20	4
oats, steel-cut	1	3½	25–30	3½
polenta, corn grits	1	4	20–25	4
quinoa	1	1¾	10–20	3½
red rice	1	2½	20–25	3
teff	1	3	15–20	3

SLOW-COOKING WHOLE GRAINS

All of the slow-cooking grains may also be cooked in ample water using the pasta method (see page 16) if you prefer. Use at least 4 cups water per 1 cup grain, and 8 cups water for 2 cups grain. Test frequently toward the end of the cooking time, drain, retaining the fragrant cooking liquid as a base for soups if you like. Return the grains to the pot, cover, and allow to steam off the heat for 5 to 10 minutes.

GRAIN	AMOUNT (CUPS)	WATER/LIQUID (CUPS)	COOKING TIME (MINUTES)	APPROXIMATE YIELD (CUPS)	TO SOAK?	SOAKING TIME (HOURS)
barley, hulled	1	2½	40–50	3	yes	overnight
barley, pearl	1	3	30–40	3½	optional	2–3
brown rice, long-grain	1	1½	35–45	3	optional	2–3
brown rice, short-grain	1	1¾	40–50	3	optional	2–3
einkorn (farro piccolo), dark	1	1¾	35–40	3	optional	overnight
emmer (farro medio), whole grain	1	2	45–60	3	yes	overnight
freekeh, whole	1	2½	25–35	3	yes	overnight
Kamut berries	1	1¾	50–60	2½	yes	overnight
oat berries (whole oat groats)	1	1¾	30–40	2½	optional	2–3
rye berries	1	1½	50–60	3	yes	overnight, up to 24 hours
sorghum	1	2	50–60	3	yes	overnight
spelt berries (farro grande)	1	1¾	45–55	2½	yes	overnight
wheat berries, hard	1	1½	50–60	3	yes	overnight, up to 24 hours
wheat berries, soft	1	1¾	40–50	3	yes	overnight
wild rice	1	2	40–50	3	optional	overnight

pick your grains—menu inspirations for the week ahead

Grains are the most versatile everyday staple. I created this table to get you inspired and to make it easy to try familiar and unfamiliar grains everyday. You can use the table in two ways: Choose a grain you'd like to try and cook a large amount of it in advance (left column). Then check your menu options for the week to see what meals you could make using the pre-cooked grain. Alternately, you could choose one delicious dish (right column) and see what other dishes you can prepare during the week using the same grain.

This table is not meant to be comprehensive. There are many recipes in the book that are streamlined to come to your table effortlessly but don't use pre-cooked grains. Look at this table as my invitation to help you explore the rich variety of mouth-watering grains.

Note: 2 cups raw grains will typically give you 5 to 6 cups cooked (7 to 8 cups for quinoa); for instructions, see the Cooking Grains table on page 22. Many recipes are forgiving, so don't fret about having the exact amount!

GRAIN CHOICES	MENU CHOICES *(The grain amount in brackets reflects the amount of cooked grain you need for the dish)*
Barley, pearl or hulled (whole-grain)	Fritatta Muffins for Any Grain (1½ cups) • Pomegranate Tomatoes for Any Grain (3 to 3½ cups) • Tangy Farro with Honey-Roasted Kumquats, Feta, and Tomatoes (3 cups) Minted Barley and Fennel Stew with Marinated Feta (2½ cups) • Roasted One-Pan Chicken with Leeks and Barley (3½ cups) • Greek-inspired Fresh Artichokes with Barley and Tomatoes (2 cups)
Bulgur	Fritatta Muffins for Any Grain (1½ cups) • Pomegranate Tomatoes for Any Grain (3 to 3½ cups) • Tangy Farro with Honey-Roasted Kumquats, Feta, and Tomatoes (3 cups) • Minted Barley and Fennel Stew with Marinated Feta (2 cups) • Roasted One-Pan Chicken with Leeks and Barley (3½ cups) • Greek-inspired Fresh Artichokes with Barley and Tomatoes (2 cups)
Einkorn, Farro Piccolo	German-Style Muesli-Yogurt (¼ cup, or more) • Farro Salad with Roasted Eggplant, Caramelized Onion, and Pine Nuts (3 cups) • Spring Salad with Asparagus Coins, Kamut, and Lemon Vinaigrette (2½ cups) • Pomegranate Tomatoes for Any Grain (3 to 3½ cups) Roasted Eggplant Fan with Tomatoes, Spelt and Mozzarella (3 cups)
Emmer, Farro Medio	German-Style Muesli-Yogurt (¼ cup, or more) • Farro Salad with Roasted Eggplant, Caramelized Onion, and Pine Nuts (3 cups) • Spring Salad with Asparagus Coins, Kamut, and Lemon Vinaigrette (2½ cups) • Kamut Salad with Oranges, Leeks, and Blue Cheese (2 cups) • Shortcut Polenta, Variation (1 cup) • Pomegranate Tomatoes for Any Grain (3 to 3½ cups) • Tangy Farro with Honey-Roasted Kumquats, Feta, and Tomatoes (3 cups) • Chicken Stew with Honey-Balsamic Squash and Farro (2 to 3 cups) • Greek-inspired Fresh Artichokes with Barley and Tomatoes (1½ to 2 cups) • Roasted Eggplant Fan with Tomatoes, Spelt and Mozzarella (3 cups) • Rum Raisin Ice Cream with Kamut Berries (½ cup)

GRAIN CHOICES	MENU CHOICES *(The grain amount in brackets reflects the amount of cooked grain you need for the dish)*
Kamut	German-Style Muesli-Yogurt (¼ cup, or more) • Fritatta Muffins for Any Grain (1½ cups) • Spring Salad with Asparagus Coins, Kamut, and Lemon Vinaigrette (2½ cups) • Artichoke and Spelt Salad with Cara Cara Citrus Boost (2 cups) • Kamut Salad with Oranges, Leeks, and Blue Cheese (2 cups) • Shortcut Polenta, Variation (1 cup) • Tangy Farro with Honey-Roasted Kumquats, Feta, and Tomatoes (3 cups) • Rum Raisin Ice Cream with Kamut Berries (½ cup)
Millet	Saffron Millet with Toasted Almonds and Cardamom (3½ cups) • Fritatta Muffins for Any Grain (1½ cups) • Baked Feta Fingers in Saffron Quinoa with Tomatoes (2 cups) • Pomegranate Tomatoes for Any Grain (3 to 3½ cups) • Creamy Millet with Greek Yogurt, Avocado, and Basil (2½ cups) • Chicken Stew with Honey-Balsamic Squash and Farro (1 to 2 cups) • Greek-inspired Fresh Artichokes with Barley and Tomatoes (1½ to 2 cups) • Roasted Eggplant Fan with Tomatoes, Spelt and Mozzarella (3 cups) • Mediterranean Meatloaf with Fresh Herbs (1½ cups)
Quinoa	Fritatta Muffins for Any Grain (1½ cups) • Baked Feta Fingers in Saffron Quinoa with Tomatoes (2 cups) • Minted Lamb Sliders with Pine Nuts and Currants (1¾ cups) • Minted Summer Couscous with Watermelon and Feta (2 cups) • Quinoa Tabouli with Purslane and Mustard Dressing (3 cups) • Creamy Millet with Greek Yogurt, Avocado, and Basil (2½ cups) • Pomegranate Tomatoes for Any Grain (3 to 3½ cups) • Quinoa Bites with Smoked Salmon and Dill (2½ cup) • Quinoa Salad with Roasted Red Beets, Blood Oranges, and Pomegranate (7 to 8 cups) • Chicken Stew with Honey-Balsamic Squash and Farro (2 to 3 cups) • Greek-inspired Fresh Artichokes with Barley and Tomatoes (1½ to 2 cups) • Roasted Eggplant Fan with Tomatoes, Spelt and Mozzarella (3 cups)
Rice, brown, red, or black	Red Rice Shakshuka with Feta Cheese (3 cups) • Red Rice and Beet Cakes with Honey Mustard (2 cups) • Minted Lamb Sliders with Pine Nuts and Currants (1¾ cups) • Chicken Stew with Honey-Balsamic Squash and Farro (2 to 3 cups) • Greek-inspired Fresh Artichokes with Barley and Tomatoes (1½ to 2 cups)
Rye or Triticale	Artichoke and Spelt Salad with Cara Cara Citrus Boost (2 cups) • Pomegranate Tomatoes for Any Grain (3 to 3½ cups) • Flemish Beef Stew with Caramelized Onions and Rye Berries (2 cups)
Spelt, Farro Grande, or Whole Wheat Berries, (preferably soft)	German-Style Muesli-Yogurt (¼ cup, or more) • Fritatta Muffins for Any Grain (1½ cups) • Spring Salad with Asparagus Coins, Kamut, and Lemon Vinaigrette (2½ cups) • Artichoke and Spelt Salad with Cara Cara Citrus Boost (2 cups) • Kamut Salad with Oranges, Leeks, and Blue Cheese (2 cups) • Shortcut Polenta, Variation (1 cup) • Pomegranate Tomatoes for Any Grain (3 to 3½ cups) • Tangy Farro with Honey-Roasted Kumquats, Feta, and Tomatoes (3 cups) • Flemish Beef Stew with Caramelized Onions and Rye Berries (2 cups) • Roasted One-Pan Chicken with Leeks and Barley (3½ cups) • Greek-inspired Fresh Artichokes with Barley and Tomatoes (1½ to 2 cups) • Roasted Eggplant Fan with Tomatoes, Spelt and Mozzarella (3 cups) • Rum Raisin Ice Cream with Kamut Berries (½ cup)
Wild Rice	Fritatta Muffins for Any Grain (1½ cups) • Warm Wild Rice Salad with Herb-Roasted Mushrooms and Parmesan (2½ cups) • Pomegranate Tomatoes for Any Grain (3 to 3½ cups) • Chicken Stew with Honey-Balsamic Squash and Farro (2 to 3 cups)

one pure aroma

We live in an age of over-the-top, exhilarating, and über-exciting food choices. We learn from blogs, magazines, revered chefs, and food heroes to constantly update, revise, rethink, and reinvent what we put on our plates and into our mouths. Maximize aroma. Marinate meat, fish, tofu, and vegetables. Brown chicken, steak, and pork loin. Roast bones before adding them to stock. Toast, rub, and sprinkle on spices and herbs as if there is no tomorrow.

I am as guilty as anyone. I have a history. I swiped anchovies off plates in Greece as soon as I could reach the rim of the table. I was fascinated by cheese, stinky and blue, long before I entered high school. Needless to say that in my own cooking, I play with salty, sweet, sour, and bitter to pursue equilibrium in a single bite, hoping to make everyone around the table swoon. Parmesan? Check. Anchovies? Check. Soy sauce? Give me more—umami that is, the deep flavor sensation we didn't even know of a decade ago.

Yet, sometimes, I long for a pause. I want to silence the screaming from my pantry. To leave the flavor tricks behind. To forget all I learned about the art of aromatics. Sometimes, I want to be a blind eater. To discover a single ingredient. To harness the darkness of a first bite. As if it were my last. Sometimes, I want my food plain.

It is then that the delirious dance of aromas in my kitchen comes to a stop. That I ignore the battalion of flavor-enhancing tools in my cupboards and cabinets. That I stop searching among my six dozen spice bottles. It is then that my hunt for the perfect oil, vinegar, or blossom water to give dinner the ultimate kick ends. It is then that I change the dial on my stove. Because I don't want my last bite lost in the storm of heat that causes browning.

I don't easily admit to my purist inclinations and single ingredient obsession, given that the food world all around me is singing the praises of toasting, roasting, searing, and browning. Of *umami this* and *more umami that.*

Yet, sometimes, I stop in my tracks. In summer, I cut slices of glistening ripe tomatoes and feel compelled to serve them dripping, on their own. With nothing but a moss-green drizzle of olive oil, leaves of basil, still warm from the sun, and uneven specks of salt. Sometimes, I place a rose-colored piece of salmon in a pan. To poach and linger—infusing it only with the fading scent of lemon zest, bay leaves, and dark peppercorn. Sometimes, I chew on a slice of dark whole grain rye bread with a smear of butter. Slowly, waiting for its sweet starches and beguiling aroma to bolt me into place.

Once I read that Jacques Pépin, a chef I adore, allows nothing but water to be added to his recipe for onion soup. Water. Not stock or broth, just H_2O. I rubbed my eyes and kept reading. Pépin explained that his mother taught him to use ordinary tap water in this recipe.

I too have learned from my mom to allow ingredients to shine in all of their simple glory. To this day, she rarely uses broth in her cooking. Nor a plethora of spices, oils, and vinegars. The determined skill with which she highlights the aroma of a whole fish, a piece of meat, or a vegetable is my inspiration when I need a break from flavor overload. I was reminded of this as I prepared her brussels sprouts recently, the much maligned vegetable that we feel compelled to roast, blacken, and brown, to top with bacon, brown sugar, or fish sauce—hoping that people will finally embrace it.

My mom's brussels sprouts are a revelation in simplicity. She gives the round knobs a boil in salted water, just enough to soften them so they retain a perfect bit of snap. Then she puts them on a platter with a generous pour of her best olive oil, an equally generous squeeze of fresh lemon juice, freshly ground black pepper, and salt. Be prepared to weep.

Greece, of course, has a long tradition of serving spectacular vegetable dishes—from seaweed to amaranth greens—in an almost monastic way, similar to my mom's brussels sprouts. Believe me, if the vegetables are of good quality, you will dance on the table for a plate of these greens. Italians embrace this tradition as well. And while it is currently highly fashionable to crisp every leaf of kale ever grown, and to roast the heck out of carrots, parsnips, and squash, I sometimes place them on my table, the Greek way—there are never any leftovers.

My sometime longing for simplicity extends to my favorite food group, ancient grains. This is why you won't find me bathing them in strong flavors every time. Why I sometimes simmer them just in water, not in stock or broth. Why I sometimes omit the simple step of toasting. While toasting can brilliantly enhance the subtle flavors of grains such as barley, millet, teff, or oats, I sometimes want my grains unadulterated.

It is then that I serve ancient grains pared down to their character. You will find them, for example, in the recipe for Barley with Faint Citrus (page 47) or for Just Tomatoes and Farro Piccolo (page 207). Because my palate wants to hover over the deep earthy scent of barley, the malty sweetness of teff, the subtle acidity of rye berries. I dream of strands of ancient wheat pasta, made from freshly milled flour, a force of nature on my fork, with a dab of butter and a few crushed flakes of salt. I want fluffy golden seeds of millet, cooked in slightly salted water and enveloped in a bit of olive oil. Or chewy textured corn in a soul-hugging polenta, sparkling with auburn flecks from a local mill.

Today, my purist soul is rewarded by the revival of the local grains economy. As more and more American farmers grow grains in areas of the country where they were long abandoned, we can now find fresh local wheat, barley, rye, and more—from New York to Vermont and Maine, from South Carolina to Arizona and California. Farmers take their harvest to local farmers' markets or offer grain shares. And these superb grains, often heirloom varieties, cook up not only splendidly but typically also faster than most of the grains you find on store shelves. They are tender and supple in your mouth, yet memorably rich—you can almost savor the soil the seeds were once sunk in.

Of course, I continue to chase aromas and coax flavors out of any new ingredient I can get my hands on. But I also push the pause button in my perpetual flavor hunt, sometimes. In this book, you will find a celebration of both, of intense aromas, concocted with all of the skills I can muster, and pure simple pleasures with a minimalist approach to seasoning. As always, all I want is ancient grains to shine.

burgundy bulgur with blueberries and orange blossom water

Of all of the grains in my pantry, intensely nutty bulgur is my go-to choice during the week. The fiber-rich grain is pleasing in a humble way yet speedy and unfussy. One morning, I tossed in all the color I could find in my kitchen to paint my bulgur a deep reddish-blue hue.

This recipe gives you two splashy breakfast variations: Unsweetened cranberry juice creates an intense burst of tanginess and a stunning dark fuchsia in your bowl in which the blueberries stand out like jewels. Pomegranate juice lets you start your day on a naturally sweeter note, with a deep burgundy hue—one is as delightful as the other. As an added benefit, this breakfast is an antioxidant powerhouse. If you have orange blossom water in your cupboard, here its fleeting floral and bittersweet scent is a boon. ♒ gluten-free option

To make the bulgur, add the pomegranate juice, bulgur, cranberries, and vanilla to a heavy 3- or 4-quart saucepan and bring to a boil, stirring once or twice. Decrease the heat to maintain a simmer, cover, and cook for 10 minutes. Stir in the blueberries and honey and continue to simmer until the berries are warmed through, about 2 minutes. Gently stir in the zest and the orange blossom water. Taste and adjust with a bit more honey and orange blossom water if you like.

Meanwhile, add the Greek yogurt and the 1 tablespoon honey to a small bowl and beat until smooth.

To finish, divide the bulgur between four bowls. Top each with ¼ cup of yogurt and garnish with pomegranate seeds. Drizzle with more honey if you like. Serve warm.

fine points

If you are new to orange blossom water, start with a little to acquaint yourself.

Leftovers reheat in the microwave—about 1½ minutes on high per serving, stirring once in between.

GLUTEN-FREE Use quinoa, preferably red for a visual treat, instead of bulgur, and cook for 18 to 20 minutes.

VARIATION Use cranberry (instead of pomegranate) juice and 1 to 2 tablespoons honey (instead of 1 teaspoon) for the bulgur, and whole milk or part-skim ricotta (instead of Greek yogurt) to finish.

BULGUR

2 cups unsweetened pomegranate juice

1 cup medium-coarse bulgur

¼ cup dried cranberries

½ teaspoon vanilla extract

1½ cups fresh or frozen blueberries (no need to defrost if using frozen)

1 teaspoon honey, or more as needed

1 teaspoon finely grated orange zest

½ to 1 teaspoon orange blossom water, or more as needed (optional)

TO FINISH

1 cup whole or low-fat Greek yogurt

1 tablespoon honey, or more as needed

¼ cup pomegranate seeds (from about ½ small fruit) or blueberries, for garnish

SERVES 4

saffron millet with toasted almonds and cardamom

About 3½ cups cooked saffron millet (1 recipe, page 135) or plain millet

1½ cups whole milk or low-fat milk, or more as needed

2 tablespoons turbinado sugar

4 tablespoons toasted slivered almonds

2 teaspoons cardamom sugar, for sprinkling (optional; see page 247)

SERVES 4

As warming bowls of breakfast go, this one is picture-perfect with its stunning deep yellow hue from saffron. And once you take a taste, its classic flavor pairings translate into something equally flawless. If you have cooked millet, even the plain grains, in the fridge, this comforting breakfast can be on the table in minutes. But be sure to try it with saffron (see "Sources," page 251) on a special day. The homemade cardamom sugar is a gentle sweet kiss.

gluten-free

Add the cooked millet, 1½ cups of the milk, and the turbinado sugar to a heavy 3-quart saucepan. Bring to a boil over medium-high heat, stirring and breaking up any lumps of millet. Decrease the heat to maintain a brisk simmer and cook, uncovered, until slightly thickened, about 3 minutes.

Add a bit more milk if you like, then spoon into four breakfast bowls. Garnish each serving with 1 tablespoon almonds and about ½ teaspoon cardamom sugar. Serve warm.

fine points

You can prepare single servings with about 1 cup cooked millet, ½ cup milk, and 2 teaspoons sugar in the microwave. Be sure to watch closely, as the millet boils over easily. Add the ingredients to a small bowl and heat on high for 1 minute. Stir, pressing down to dissolve any lumps of millet, and heat again at 50 percent power until it just boils up once, another 1 minute. Or simply heat in a small saucepan over medium heat, stirring as described above.

Leftover single servings reheat well in the microwave as well. Just stir in 1 tablespoon milk or so, and heat on high for about 1½ minutes.

coconut buckwheat porridge with cinnamon and buttered dates

If you have a hard time eating a nourishing breakfast unless it tastes like dessert, this is your bowl. This simple morning fare doesn't have added sweeteners—its heavenly sweetness is entirely natural and comes just from toasting the ingredients and from sizzling a few dates in a dab of butter for a little luxury. I like my porridge unadorned, but sliced bananas on top are a treat.

If you want to create new buckwheat fans, serve this for brunch and top each bowl with a dollop of lightly maple-sweetened whipped cream. gluten-free

Place a heavy 3- or 4-quart saucepan over medium heat and add the buckwheat. Toast, stirring occasionally but watching closely, until the seeds turn golden brown in spots and emit a toasty scent, 3 to 4 minutes.

Add the cinnamon to give it a brief toasting until fragrant, 15 to 20 seconds, stirring continuously (don't walk off) and right away pour in the coconut water (it will splatter!). Add 2 tablespoons of the shredded coconut and a pinch of salt and bring to a boil. Decrease the heat to maintain a simmer, cover, and cook until the buckwheat is tender and the liquid is absorbed, 15 to 17 minutes.

Meanwhile, cut 2 of the dates lengthwise into thin strips and set them aside for garnish. Finely chop the remaining 4 dates, until you have about 3 tablespoons. Melt the butter in a small heavy saucepan over medium-low heat until foamy. Add the chopped dates and cook, undisturbed, until they sizzle, about 1 minute. Stir, sprinkle with the remaining pinch of salt, and remove from the heat. Set aside.

Stir the buttered dates and the lime zest into the buckwheat. If you like a more soupy porridge, add a bit more coconut water.

To finish, spoon the porridge into four bowls. Top with bananas and sprinkle with some of the remaining shredded coconut. Garnish with the slivered dates and a dash of cinnamon and eat warm.

fine points
Coconut water adds a delicate sweet note and is worth looking for here. Light coconut milk may be substituted.

1 cup raw buckwheat groats (do not use kasha)

½ teaspoon ground cinnamon, plus more for garnish

2 cups coconut water, or more as needed

3 to 4 tablespoons unsweetened shredded toasted coconut

2 pinches of fine sea salt

6 small firm dates, preferably Deglet Noor

2 teaspoons unsalted butter

1 teaspoon finely grated lime zest

Sliced bananas, for serving (optional)

SERVES 4

orange-scented amaranth porridge with apricots and pine nuts

AMARANTH

1 cup amaranth grains

3 tablespoons chopped dates (about 4)

½ cinnamon stick (about 1½ inches)

1½ cups boiling water

TO FINISH

1 cup whole milk, or more as needed

3 tablespoons chopped soft dried apricots (see Fine Points)

Pinch of fine sea salt

1 tablespoon honey, or more as needed

1 teaspoon finely grated orange zest

2 tablespoons lightly toasted pine nuts, for garnish

SERVES 4

This simple porridge is an enticing introduction to tiny golden amaranth. It makes for a comforting, creamy breakfast with a gentle crunchiness. The Two-Step Method not only speeds up cooking time on busy mornings but also prevents the grains from becoming overly sticky, a common problem when cooking amaranth. And don't forget to take a look at the minuscule seeds when you add the water—it's beautiful how they sink to the bottom, in blossomlike clusters, with a layer floating on top.

This is a light breakfast I enjoy year-round. In the summer months, I allow a dollop of cool Greek yogurt to melt on top. ⁂ gluten-free

step one

Start the amaranth the night before: Add the amaranth, dates, and cinnamon stick to a heavy 3- or 4-quart saucepan. Pour the boiling water over it, cover, and allow to sit at room temperature overnight (or chill, covered, for up to 2 days).

step two

The next morning, finish the porridge: Add the milk, apricots, and salt to the saucepan, cover, and bring to a boil. Uncover, stir well with a wooden spoon once, decrease the heat to maintain a lively bubble, and cook until the mixture starts to thicken, about 8 minutes. Stir thoroughly, scraping the bottom, and continue cooking at a simmer, stirring often, until the amaranth is creamy, about 2 more minutes. The grains will swell and become translucent but maintain a little crunchiness.

Remove from the heat, discard the cinnamon stick, and stir in the honey and orange zest. Taste and adjust sweetness with a bit more honey and milk, if desired. If you have time, cover and allow to sit for 2 minutes. Spoon into bowls and serve warm, garnished with pine nuts.

fine points

Adding dates in step 1 naturally sweetens the porridge, so you might not need much honey in the end.

Avoid Blenheim apricots, as their sourness can lead to curdling.

If you have time in the morning: Bring the amaranth with 2 cups water and 1 cup milk to a boil and cook, covered, at a low simmer, 20 to 25 minutes, until creamy—add the dates and cinnamon stick from the start and the remaining ingredients in the last few minutes when you stir nonstop. Add a bit more milk if you like.

creamy bulgur with honey and tahini

This supersimple warming breakfast is inspired by the flavors of my Greek childhood. It is easy enough for busy mornings yet still has a nicely indulgent feel to it. Quick-cooking bulgur is nourishing with a slight chewiness, and aromatic tahini adds a creamy quality to make it a treat. I was raised on of this earthy sesame butter, the peanut butter of the eastern Mediterranean.

1½ cups water

1 to 1½ cups whole or low-fat milk, or more as needed

1 cup medium-coarse bulgur

2 tablespoons honey, or more as needed

¾ teaspoon ground cinnamon, plus more for sprinkling

Pinch of fine sea salt

¼ cup tahini

Sesame seeds, for sprinkling (optional)

SERVES 4

Add the water, 1 cup of the milk, the bulgur, 1 tablespoon of the honey, the cinnamon, and salt to a heavy 3- or 4-quart saucepan and bring to a boil, stirring once or twice with a wooden spoon. Decrease the heat to maintain a simmer, cover, and cook until the bulgur is tender with a slight chew, 10 to 15 minutes. Not all of the liquid will be absorbed at this point.

Add the tahini and the remaining 1 tablespoon honey and stir very well, until the ingredients are amalgamated. At this point stir in a bit more milk, ¼ to ½ cup or to your liking. Remove from the heat, taste for sweetness, and stir in a bit more honey if you like.

Spoon the bulgur into four bowls, sprinkle with sesame seeds and a dash of cinnamon, and enjoy warm.

fine points

On Sundays, melting a little heavy cream from my morning coffee into my warm bulgur is mandatory.

MAKE AHEAD You can make the creamy bulgur up to 3 days ahead. It reheats beautifully in the microwave or on the stove top. It will thicken, so you have to add a bit of milk or water, 2 to 3 tablespoons per bowl. Heat on high, in a microwave-safe bowl, until hot, about 1½ minutes per serving, stirring once in between. Or reheat in a small saucepan over medium heat, stirring frequently, until warmed through, about 3 minutes.

cardamom-infused black rice porridge
with blueberries and pistachios

BLACK RICE

¾ cup black rice

2 whole green cardamom pods (optional; see Fine Points)

1½ cups boiling water

PORRIDGE

1 cup half-and-half, plus more as needed

3 tablespoons maple syrup, or more as needed

¾ teaspoon ground cardamom

1 cup fresh or frozen blueberries (do not thaw when using frozen)

4 to 6 tablespoons pomegranate seeds (from about ½ fruit), for garnish (optional)

2 tablespoons lightly toasted chopped plain pistachios, for garnish

SERVES 4 TO 6

fine points

Whole milk can be used instead of half-and-half, but the porridge won't be as lush.

If not using cardamom pods, increase the ground cardamom to 1 teaspoon.

Gently reheat over medium heat, adding about a scant ¼ cup of milk per serving. Or add 1 serving to a microwave-safe bowl and heat on high, covered, for about 1 minute, stirring once in between.

In this glorious speedy porridge, my new home of New England meets my husband's India with a detour to China. The starring role belongs to soft-textured black rice, scented with cardamom and intermingled with wild Maine blueberries and a touch of maple syrup. A few glistening pomegranate seeds and the green hue of pistachios make this a feast for your eyes as well as your taste buds.

Black rice, also called purple rice, is a whole grain rice with a mesmerizing gentle chew. Furthermore, it turns a deep burgundy when cooked—no wonder it was once reserved for the tables of China's emperors. My favorite brand is from Lotus Foods, which specializes in sustainable heirloom rice varieties. Their trademarked Forbidden Rice has become more widely available and is worth seeking out (see "Sources," page 251). gluten-free

step one

Start the rice the night before: Add the rice and cardamom pods to a large heavy saucepan. Pour over the boiling water, cover, and let sit at room temperature overnight (or chill, covered, for up to 2 days).

step two

The next morning, make the porridge: Add 1 cup of the half-and-half, the maple syrup, and ground cardamom to the saucepan with the rice, cover, and bring to a boil over medium-high heat. Uncover, decrease the heat to retain a lively simmer, and cook, stirring once in a while, until the rice is tender with a slight chew, 5 to 7 minutes. Remove the cardamom pods, if you like (in India I learned not to bother!). Add the blueberries and simmer gently until they are warmed through, 1 to 2 minutes more.

To finish, add ¼ to ½ cup more half-and-half to reach a consistency you like. Taste for sweetness and adjust with a bit more maple syrup if needed. Divide between four to six breakfast bowls. Top each bowl with 1 tablespoon of the pomegranate seeds and 1 teaspoon of the pistachios. Serve warm.

my muesli, a formula

3 cups rolled oats or any other grain flakes such as rye, barley, quinoa, spelt, wheat, or a mixture (gluten-free if desired; see "Fine Points," page 41)

¾ cup chopped nuts such as almonds, walnuts, hazelnuts, or a mixture

½ cup seeds such as sesame, flax, pumpkin, or a mixture

1 cup chopped dried fruit such as apricots, figs, dates, prunes, or raisins

Pinch of fine sea salt

MAKES ABOUT TEN ½-CUP SERVINGS

I have never understood why people are willing to spend top dollar for muesli. Of course sometimes our shelves are bare. But for me making muesli is really an everyday opportunity to clean out my pantry from any leftover bits of rolled cereals, nuts, seeds, and dried fruit—and to get a prime breakfast in return. I might chop up a few forlorn dried figs or apricots, toss in a handful of forgotten raisins from a jar in the back, add the remaining slivered almonds I bought for a cake, and use up the rye flakes from making bread last week. Making muesli is a great way to get creative—in fact, some of my best mueslis were the result of such cleanouts. I have since learned to always write the best ones down.

Here is a basic ratio of ingredients you can use to get started. Vary it to your preference by adding more or less nuts or dried fruit. Or make a dried fruit muesli or a pure nut muesli someday. And then you can start selling it!
🐛 gluten-free option

Add all of the ingredients to a large bowl or combine them directly in a tall glass jar with a tight-fitting lid, shaking or stirring with a soup spoon. Muesli will last at room temperature for at least 4 weeks.

There are as many ways to enjoy muesli for breakfast as there are people in the German-speaking areas of Switzerland, Germany, and Austria.

Classic Muesli: Add ½ cup of the mixture to a small bowl and stir in ¼ cup yogurt, kefir, milk, or cream (yes!). Cover and place in the fridge overnight to soften the grain flakes. In the morning, stir in a freshly grated apple (preferably unpeeled), top with more fruit if you like, and squeeze on a bit of fresh lemon juice.

My Everyday Muesli: Add ½ cup of the mixture to a small bowl and pour about ¼ cup boiling water over it to soften the grain flakes. After 5 minutes or so, add a bit of whole milk, buttermilk, kefir, or yogurt, top with any fresh fruit on hand, and *Guten Appetit*! On Sundays, I often add a dollop of freshly whipped cream.

anise-scented muesli with toasted pine nuts and almonds

Muesli is a staple in our house and I always make it on the fly, from leftover tidbits in my kitchen (see "My Muesli, A Formula," opposite). However, sometimes tossing this and that into a Mason jar and calling it muesli ends up a splendid little concoction, and this is what happened here. Then I went further and lightly toasted the nuts with a few spices, adding a luxurious touch to this pedestrian Alpine breakfast.

I always leave a soup spoon inside my muesli jar because ingredients tend to settle—the spoon allows me to mix them through before removing a portion.

gluten-free option

Have a plate at the ready next to the stove. Add the almonds, pine nuts, and sunflower seeds to a medium skillet over medium heat and cook, stirring frequently, until they are just lightly toasted, about 2 minutes. Add the anise seeds, and toast, stirring all the while, until fragrant, about 30 seconds. Sprinkle with the cinnamon and stir for 20 more seconds just to unleash the aroma. (Be on alert all the while as to not burn the nuts or spices!) Immediately scrape the mixture onto the plate, sprinkle with the salt, and allow to cool completely.

Once the nut mixture has cooled, combine all of the ingredients in a large bowl or add them straight to a tall glass jar or other container with a tight-fitting lid. Stir to combine. Muesli will last at room temperature for at least 4 weeks.

½ cup slivered almonds

¼ cup pine nuts or chopped raw pistachios

¼ cup sunflower seeds

1 teaspoon whole anise seeds (see page 44) or whole fennel seeds

¼ teaspoon ground cinnamon

Pinch of fine sea salt

3 cups old-fashioned rolled oats or a mixture of rolled cereal

½ cup dark raisins or chopped sweet Turkish apricots (¼-inch pieces)

MAKES NINE ½-CUP SERVINGS

fine points

This muesli uses only one type of dried fruit to highlight the combination of toasted nuts and spices.

Here are some of my favorite rolled cereal mixtures: Use 2 cups supremely chewy rye flakes and 1 cup tender quick-cooking rolled oats. Or combine 1½ cups old-fashioned rolled oats with 1½ cups barley flakes. Or simply use a store-bought rolled cereal mixture, which are becoming more widely available.

GLUTEN-FREE Mix 2 cups gluten-free rolled oats and 1 cup quinoa flakes.

breakfast polentina with strawberries, poppy seeds, and lime

Serve this eye-catching bowl of golden cornmeal on a chilly morning in late spring when the first strawberries show up in stores. Italians cherish their polenta. Polentina is a creamier version typically served in the morning. This is a nourishing breakfast with the sunny feeling of dessert. On lazy Sundays, I go all the way and top my bowl with a dollop of softly whipped cream. ✹ gluten-free

---

step one

Start the polentina the night before: Add the polenta and the poppy seeds to a large heavy saucepan and whisk in the boiling water. Cover and let sit at room temperature overnight (or chill, covered, for up to 2 days).

step two

The next morning, finish the polentina: Add the milk, 2 tablespoons of the honey, and the salt to the saucepan with the polenta and whisk well to loosen, breaking up any clumps. Bring to a boil over medium-high heat, whisking occasionally. Cook, whisking continuously and adjusting the heat to maintain a gentle bubble until the mixture thickens, about 2 minutes (beware of splatters!).

Decrease the heat to low to maintain a simmer. Cover and cook, stirring vigorously with a wooden spoon every couple of minutes and scraping the bottom until the polenta becomes creamy and thick (cornmeal remains a little softer), 10 to 12 minutes. The polenta granules will swell and become tender, and the polenta should retain an appealing toothsomeness.

Meanwhile, add the strawberries to a small bowl and stir in the 2 teaspoons honey and the lime juice, tasting and adding more of either to adjust. Set aside to macerate, stirring once or twice, while the cornmeal simmers.

Remove from the heat, stir in the lime zest, and add a bit more milk if you like a looser polentina. Taste for sweetness and adjust with honey as needed. Spoon into four breakfast bowls, top with the strawberries, arranging them like flower petals in the center of the bowl. Or, if you like more fruit, just pile them on. Serve at once.

POLENTINA

1 cup (5.5 ounces) polenta or stone-ground cornmeal, preferably medium grind

2 tablespoons poppy seeds

1½ cups boiling water

TO FINISH

1½ cups whole or low-fat milk (1 cup for cornmeal), or more as needed

2 tablespoons plus 2 teaspoons honey, or more as needed

Pinch of fine sea salt

1½ cups (6 ounces) quartered fresh strawberries, preferably organic (see page 248)

½ to 1 teaspoon lime juice

1 teaspoon finely grated lime zest, preferably organic

SERVES 4

fine points

For types of polenta, see page 8 and be sure to use weight measures as volume can vary widely, especially when using cornmeal.

Adding hot milk in step two will further speed up your breakfast.

Fresh strawberries are a nice contrast on top, but sliced bananas or blueberries work well too.

If you have leftover cooked wheat berries or farro, add ½ cup with the zest for a nice chew.

porridge in pink with raspberries and greek yogurt

STEEL-CUT OATS

1 cup steel-cut oats (gluten-free if desired)

¼ cup dried cranberries

1 (2-inch) cinnamon stick (optional)

1½ cups boiling water

PORRIDGE

1 cup whole or low-fat milk

1 cup water

1½ cups fresh or frozen raspberries (no need to thaw if frozen), plus a few for garnish

¼ cup dried barberries, sour cherries, or cranberries (see "Sources," page 251)

1 to 2 tablespoons turbinado sugar, plus extra for sprinkling

Pinch of fine sea salt

1 to 1½ cups whole or low-fat Greek yogurt

About 2 tablespoons chopped lightly toasted shelled pistachios

Ground cinnamon, for sprinkling

SERVES 4 TO 6

fine points

Adding dried fruit in two stages releases some of their sweetness overnight, while the fruit added in the morning retains an appealing chew.

Pedestrian steel-cut oats don't have the color of my dreams. But what if they had a magnificent hue? That's why one day I decided to go overboard with raspberries and turn my everyday oatmeal into a pink sensation. Add a dollop of tangy Greek yogurt, and this warm breakfast will power everyone in your family through the morning. Even your kids might be fascinated enough by the bold color to eat a good amount of fruit without having to be prodded.

I never hesitate to use frozen berries, especially during the cooler months of the year when they are not in season—I always stash a few bags in my freezer. If you can get your hands on Iranian barberries (see "Sources," page 251), try them here; their brazen sourness is unsurpassed. The Two-Step Method is my favorite way of cooking steel-cut oats, resulting in tender and creamy grains with just the right chewiness in a snap. The color depends on the oats—sometimes bold, sometimes subdued. ◢ gluten-free

step one

Start the steel-cut oats the night before: Add the oats, cranberries, and cinnamon stick to a heavy 4-quart saucepan. Pour over the boiling water, stir once, cover, and let sit at room temperature overnight (or chill, covered, for up to 2 days).

step two

The next morning, make the porridge: Add the milk, water, raspberries, barberries, 1 tablespoon of the sugar, and the salt to the saucepan with the oats. Partially cover and bring to a boil over medium-high heat, stirring occasionally. Uncover, decrease the heat to maintain a steady but gentle bubble, and cook, stirring occasionally, until the oats are creamy but still slightly chewy, about 7 minutes.

To finish, remove the cinnamon stick (if you haven't used one, add 1 teaspoon ground cinnamon). Taste for sweetness and add the remaining tablespoon of sugar if you like. Divide the oatmeal among four to six bowls. Top each with about ¼ cup of the yogurt and 1 teaspoon of the pistachios. Garnish with raspberries, a sprinkle of turbinado sugar, and a dash of ground cinnamon. Serve right away.

last-minute porridge in pink

Sometimes life is so fast that I forget to start my steel-cut oats the night before. While they don't have the same lovely mouthfeel, quick-cooking steel-cut oats (see "Sources," page 251) are a great last-minute alternative. For total liquid (water and milk combined), use package directions.

Add the water, milk, oats, raspberries, cranberries, 1 tablespoon of the sugar, the cinnamon, and salt to a heavy 4-quart saucepan and bring to a boil over medium-high heat, stirring occasionally with a wooden spoon. Reduce the heat to maintain a lively bubble and cook, uncovered and stirring often, until the oats are creamy but maintain a little chewiness, 5 to 7 minutes. Depending on your preference, add more milk and stir in the remaining tablespoon of sugar.

Divide between four to six bowls and top with a dollop of yogurt. Sprinkle with a few raspberries and pistachios. Sprinkle with a bit more sugar if you like and a dash of cinnamon.

CINNAMON VERSUS REAL CINNAMON

If you can get your hands on real Ceylon cinnamon, also called Mexican cinnamon (Cinnamomum zeylanicum), please do. After I moved to the United States, I never understood why I couldn't re-create the flavorful milk rice of my Greek grandma, always served with a sprinkle of cinnamon. Only when I became a food writer did I learn that most cinnamon in the United States is of the cassia variety. Cassia is not real cinnamon but the bark of a tree with a similar flavor. It has a stronger yet more one-dimensional aroma. Take my word for it: using real cinnamon will give you a whole new appreciation for this intriguing spice.

1 or 2 cups water, depending on the brand (see headnote)

1 cup whole or low-fat milk

1 cup quick-cooking steel-cut oats

1½ cups fresh or frozen raspberries (no need to thaw if frozen), plus a few for garnish

½ cup dried cranberries or sour cherries or a mixture

1 to 2 tablespoons turbinado sugar, or more as needed, plus extra for sprinkling

1 teaspoon ground cinnamon, plus more for sprinkling

Pinch of fine sea salt

1 to 1½ cups whole or low-fat Greek yogurt

About 2 tablespoons lightly toasted chopped shelled pistachios (optional)

SERVES 4 TO 6

minute-oatmeal puffs with anise and grapes

DRY OATMEAL MIX

2 cups old-fashioned rolled oats (use gluten-free if desired) or mixed rolled grains

⅔ cup golden raisins

2 teaspoons anise or fennel seeds

1¼ teaspoons baking powder

MAKES 1 SERVING, WITH ENOUGH DRY OATMEAL MIX TO SERVE 8

PER OATMEAL PUFF

⅓ cup or ½ cup whole milk or low-fat milk (see "Fine Points")

1 tablespoon maple syrup

⅛ teaspoon vanilla extract

1 large egg

A few fresh grapes, plus a few for garnish

Ground cinnamon, for dusting

Until a few years ago, I had never owned a microwave. I have since learned to appreciate its convenience and speed for certain tasks in the kitchen. This breakfast on the go, fortified with an egg, is one of them. It is a warming anise-scented oatmeal and an omelet all rolled into one—perfect for chilly winter days when you need something real to carry you through the morning.

My recipe is inspired by the countless mug cakes and mug muffins that have been making the rounds in the blogosphere. Ultimately, the idea won me over because this breakfast puffs up adorably in your morning mug. Even with company, I prefer making individual servings because they look so cute.

gluten-free

To prepare the dry oatmeal mix, add all of the ingredients to a bowl and combine well with a fork. Transfer to an airtight container and store at room temperature for up to 4 weeks.

step one
The night before, combine ⅓ cup of the dry oatmeal mix with the milk, maple syrup, and vanilla in a microwave-safe mug or bowl (11- to 14-ounce capacity) and chill, covered.

step two
The next morning, add the egg to a small bowl and beat with a fork until well blended, about 30 seconds. Gently stir into the mug with the oat mixture to combine. Stir in 3 or 4 grapes.

Place the mug in the microwave and cook on high for 1 minute 20 seconds—the oatmeal will rise beautifully, maybe briefly above the rim, but not spill over. Insert a cake tester or wooden skewer into the center; it should come out clean. Otherwise cook 10 seconds more and check again. Allow to sit for a few minutes; then top with a few more grapes, dust with cinnamon, and spoon in.

fine points
Soaking the oats in milk overnight makes for a softer, more appealing texture. Less milk (⅓ cup) gives a firmer spoonful while ½ cup milk results in a creamier breakfast.

Whole anise seeds add a delicate note of sweet licorice. Milder fennel seeds can be used instead.

VARIATIONS I enjoy dried figs with fresh pear, or combine dried cranberries and fresh apples, dried apples and fresh blueberries, or chopped prunes with bananas.

one good grain: barley with faint citrus

Sometimes, I long for my grains to emerge from the pot with the elusive scent of citrus orchards. During long car rides when my parents had only Byzantine churches in mind, a stop in the midst of fragrant lemon or orange groves, heavy with fruit, was paradise. Or pretty close.

With this recipe, I try to infuse whole grain berries with the perfume of those orchards. Their scent is captivating in a slow way, fleeting, and faint. It is an experiment with which I remind myself how special certain aromas are that we take for granted today (see "One Pure Aroma," page 28).

I make these grains on a quiet day for use in fruity desserts or toss a handful into a leafy green salad. But by far my favorite way to use them, during the warmer months, is in a simple German-style muesli-yogurt (see page 48).

2½ cups water

1 cup hulled (whole grain) barley, soaked overnight and drained

Peel of 1 large lemon, preferably organic (in several strips, about ½ to ¾ inch wide, with a total length of about 20 inches; a lacing of white pith is fine)

1 bay leaf

Good pinch of salt

MAKES ABOUT 2¾ CUPS SCENTED GRAINS

Add the water, barley, lemon peel, bay leaf, and salt to a heavy 2-quart saucepan and bring to a boil over medium-high heat. Decrease the heat to maintain a simmer, cover, and cook until the grains are tender with a slight chewiness, 50 to 60 minutes.

Remove the pot from the heat, cover, and allow to steam for at least 10 to 15 minutes, or until completely cool. With the back of a spoon, press onto as many peels as you can easily find to release all of the lemon scent. Drain any remaining liquid. If you don't need it right away, chill the barley—the flavors will stay subtle but intensify. I often remove the bay leaf and the peels only when I'm ready to eat, as they continue to infuse the grain.

fine points

Any citrus is lovely here, from oranges to tangerines. To pack the most punch, look for fresh and fully ripe fruit. (The fruit should feel heavy in your hand with tight skin. Smell it while rubbing the skin: it should give off a nice scent.)

VARIATION If you can find fresh local grains, even better, because they are softer and the scent can penetrate the kernels. Soft wheat berries are lovely as well, or try spelt, Kamut, or emmer wheat (farro).

german-style muesli-yogurt

1 cup plain whole milk yogurt

¼ cup cooked scented barley or other grain, or more as needed (see recipe page 47)

2 tablespoons finely chopped dried figs, apricots, or golden raisins

Maple syrup, preferably Grade B, or good-quality honey, for drizzling

1 fresh fig, cut into wedges (optional)

MAKES 1 SOUL-LIFTING SERVING

Germans are pretty crazy about muesli, I sometimes think maybe even more so than the Swiss. The invention of muesli-yogurt was only a matter of time. It is yogurt with some whole grain berries, raisins, or other dried fruit. Muesli-yogurt is a treat, refreshing, comforting, *and* good for you, and nothing could be easier to make at home. With the scented grains it becomes a special snack or breakfast.

From all of the types of widely available yogurt, nothing comes close to Trader Joe's organic whole milk European-style yogurt. Its rich, balanced creaminess is sensational. Even my own homemade yogurt bows down in front of it, and I recommend it here.

Add the yogurt to a bowl. Top with the grains and dried fruit, and drizzle with the sweetener of your choice, but not too much. You can always add more. Top with the fresh fig.

Spoon in and chew on some of the scented grains. Take note, then stir a bit more, and slowly pull up your next spoon. Linger on the toothsome kernels and dried fruit, now enveloped in a white, creamy coat. Who needs dessert?

fine points

VARIATION Any leftover cooked whole grains are splendid here, e.g., whole wheat berries, spelt, Kamut, emmer (farro), and einkorn.

slow mornings
brunch, lunch, and breakfast-for-dinner

cooking without knife skills

If you come to my house on a Tuesday night, don't expect to be served a perfectly composed dinner plate, restaurant-style. Much of my weekday cooking is fast, easy, and restrained—a quick wholesome pasta, fish and vegetables with leftover grains, or a toss-it-all-in soup or grains salad. My cooking during the week is often improvised and so low-key that, as a professional food writer, I should be embarrassed. But I believe in home cooking. I was raised on it, and today I pride myself on it.

So how do I cook every day? Mostly I prepare modest and practical meals, trying to bring dinner to the table without exhausting myself. I never went to cooking school. I learned by doing, mostly by failure. And I reserve complicated and more elaborate preparations for a slow weekend when I am bored or when I look for a challenge. I learned much of it from my mom, but also from observing home cooks the world over when I travel. Because people who cook to feed themselves do essentially the same everywhere.

Cooking every day is a compromise and a lesson in simplicity. During the week, I have no time to cook up complicated sauces or spend an hour washing piles of dishes in the sink. Instead I rely on the basics: my hands and a few sturdy pots and pans. So, if you struggle to prepare a home-cooked meal more often, here are a few things I hope will ease your life at the stove. It is a no-nonsense laundry list of things you don't need to worry about.

First, please don't fret about your knife skills. You don't have to attend classes on wielding large chef's knives to become a solid home cook. My mom doesn't have any knife skills and, boy, does she cook. Neither does my Indian mother-in-law, who has prepared elaborate meals for a crowd of thirty all her life, with not much more than a beat-up paring knife.

I must admit that I have no knife skills myself. None whatsoever. I tried to hide this when my first cookbook came out. I have since learned not to pretend anymore. I cut my onions differently than you learn in cooking school, but fast and, may I add, just as well. Certainly good enough for dinner. I never went out of my way to practice cutting carrots or potatoes into chunks of similar size. I simply learned it over time *by doing*, especially when I noticed that differently sized pieces cooked unevenly. So just get started with any knife you have. And if you want to learn to use a chef's knife, go ahead. Just know that it's not mandatory.

In my kitchen, the humble fork and a solid whisk are the blending tools of choice. I perform most tasks working out of a bowl, small or big, and using my hands. It is easy, fast, and efficient—and the cleanup? Minimal. I beat dips, omelets, dressing, and more with a fork. I often use a fork to bring together dough for soda bread, scones and batter for pancakes (see, for example, "Farro Scones with Almonds, Apples, and Thyme," page 57, and "Irish Soda Bread with Amaranth, Cranberries, and Rosemary," page 68). In fact, it is sometimes the best mixing tool because it forces me to be gentle. Whipping cream, anyone? I used to pull out a hand blender until I bought myself a good balloon whisk and found the task easy and enjoyable. Yes, I find it satisfying to do things by hand. I marvel every time I travel to see how many things we can actually do by hand in the kitchen.

As a result, my food processor doesn't get a workout every day. Not because I don't appreciate the efficiency and sheer force of it. I love using a food processor to grind half a pound of nuts, or to see pie dough come together in a cinch. But why blend 5 tablespoons of tahini, a few tablespoons of water, and a drizzle of lemon juice in it? Yes, it is fast but not so fast—if you add the washing up, the clutter in the sink, the space it eats in the dishwasher to all of the other things you have to do—all for a little sauce? And, until very recently, a hand mixer and my hands did all the work of a baker, mixing and kneading everything from breads to rolls, cakes, and more.

I love greens as much as anyone, but they too don't get the red-carpet treatment on a Monday. Do you feel pressured to blanch vegetables and cool them down in an ice bath for intense green color? I used to. Not anymore. All in all, I can count on two hands how often I have blanched vegetables in my life. I have no time for this extra step during the week, and it creates one more pot and one more bowl to wash. In my kitchen, I just sauté my broccoli rabe or my broccoli, and then I add a splash of water or broth to the skillet to allow the vegetables to soften, and then I enjoy my meal—in a subtle green. It always tastes perfect.

I'm rather plain and old-fashioned too with my pans: for weeknight cooking, I rely on a set of three good-quality pots and a couple of cast-iron skillets (see "Equipment," page 20). I long ago gave up on fancy skillets with special coatings or beautiful pots that need extra care and attention. My cast-iron skillets are essentially indestructible and can do anything and more. Their heavy bottoms deliver great browning over high heat and nice even cooking, perfect for frying fish and steak. Admittedly, browning a steak first in a skillet and finishing it in the oven will bring you perfection. Yet normally this is one step too much. Plus, it uses a lot more energy for a simple weeknight meal. I reserve this double take for special occasions or for a pricey piece of meat where the even heat of the oven matters.

Last but not least, my favorite food group, grains. During the week you won't find me placing spelt berries or barley in the oven on large baking sheets to toast to perfection. Of course I enjoy coaxing flavor out of my grains, on Sundays! But when I'm hungry, they just go into a pot of water or broth, with some olive oil or butter and a pinch of salt, and I'm as happy as anyone. Because if your grains are fresh, they taste mighty good pretty much left alone.

In this spirit, I very much hope you will start cooking, more often, with confidence and courage, knowing that your skills will improve over time—and by cooking. You will learn what works for *you* in *your* kitchen. What tasks you enjoy and which less so. What you want to streamline and how. And I hope you won't hesitate to try and to do it your own way.

I was raised by a mom who wanted to do *anything but* be in the kitchen. Yet she has demanding taste buds that made her into a marvelous home cook. I learned from her how to cook, and *fast*. And good enough to please my taste buds. Now I hope you cook, often. And keep it simple.

oatmeal butternut pancakes with browned buttered nuts

These delectable pancakes with their saffron hue from roasted autumn squash are such a fantastic way to eat your oatmeal—stacked high on the table. They are thick, nourishing, and substantial, making them hard to resist, even more so with the browned buttered nuts. Best of all, you can assemble them in minutes in a food processor.

Serve them with a dollop of Greek yogurt or ricotta and a drizzle of maple syrup. I like adding these to a brunch table in the colder months of the year. In my house they make great dinner fare too. ~~~ gluten-free

step one

Start the batter the night before, or at least 30 minutes ahead: Add the oats, nutmeg, baking powder, baking soda, and salt to the bowl of a food processor fitted with a steel blade. Process until you have oat flour, about 30 seconds.

Tip in the eggs and the squash puree and pour in the milk, syrup, and vanilla. Pulse until just blended and no chunks of squash remain, about five 1-second pulses. Transfer the batter to a large bowl, cover with plastic wrap, and allow to sit at room temperature for 30 minutes (or chill overnight).

step two

When you are ready to make the pancakes, prepare the nuts. Add the butter to a 10-inch skillet or a medium saucepan, preferably stainless steel, and melt over medium heat. Cook, watching attentively, until the color turns golden brown, the butter smells deeply nutty, and the bottom of the pan fills with brown specks, 3 to 5 minutes. Add the pecans, almonds, sesame seeds, nigella seeds, Aleppo pepper, and cayenne and cook, stirring, until fragrant, about 1 minute. Immediately transfer the buttered nuts to a small serving bowl and sprinkle with salt to taste.

Place a wire rack inside a large rimmed baking sheet and transfer the sheet to the center rack of the oven—this will keep the pancakes from getting soggy. Preheat the oven to 200°F. Check the consistency of the batter. It will have thickened considerably. Gently stir in a few tablespoons more milk with a spatula until you have a thick, pourable consistency.

To finish the pancakes, heat a large cast-iron skillet or a griddle pan over medium heat. Lightly grease the pan with olive oil. When a drop of water sizzles and briskly evaporates on the surface, add ¼ cup batter per pancake, leaving space in between so you can flip them. Cook until the edges of the pancakes start to look dry and the

PANCAKES

2 cups plus 3 tablespoons (200 g) old-fashioned rolled oats (gluten-free if needed)

1¼ teaspoons ground nutmeg, preferably freshly ground

1 teaspoon baking powder

¼ teaspoon baking soda

½ teaspoon fine sea salt

4 large eggs

1 cup (225 g) mashed roasted kabocha or butternut squash

¾ cup whole or low-fat milk, plus up to ¼ cup more as needed

1 tablespoon maple syrup, plus more for serving

½ teaspoon vanilla extract

BROWNED BUTTERED NUTS

¼ cup (½ stick) unsalted butter

¼ cup coarsely chopped toasted pecans

¼ cup toasted slivered almonds

1 tablespoon golden or black sesame seeds

1 tablespoon nigella seeds (see page 248) or more sesame seeds

½ teaspoon Aleppo pepper, or ⅛ teaspoon dried chile flakes

Pinch of cayenne pepper

Fine sea salt

8 ounces soft mild goat cheese or cream cheese (optional), cut into ½-inch slices

MAKES 12 TO 14 PANCAKES, TO SERVE 4 TO 6

continued >

bottoms turn golden brown, 2 to 3 minutes. Decrease the heat to medium-low if they brown too quickly. Flip and cook until golden and puffy, almost 2 minutes more. Transfer to the baking sheet in the oven to keep warm. Do not stack. Continue until all of the batter is used, greasing the pan lightly in between as necessary.

Serve each pancake with a slice of goat cheese and a teaspoon or two of the buttered nuts on top, passing the maple syrup around.

fine points

If you have leftover oven-roasted squash, this is a great place to use it. If your squash is a little blah, you may add a bit more maple syrup to round out the flavor.

Omit the hot spices, Aleppo and cayenne, when making this for children.

MAKE AHEAD As in so many whole grain recipes, allowing the batter to rest overnight improves the texture and makes for a more enticing soft pancake.

You can make the buttered nuts 1 day ahead. Reheat in a small heavy pot over low heat, or in a microwave-safe bowl at 50 percent power, until the butter is hot and the nuts are warm, about 3 minutes, stirring a few times in between.

farro scones with almonds, apples, and thyme

British-style scones are in a class of their own. More crumbly and less sweet than their American cousins, I could eat them all day long. I created these lemon and thyme-scented treats to let the mild sweet wheatiness of emmer flour (better known as farro) shine. Bluebird Grain Farms sent me samples for testing, and if you have the time, seek out their remarkable American-grown flour (see "Sources," page 251). These scones, not overly sweet, have a bit of texture from ground almonds and a pleasant chewiness from dried apples. Serve them for brunch, with jam or with a selection of cheese and perhaps a glass of Prosecco or a fruity dry Riesling. Of course, they are just as enticing on their own with a dab of butter.

Position a rack in the center of the oven and preheat to 400°F. Lightly butter a baking sheet or line with parchment paper. Lightly flour your work surface.

Whisk together the emmer flour, almond meal, sugar, baking powder, and salt in a large mixing bowl (be sure to loosen any clumped almonds with your fingers). Scatter the butter on top. Using a pastry blender or your fingers, quickly rub the butter into the flour mixture until it resembles coarse meal with some uneven pebbles. Stir in the apples. Make a well in the center.

Add the cream and the applesauce to a 2-cup liquid measure; beat in the zest and the thyme with a fork. Add the mixture to the center of the flour mixture. Gently combine with a fork or fold in with a rubber spatula until a rough patchy and shaggy dough just comes together. If a fair bit of flour remains, add cream by the tablespoon to just gather the dough with your lightly floured hands. Give the dough four to six gentle turns inside the bowl.

Cut the dough in half and transfer to the work surface. Pat each half into a 5-inch circle, about 1 inch high. Using a long, sharp knife, dipped in flour, cut each circle into 6 small wedges. Be sure to cut straight down, and forcefully. Place the wedges 2 inches apart on the baking sheet. Brush the scones with cream and sprinkle with a bit of sugar.

Bake until the scones turn golden brown with brown edges and are firm to the touch, rotating the baking sheet halfway, 16 to 18 minutes. Transfer to a wire rack to cool a bit. Eat warm or at room temperature.

2 cups minus 1 tablespoon (225 g) whole grain emmer (farro) flour

½ cup plus 1 tablespoon (50 g) lightly packed almond meal (see page 247)

2 tablespoons (25 g) sugar, plus extra for sprinkling

2½ teaspoons baking powder

½ teaspoon fine sea salt

5 tablespoons (70 g) chilled unsalted butter, cut into ½-inch pieces

½ cup (40 g) chopped dried apples

½ cup chilled heavy cream, plus a few tablespoons more as needed, plus extra for brushing

¼ cup unsweetened applesauce

1 tablespoon finely grated lemon zest (from about 2 lemons)

1 tablespoon fresh thyme leaves

MAKES 12 MINI SCONES

fine points

Whole grain spelt flour may be used, or a mixture of white whole wheat flour and whole wheat pastry flour—for best results be sure to weigh the flour.

You can add up to ¼ cup sugar (instead of 2 tablespoons) if you like a sweeter scone.

MAKE AHEAD You can prepare scones the night before, cover with plastic wrap, and chill—but don't yet brush them with cream and sprinkle with sugar. Do this the next morning and bake in a preheated oven straight from the fridge. They will need a few extra minutes. The scones freeze well for 1 month.

lemon pancakes with millet and amaranth

If you like fluffy pancakes, these are for you. If you like wholesome pancakes with appealing texture, these are for you as well—because these breakfast treats are a hybrid of sorts, surprisingly delicate yet with satisfying character. Leftover cooked amaranth, slipped in on a whim, is responsible for the light, nourishing quality.

We enjoy these with ricotta and a drizzle of honey. But I find them equally tempting with Greek yogurt, or with butter and bittersweet yuzu marmalade.

step one

Start the batter the night before or at least 30 minutes ahead: Whisk together the whole wheat flour, millet flour, baking powder, baking soda, and salt in a large bowl. Make a well in the center. In a medium bowl, whisk together the buttermilk, eggs, honey, olive oil, zest, and vanilla until blended. Pour the buttermilk mixture into the center of the dry ingredients and stir with a spatula or wooden spoon until just combined—the batter should have many lumps. Using a fork, loosen the amaranth if needed and gently stir in. Do not overmix. The batter will be thick. Let it sit at room temperature for 30 minutes to soften the bran (or chill, covered, overnight or up to 24 hours).

step two

When you are ready to make the pancakes, place a wire rack inside a large rimmed baking sheet and transfer the sheet to the center rack of the oven—this will keep the pancakes from getting soggy. Preheat the oven to 200°F.

To finish the pancakes, heat a griddle pan (see Fine Points) over medium heat. Lightly grease the pan with olive oil. When a drop of water sizzles and briskly evaporates on the surface, add ⅓ cup batter per pancake, leaving enough space in between to flip them. Cook, undisturbed, until the edges of the pancakes start to look dry, bubbles break on the surface, and the bottoms turn golden, a scant 2 minutes. Flip and cook until golden, about 1½ minutes more. Lower the heat a bit if the pancakes brown too quickly. Transfer to the oven, for up to 20 minutes, but do not stack the pancakes. Continue until all of the batter is used, greasing the pan lightly in between as necessary.

Serve the pancakes with ricotta and a drizzle of honey on top.

1½ cups (180 g) white whole wheat flour or whole grain spelt flour

½ cup (60 g) whole grain millet flour

1½ teaspoons baking powder

½ teaspoon baking soda

¼ teaspoon fine sea salt

1½ cups low-fat buttermilk, well shaken

3 large eggs, lightly beaten

2 tablespoons honey, plus more for serving

¼ cup extra-virgin olive oil or vegetable oil

2 tablespoons finely grated lemon zest (from about 3 lemons)

1 teaspoon vanilla extract

1 cup cooked amaranth (see page 22)

Whole milk or part-skim ricotta, for serving

MAKES ABOUT TWELVE 5½-INCH PANCAKES, TO SERVE 6

fine points

I like these pancakes a bit more sizable—a griddle pan gives you enough space to flip them. Otherwise use ¼ cup batter for about eighteen 4-inch pancakes.

overnight waffles with teff, coriander, and caramelized pineapples

1 cup plus 1 tablespoon (120 g) whole grain spelt flour or white whole wheat flour

¾ cup plus 1 tablespoon (115 g) whole grain teff flour

3 tablespoons coriander sugar (see page 247), plus extra for sprinkling

1½ teaspoons instant or rapid-rise yeast

¼ teaspoon fine sea salt

2 large eggs

2¼ cups whole or low-fat milk

4 teaspoons finely grated orange zest (from 1 large orange), preferably organic

½ teaspoon vanilla extract

¼ cup extra-virgin olive oil or vegetable oil

4 (½-inch-thick) pineapple rings (from about half a 4-pound fruit)

1 to 2 cups whole or part-skim ricotta, for serving

MAKES ABOUT FOUR 7-INCH BELGIAN-STYLE WAFFLES, TO SERVE 6

Sometimes grabbing the wrong spice jar is the right thing to happen to a recipe. With an absent mind, I was combining orange and cardamom, a classic pairing, when I found myself grinding whole coriander seeds instead. Knowing teff's unusual character, I decided to give the accidental pair a try. And indeed, when the crisp tangy waffles emerged, coriander's earthy lemony scent hit all the right notes with the caramelly sweetness of the dark grain flour. Olive oil adds subtle fruitiness.

These are delicious topped with chunks of ricotta, mixed fresh fruit, and a sprinkle of coriander sugar. Broil some pineapple rings, and you have a Sunday feast!

---

step one

Start the batter the night before, or at least 8 hours: Add the spelt flour, teff flour, 2 tablespoons of the coriander sugar, yeast, and salt to a large bowl (at least 4 quarts) and thoroughly whisk together.

Add the eggs to a medium bowl and lightly whisk to combine. Gently whisk in the milk, zest, and vanilla. Gradually whisk the egg mixture into the flour mixture until smooth, followed by the olive oil. Tightly cover the bowl with plastic wrap and chill overnight, or up to 24 hours.

step two

The next morning, remove the batter from the fridge. Position a rack about 4 inches away from the broiler and preheat for 5 minutes on high. Lightly grease a large rimmed baking sheet with olive oil or cooking spray. Place the pineapple rings on it and sprinkle them with the remaining tablespoon of coriander sugar.

Broil until the slices caramelize and are blistered in spots, 12 to 15 minutes. Turn off the broiler, then transfer the sheet with the pineapples to a low oven rack. Loosely cover with aluminum foil. Place a wire rack inside a large baking sheet and transfer the sheet to the center rack of the oven—this will keep the waffles from getting soggy.

When the pineapple slices are almost done, preheat the waffle iron, preferably non-stick. Gently whisk the batter to combine; it will be thin. Grease the waffle iron with oil or coat it with cooking spray. When a drop of water sizzles and briskly

continued >

evaporates on the surface, add a scant 1 cup of the batter to the center (or as specified in the manufacturer's instructions). Close the lid and cook until the waffle emits a toasty scent, turns golden brown, and can be removed easily using tongs, 4 to 5 minutes. Place on the wire rack to keep warm. Continue until all of the batter is used, lightly greasing the waffle iron in between as needed.

To finish, place a broiled pineapple ring onto each waffle (or cut into quarters to place onto waffle segments). Top with a good dollop of ricotta and sprinkle with coriander sugar. Serve at once.

fine points

In a hurry, use plain turbinado sugar and add 1 teaspoon ground coriander to the flour mixture.

You will need to adjust the preheating and cooking times as well as the amount of batter needed according to the manufacturer's directions for your waffle iron.

instant quinoa and olive oil granola

Slowly toasting the ingredients in the oven is the key to a good granola—my problem is that I sometimes can't wait. This crisp, crunchy, and intensely fragrant granola is what I make on my impatient days. It uses a no-bake method and comes together almost as fast as a breakfast omelet. Serve warm in a bowl, with milk or yogurt, or just grab a handful for a snack. If you are firmly in the chunky granola camp, we've got you covered too!

⁙ gluten-free

Add the oats, quinoa, sunflower seeds, sesame seeds, cardamom, cinnamon, and salt to a medium bowl and stir well to combine. For an instant treat, have a large heatproof bowl ready next to the stove. For a slower, chunky granola, grease an 8 by 8-inch square metal baking pan with olive oil or cooking spray.

Add the olive oil to a 10-inch skillet (cast-iron works great here) and heat over medium heat until shimmering. Add the oat mixture. Cook, stirring frequently with a wooden spoon and making sure all of the ingredients are coated, until the cereal turns golden and smells fragrant, 3 to 4 minutes. Watch closely and turn down the heat to medium-low if the mixture starts to burn.

Reduce the heat to medium-low, if you haven't already done so. Drizzle the maple syrup across (it will hiss!) and cook, stirring continuously until all of the ingredients are coated and the syrup has been completely absorbed. The bottom of the skillet should turn dry and the cereal will turn nicely golden brown and very aromatic, 2 to 3 minutes more. Watch closely because at this point the mixture can burn fast.

For instant gratification: Immediately transfer the cereal to the heatproof bowl. Allow to cool a little, then stir in the dried fruit and eat warm.

For a treat later: Immediately spread the cereal mixture evenly into the prepared baking pan. Using the bottom of a measuring cup, press it with a gentle but firm hand into an even layer. Leave to cool completely, about ½ hour, during which time the mixture will become firm. Once cooled, I like to cut mine into 8 rectangular pieces and remove them with a spatula, breaking each into chunks. Stir in the dried fruit and store in an airtight container.

1 cup old-fashioned rolled oats (use gluten-free if needed)

1 cup quinoa flakes

¼ cup sunflower seeds

¼ cup hulled or unhulled sesame seeds

1 teaspoon cardamom, preferably freshly ground

½ teaspoon ground cinnamon

¼ teaspoon fine sea salt

¼ cup extra-virgin olive oil or vegetable oil

¼ cup maple syrup, preferably Grade B

¾ cup dried fruit, chopped finely (try a mix of golden raisins, dried cranberries, and figs)

MAKES ABOUT TEN ½-CUP SERVINGS

fine points

Delicate gluten-free quinoa flakes have a grassy sweetness, worth seeking out. Look for them in health food stores or online (see "Sources," page 251).

No cardamom? Just use 1½ teaspoons ground cinnamon instead.

VARIATIONS Fiber-rich rye flakes (instead of rolled oats) give the granola a supreme chewiness, but it will *not* be gluten-free anymore.

MAKE AHEAD Yes! The granola can be stored for at least 1 week.

orange-scented rye muffins with walnut streusel

STREUSEL

¼ cup (4 tablespoons) unsalted butter, cut into a few pieces

½ cup (50 g) old-fashioned rolled oats

¼ cup plus 2 tablespoons (40 g) white whole wheat flour

¼ cup (50 g) packed light brown sugar

⅓ cup (35 g) finely chopped walnuts

1 teaspoon ground cinnamon

Pinch of salt

MUFFINS

2 tablespoons unsalted butter or extra-virgin olive oil

1 cup (100 g) old-fashioned rolled oats

1 cup (100g) rye flakes

2 cups (240 g) white whole wheat flour

1 teaspoon baking powder

½ teaspoon baking soda

½ teaspoon fine sea salt

1 cup (200 g) packed light brown sugar

¼ cup plus 2 tablespoons extra-virgin olive oil or vegetable oil

2 tablespoons finely grated orange zest (from 2 oranges)

2¼ cups well-shaken low-fat buttermilk

2 large eggs, at room temperature, lightly beaten

MAKES 12 MUFFINS

Rye and orange is an intriguing flavor pairing. These nourishing oatmeal muffins have a crisp streusel topping and a good size to keep you going through long mornings. Olive oil, used by bakers in the Mediterranean for centuries, adds a delicate floral aroma. Don't hesitate to use it here.

Dan Souza's oatmeal muffins in *Cook's Illustrated* were the initial inspiration before I gave them a whole grain makeover and a Mediterranean twist. Enjoy them on their own or with butter and orange marmalade.

step one

The night before, or at least 1 hour ahead, first prepare the streusel: Melt the butter in a large skillet over low heat, swirling the pan a few times. Remove from the heat and allow to cool for 5 minutes. Meanwhile, add the oats, flour, sugar, walnuts, cinnamon, and salt to a medium bowl and combine well with a fork. Drizzle the butter over the streusel ingredients and stir until crumbly and moistened. Cover and chill. Do not clean the skillet.

To prepare the batter, have a plate at the ready next to the stove. In the same skillet melt the butter over medium heat. Add the oats and rye flakes and cook, stirring frequently, until the flakes smell fragrant and turn golden brown in places, 3 to 5 minutes. Watch closely so as not to burn them. Immediately transfer to the plate and spread to cool, about 15 minutes.

Add the flake mixture to the bowl of a food processor fitted with a steel blade. Process until you have a fine meal, 40 to 50 seconds, scraping the sides once or twice in between. Add the flour, baking powder, baking soda, and salt and pulse to combine, about eight 1-second pulses. Transfer the dry ingredients to a medium bowl.

Add the sugar, olive oil, and zest to a large bowl and combine with a large whisk until no dry spots remain. Gently whisk in the buttermilk and the eggs until smooth. Add the flour mixture in four additions (a 1-cup measure helps) and gently whisk to combine, using a folding motion, until no streaks of flour remain. At this point, the batter will be thick but pourable. Cover the bowl with plastic wrap and allow the batter to rest for 1 hour at cool room temperature (or chill overnight).

step two

When you are ready to bake the muffins, position a rack in the center of the oven and preheat to 375°F. (Remove the batter and the streusel mixture from the fridge if making ahead. The batter will now resemble firm oatmeal and will not be pourable.) Lightly butter the cups *and* rims (these muffins expand!) of a standard-size 12-cup muffin pan, preferably nonstick, or coat with baking spray.

Using a ½-cup measure, add the batter to the muffin cups, filling them almost full. Break up the chilled streusel with a fork. Evenly sprinkle 2 tablespoons of streusel on top of each muffin and gently press to adhere.

Bake until the muffins turn golden brown with nice domes, the tops spring back when gently pressed, and a toothpick inserted into the center comes out with a smidgen of batter or clean, 18 to 20 minutes for batter that has rested for 1 hour, or 23 to 28 minutes for batter that has rested overnight, rotating the pan halfway. Transfer to a wire rack to cool for 5 to 7 minutes, then cup the top of each muffin with your palm and gently jiggle until it comes loose and can be pulled out. Transfer to a wire rack to cool, or eat warm.

fine points

Look for rye flakes, aka rolled rye, in health food stores or well-stocked markets (see "Sources," page 251). Regular whole wheat flour can be used instead of white whole wheat but will impart its hearty aroma.

I highly recommend allowing the batter to rest overnight and up to 24 hours (the batter will darken)—you will be rewarded with a more appealing soft texture and beautifully domed muffins.

Finely ground oats have a tendency to create lumps. The folding method for combining the ingredients gives you the most tender muffin.

olive oil biscuits with cracked pepper and honey glaze

BISCUITS

¼ cup extra-virgin olive oil

2 cups (230 g) whole wheat pastry flour

2 teaspoons baking powder

½ teaspoon baking soda

¼ teaspoon fine sea salt

⅔ cup chilled well-shaken low-fat buttermilk, plus a bit more as needed

GLAZE

1 tablespoon extra-virgin olive oil

1 tablespoon honey

½ teaspoon freshly cracked or very coarsely ground black pepper

MAKES 10 TO 12 TWO-INCH BISCUITS

Even though I came to biscuits late, only after moving to this country, I love them as much as anyone raised on them. But to please my German heart, a whole grain biscuit was in order, and olive oil had to play first fiddle in honor of my Greek baker's soul.

These biscuits have delicious crisp bottoms and golden-brown tops. The pepper glaze, balanced by a touch of honey, adds a nice kick, enhancing the flavor of the whole grain. If you're in a hurry, just brush them with a bit of buttermilk for shine. Because of the olive oil, they are less crumbly than a butter biscuit, a bit more tender and cakelike. I often make these for brunch. We also love them alongside soups or on their own, split and drizzled with a bit more olive oil and served with goat cheese or serrano ham. Even salty feta sings here, contrasting nicely with the sweet heat of the glaze.

To make the biscuits: Put the olive oil into a small bowl and place it in the freezer for 20 to 30 minutes as you prep your ingredients and preheat the oven. Position a rack in the center of the oven and preheat to 500°F. Line a baking sheet with parchment paper.

Whisk together the flour, baking powder, baking soda, and salt in a large bowl. Make a well in the center. Remove the olive oil from the freezer. Add the buttermilk to a 2-cup measuring cup, gradually beat the olive oil into the buttermilk, using a fork, then pour all but 2 tablespoons of it into the center of the flour mixture. With a fork, and starting from the center, gently stir and fold the ingredients together until you have a shaggy dough with some flour remaining at the bottom. Slowly add just enough of the remaining buttermilk, by the tablespoon or a bit more as needed, to gather the dough with your hands. It will have lumps and look shaggy.

Put a generous amount of flour into a small bowl. Use it to lightly flour your work surface and your hands. Transfer the dough to the work surface and gently flatten it into a ½- to ⅓-inch thick round. Fold one half of the dough over the other half, then gently pat into a round again, using flour sparingly.

Now pat the dough into a 7-inch circle, about ¾ inch thick. Brush any visible flour from the top. Using a 2-inch biscuit cutter, dipped into the reserved flour, cut out biscuits—start from the outer edge and cut close together, being sure to press firmly downward and not to twist the cutter. Place the biscuits about 2 inches apart on the prepared baking sheet. Gently pat the dough scraps together into a ¾-inch thick rectangle, don't refold, and cut out as many biscuits as you can from it. Place on the sheet.

Bake the biscuits for 5 minutes.

Meanwhile, make the glaze: Add the olive oil, honey, and pepper to a small saucepan and briefly warm over low heat, stirring until blended.

Remove the biscuits from the oven and brush with the glaze. Rotate the baking sheet and return the biscuits to the oven. Bake until the tops turn golden brown and the sides have crisped up, 4 to 5 minutes more. Transfer the biscuits to a wire rack to cool a bit and serve at once.

fine points

You can always double the recipe and make large (or more) biscuits.

Placing the olive oil in the freezer slightly thickens it and makes for a better rise. But don't let it freeze completely, because unlike butter, it can't be grated but will just melt into your hands.

MAKE AHEAD The biscuits can be cut and placed on the baking sheet 1 day ahead. Cover with plastic wrap and chill the baking sheet with the biscuits. Bake straight from the fridge. The fully baked biscuits can be frozen for 1 month. Thaw at room temperature for about 30 minutes, then add to a preheated 400°F oven for 5 to 7 minutes. If I'm in a hurry, I stick them in the microwave straight from the freezer and heat on high for 30 seconds per piece.

irish soda bread with amaranth, cranberries, and rosemary

½ cup (70 g) dried cranberries, chopped

2 cups (240 g) white or regular whole wheat flour, plus extra for the work surface, and for dusting

1 cup plus 1 tablespoon (110 g) whole grain amaranth flour

¼ cup (55 g) uncooked amaranth seeds

2 tablespoons turbinado sugar

1 tablespoon minced fresh rosemary (from about three 3-inch sprigs)

1¼ teaspoons baking soda

¾ teaspoon fine sea salt

4 tablespoons (¼ cup, 55g) chilled unsalted butter, cut into ¼-inch pieces

1¼ cups chilled low-fat buttermilk, well shaken, plus a few tablespoons more as needed

MAKES 8 TO 12 WEDGES

fine points

White whole wheat flour, naturally sweet, is my first choice here.

VARIATIONS Use ¾ cup (35 g)barberries in place of cranberries and increase turbinado sugar to ¼ cup (50 g).

MAKE AHEAD This loaf tastes best on the day it is made. Leftovers freeze well for 1 month. Defrost individual wedges at room temperature, and briefly warm in a microwave for about 20 seconds, or in a 300°F oven.

This richly textured bread, infused with the scent of rosemary and flecked with ruby-red cranberries, was a wonderful accidental kitchen discovery. Two forms of amaranth—tiny golden seeds and dense but intensely nutty-sweet flour—are behind its appeal.

This is a soda bread in the American tradition, more cakelike with a bit of butter and a hint of sweetness, compared to traditional austere Irish soda breads. Serve it for brunch or late breakfast or paired with a warm bowl of soup made from roasted squash or tomatoes. Of course, it can't be beat with creamy rich Irish butter.

Position a rack in the center of the oven and preheat to 425°F. Place a piece of parchment paper on a large rimless baking sheet. Lightly flour your work surface.

Add the cranberries to a small bowl and cover them with warm water for 10 minutes, drain, and gently pat dry with a paper towel.

Whisk together the flours, amaranth seeds, sugar, rosemary, baking soda, and salt in a large bowl. Using your fingertips or a pastry blender, quickly rub the butter pieces into the dough until it resembles coarse meal with small pebbles. Sprinkle the cranberries across and make a well in the center. Add a bit more than 1 cup of the buttermilk to the center of the flour mixture. Using a fork or a spatula, and starting from the center, gently stir until much of the flour is incorporated and a lumpy dough starts to form. Lightly flour your hands and gather any remaining flour at the bottom, drizzling on just enough of the remaining buttermilk until a patchy, slightly tacky dough just comes together.

Transfer the ball to the work surface and give it four to six turns while gently shaping it into a mound; the surface will not be smooth. Place onto the baking sheet and pat it down gently to flatten to about 7 inches across and 2 inches tall. Using a sharp knife, cut a cross into the top, going across the whole length of the loaf, about ¼ inch deep. This will contribute to a beautiful rise. Dust with flour, from about a foot above the loaf, for a nice rustic touch.

Bake until the bread turns golden brown around the edges, has a crusty top, and a cake tester or toothpick inserted into the center comes out clean, 30 to 35 minutes. Remove and slide the parchment paper with the bread to a wire rack. Peel off the paper and cool until warm, about 15 minutes. Cut into 8 or 12 wedges with a large serrated knife and serve right away or on the same day.

dark chocolate spelt waffles with chile and warm raspberry sauce

Chocolate, chile, and raspberries—no one needs to make a pitch for this trio of ingredients. Get ready for intense bittersweet waffles, with the occasional chunk of soft chocolate to bite into. They bake up with crisp edges and soft centers, thanks to a nice glug of extra-virgin olive oil—don't be tempted to reduce the amount. I've tried it, and you'll regret it.

For a brunch table, I suggest you offer both yogurt *and* cream. Your guests will be back next week. These luscious waffles can even be dessert. And adults can take them up a notch with a fine Scotch—this comes highly recommended from Joe, my splendid recipe tester's husband.

---

step one

Prepare the batter the night before, or at least 30 minutes ahead: Add the spelt flour, cocoa, sugar, baking powder, baking soda, chile flakes, and salt to a large bowl and whisk well to combine. Make a well in the center. Add the milk, eggs, and vanilla to a medium bowl and whisk until blended, followed by the oil. Add the wet ingredients to the center of the dry ingredients and stir. I always use a dough whisk (see page 21) or a fork, but a spatula works fine. Do not overmix; the batter should have a pebbled look, with many lumps. Fold in the chocolate. Cover the bowl with plastic wrap and set aside for 30 minutes (or chill overnight or up to 24 hours).

While the batter rests, prepare the raspberry sauce: Add the raspberries, water, and sugar to a small, heavy pot (it will be full). Cover and bring to a boil over medium heat, stirring once. Uncover, decrease the heat to maintain a brisk simmer, and cook, stirring occasionally, until fallen apart and thickened, about 25 minutes. Stir in the limoncello, cover, and set aside.

step two

When you are ready to make the waffles, place a wire rack inside a large rimmed baking sheet and transfer the sheet to the center rack of the oven—this will keep the waffles from getting soggy. Preheat the oven to 250°F.

Preheat the waffle iron. Lightly grease it with oil or coat it with cooking spray. Gently stir through the batter if made the day before. When a drop of water sizzles and briskly evaporates on the surface, add a scant 1 cup batter to the center and level with a spatula to distribute (or as specified in the manufacturer's instructions). Close the lid and cook until the waffles are golden and can be removed easily using tongs, 3½ to 4 minutes. Place on the wire rack and loosely cover with aluminum

continued >

WAFFLES

1½ cups plus 2 tablespoons (185 g) whole grain spelt flour

½ cup (45 g) Dutch-process unsweetened cocoa powder

¼ cup (50 g) turbinado or granulated sugar

1¾ teaspoons baking powder

¼ teaspoon baking soda

½ to 1 teaspoon red chile flakes (optional)

½ teaspoon fine sea salt

2 cups low-fat milk

3 large eggs, lightly beaten

1 teaspoon vanilla extract

¼ cup plus 2 tablespoons extra-virgin olive oil or vegetable oil

About ¾ cup (115 g) chopped dark chocolate with 70% cocoa content

RASPBERRY SAUCE

1 pound fresh or frozen raspberries (no need to thaw if frozen)

1 tablespoon water

1 tablespoon turbinado or granulated sugar, plus more as needed

1 tablespoon limoncello (optional)

Confectioners' sugar, for sprinkling

Softly whipped heavy cream or Greek whole-milk yogurt, for serving

Maple syrup, preferably Grade B, for drizzling

MAKES FOUR 7-INCH BELGIAN-STYLE WAFFLES, TO SERVE 6

foil until ready to serve. Do not stack the waffles, as they will become soggy. Continue until all of the batter is used, lightly greasing the waffle iron in between as needed.

To finish, sprinkle the waffles with confectioners' sugar. Place one waffle or a segment onto each plate and spoon a nice dollop of softly whipped cream on top, followed by warm raspberry sauce. Don't forget a drizzle of maple syrup. Serve at once.

fine points

Ingredients really matter here: use good-quality chocolate with 70 percent cocoa content, and I recommend Dutch-process cocoa.

Turbinado sugar with its caramel notes offsets the natural bitterness of dark chocolate and enhances the subtle nuttiness of spelt.

The amount of chile depends on your liking and the freshness of the spice in your cupboard: ½ teaspoon adds a spicy kick—my choice—but go ahead and use 1 teaspoon if you want more. Please don't use chile if making the waffles for children; they might also prefer a sweeter chocolate.

If you're in a hurry, you can just simmer the berries for the sauce for a few minutes until they are warmed through.

You will need to adjust the preheating and cooking times as well as the amount of batter needed according to the manufacturer's directions for your waffle iron.

MAKE AHEAD Raspberry sauce can be made up to 2 days ahead. Chill, covered. Gently reheat over medium heat until warm.

whole grain rye waffles with parmesan and rosemary

During cold dark winter months, many of us long for heartier fare. These savory waffles hit the spot and provide stamina, with their nourishing combination of whole grain rye and whole wheat flour, and scented with rosemary and umami-rich Parmesan. If you want to go the extra mile, sauté some mushrooms too—which is what one of my testers started dreaming about when the waffles hit her plate . . .

step one
Prepare the batter the night before, or at least 1 hour ahead: Add the flours, sesame seeds, baking powder, baking soda, salt, and pepper to a large bowl and thoroughly whisk together. Whisk in the cheese, rosemary, and chile and make a well in the center. In a medium bowl, whisk the eggs with the buttermilk and olive oil until well blended. Add the wet ingredients to the center of the dry ingredients and combine with a dough whisk (see page 21) or a spatula. Do not overmix; the batter should have a few lumps. Cover the bowl with plastic wrap and chill for 1 hour or up to 24 hours.

Meanwhile, prepare the rosemary oil: Heat the olive oil with the rosemary sprigs in a small saucepan over medium-low heat until the oil starts to sizzle. Cook for 1 minute, pressing on the sprigs with a wooden spoon to release their etheric oils. Remove from the heat and set aside until ready to use, at least 20 minutes (or chill if making ahead). Before serving, take out the sprigs but don't bother with any loose needles—they add character. Pour the oil into a small serving bowl.

step two
When you are ready to make the waffles, preheat the waffle iron. Place a wire rack inside a rimmed baking sheet and transfer the sheet to the center rack of the oven—this will keep the waffles from getting soggy. Preheat the oven to 200°F.

Lightly grease the waffle iron with oil or coat it with cooking spray. When a drop of water sizzles and briskly evaporates on the surface, add about 1 cup batter to the center and level with a spatula to distribute (or as specified in the manufacturer's instructions). Close the lid and cook until the waffles are crisp and golden brown and can be removed easily using tongs, about 4 minutes. Transfer the waffles to the baking sheet until ready to serve. Do not stack them, as the waffles will become soggy. Continue until all of the batter has been used, lightly greasing the waffle iron in between as necessary.

Serve each waffle or waffle section with a dollop of sour cream and a drizzle of the rosemary oil.

continued >

WAFFLES

1 cup (105 g) whole grain rye flour

1 cup (120 g) whole wheat flour

¼ cup lightly toasted sesame or flax seeds or a mixture

1½ teaspoons baking powder

½ teaspoon baking soda

¼ teaspoon fine sea salt

¼ teaspoon freshly ground black pepper

1 cup finely grated Parmesan

1 tablespoon minced fresh rosemary

1 to 2 teaspoons minced serrano chile, veins and seeds removed for less heat (optional)

2 large eggs, lightly beaten

2½ cups well-shaken low-fat buttermilk

¼ cup plus 2 tablespoons extra-virgin olive oil or vegetable oil

ROSEMARY OIL (OPTIONAL)

¼ cup extra-virgin olive oil

Four 3-inch sprigs fresh rosemary, rinsed and patted dry

1 cup plain or low-fat sour cream, for serving

MAKES ABOUT FOUR 7- OR 8-INCH BELGIAN-STYLE WAFFLES, TO SERVE 6

fine points

Oil creates crispness—don't be tempted to reduce the amount of it here.

MAKE AHEAD The rosemary oil can be prepared up to 1 week ahead. Chill, covered. Bring to room temperature before serving. It is also delicious drizzled on grains and vegetables, grilled fish, or meat, so don't hesitate to double the amount.

Why resting matters? See "Baking," page 3.

You will need to adjust the preheating and cooking times as well as the amount of batter needed according to the manufacturer's directions for your waffle iron.

red rice shakshuka with feta cheese

This one-skillet meal, originally from North Africa, gets a Greek makeover in my kitchen and a nourishing boost from spectacular red rice. With bright eggs shining in a deep red tomato sauce, this is already a stunning dish. The light burgundy hue of red rice enhances its visual appeal. Serve this all-around satisfying meal for a late brunch, lunch, or dinner. I always have some baguette on hand to dip into the soft yolks. And don't forget to put a bottle of Sriracha chile sauce on the table—here it is almost mandatory. gluten-free

Heat a heavy 12-inch skillet—cast iron works well—over medium heat. Swirl in the olive oil and wait until it shimmers. Add the onion, bell pepper, and salt. Cook, stirring occasionally, until the vegetables turn golden and start to brown, about 7 minutes. Add the garlic, oregano, and Aleppo pepper and cook, stirring, until fragrant, about 1 minute. Stir in ¼ cup of the parsley, followed by the tomatoes, rice, water, and pepper. Cook, uncovered and at a lively simmer, until the tomato sauce thickens a bit, 8 to 10 minutes. Taste and season with salt and pepper (keeping in mind that you will add salty feta).

Decrease the heat to medium-low. Crack one of the eggs into a small bowl. Using the rounded side of a spoon, make a shallow indentation in the center of the rice mixture and slide the egg into it. Repeat 5 more times all around the first egg. Sprinkle the feta in the space around the eggs.

Cover the pan with a lid and cook, at a gentle simmer until the whites are opaque and just set but the yolks remain delightfully runny, 6 to 8 minutes. Sprinkle with a bit more Aleppo if you like and scatter the remaining ¼ cup parsley across. Allow to sit for a few minutes before serving—the slight cooling brings all of the flavors to the forefront.

fine points

On supermarket shelves, you can now find beautiful, colorful whole grain rice varieties. For this dish, I recommend Bhutanese red rice from Lotus Foods for its rewarding supple-soft texture (see "Sources," page 251). But don't hesitate to use any cooked whole grain rice.

As a home cook with frugal kitchen habits, I rarely turn on the oven for a simple dish like this. But you can, of course, finish your shakshuka in the oven for chef-style perfection. Be sure to preheat the oven from the start to 375°F and carefully slide in the skillet once you have added the eggs and the feta. Bake, uncovered, for 8 to 11 minutes, until the whites are just set.

2 tablespoons extra-virgin olive oil

1 yellow onion, cut into ¼-inch dice (about 1½ cups)

1 red or yellow bell pepper, cored, quartered, and chopped into ½-inch pieces (about 1¼ cups)

¼ teaspoon fine sea salt

2 cloves garlic, minced

1 tablespoon chopped fresh oregano, or 1 teaspoon crumbled dried oregano

1 teaspoon Aleppo pepper, or 1 teaspoon sweet paprika and ⅛ teaspoon cayenne pepper (optional)

½ cup chopped fresh flat-leaf parsley or basil

1 large (28-ounce) can whole peeled tomatoes with their juices, crushed

3 cups cooked red rice or brown rice (see page 22)

½ cup water

¼ teaspoon freshly ground black pepper

6 large eggs

1 cup crumbled mild feta, preferably sheep's milk

SERVES 4 TO 6

frittata muffins for any grain

1½ cups cooked quinoa, preferably black or red (see page 22)

2 cups fresh or frozen green peas (do not thaw)

¾ cup (3 ounces) shredded Grana Padano cheese, Parmesan, or sharp Cheddar, plus ¼ cup finely grated, for sprinkling

½ cup finely chopped green onions (about 3)

½ cup loosely packed finely chopped fresh herbs, such as a mixture of mint and parsley or dill and mint

1 to 2 teaspoons minced serrano chile, veins and seeds removed for less heat (optional)

7 large eggs

¼ to ½ teaspoon fine sea salt

¼ teaspoon freshly ground black pepper

12 pitted salt-cured black Moroccan or green olives (optional)

MAKES 12 MUFFINS, TO SERVE 4 TO 6

These nourishing egg muffins, similar to mini frittatas, are leftover heroes in my kitchen—use any greens and grains you have on hand. Don't hesitate to make them for dinner on a busy weeknight—they are flavorful, fun, and easy as pie. Leftovers transport well in your lunch bag the next day.

The version here with green peas, fresh mint, and quinoa is gluten-free and makes a lovely addition to a spring brunch or an Easter table. I have also made these with barley, spelt, Kamut, wild rice, and millet (the last one soaks up a fair bit of liquid, so add an egg for a total of 8). Their consistency and chewiness will vary depending on the grains used, and sometimes they puff up a bit more. Serve them with a bit of ketchup, spiced up with chile sauce for adults, and a simple salad. ⟫ gluten-free

Position a rack in the center of the oven and preheat to 400°F. Grease a standard 12-cup muffin pan, preferably nonstick, with olive oil or coat with cooking spray.

Add the quinoa, peas, shredded cheese, green onions, herbs, and chile to a medium bowl and combine well with a fork (if using previously cooked grains, be sure to separate any clumps). Divide the grain mixture equally among the muffin cups, about ⅓ cup for each, filling them almost full.

Add the eggs to a large bowl and season with ½ teaspoon salt (¼ teaspoon if using previously cooked salted grains and greens) and pepper. Beat vigorously, using a large whisk, until foamy, about 30 seconds. Divide the egg mixture into the cups, using a scant ¼ cup for each. Sprinkle each muffin with about 1 teaspoon of the finely grated cheese and gently press in 1 olive.

Bake until the frittata muffins have puffed up and turn light golden on top and golden brown around the edges, 20 to 25 minutes. Transfer the pan to a wire rack to cool for about 5 minutes. Run a thin rubber spatula or a knife around each muffin cup to release. Eat warm or at room temperature.

fine points

You can reduce the amount of eggs to 5 (instead of 7), adding ½ cup whole or low-fat milk instead; the egg muffins will just dome a bit less.

MAKE AHEAD You can prepare the mixture and fill the muffin pan the night before. Loosely cover the pan with plastic wrap and chill. Remove the muffins while you preheat the oven; they might take a few minutes longer to bake. These freeze well for up to 1 month.

giant spelt pancake with squash blossoms

My German dad was a competitive pancake gobbler—to call him a pancake eater would do the term injustice. But he certainly loved pancakes, and the ones he made for us children were always huge, the size of a skillet. As is traditional, he used no chemical leaveners, just the power of eggs to give them a lift. This recipe, almost a cross between pancakes and omelets, is inspired by German-style pancakes to which I add lots of fresh herbs and tender squash blossoms.

I often serve them for brunch, but add a simple salad of spinach leaves or bitter greens, and it is just as good for dinner.

step one

Prepare the batter the night before, or at least 30 minutes ahead: Add the flour to a medium bowl. Lightly whisk the egg yolks in a 2-cup liquid measuring cup. Add the milk, water, salt, and pepper and whisk until blended. Gradually whisk the egg mixture into the flour, starting from the center, until smooth. Set aside for 20 to 30 minutes, covered. Place the egg whites in a bowl in which you can whisk them later. (If making the night before, cover the egg whites as well and chill both bowls, up to 24 hours.)

step two

When you are ready to make the pancakes, remove both bowls from the fridge about 30 minutes ahead (up to 1 hour for the egg whites for best volume). Briefly swish the squash blossoms in a bowl of cold water, then place on a clean dish cloth to drain and gently pat dry. Trim the stems to a length of about 1 inch. Very gently pry each blossom open and remove the stamen in the center, using tweezers. Don't worry if the petals tear a bit; just twist them gently to close at the top.

Add a pinch of salt to the egg whites and beat them with a hand blender or with a balloon whisk until soft peaks form. Stir the batter briefly to blend with a fork. If it has become thick, add a little water by the tablespoon—it should have the consistency of buttermilk (or heavy cream if you're using Kamut flour). Set aside 2 tablespoons of the herbs for garnish. Stir the remaining herbs and half of the cheese into the batter. Gently fold in the egg whites, in three additions.

Place a rack 4 inches away from the broiler and preheat on high. Set a large platter or plate next to the stove and have a piece of aluminum foil handy to cover it.

Heat a 10-inch cast-iron or other heatproof skillet for 2 minutes over medium heat. Swirl in 2 teaspoons of the olive oil and wait until it shimmers. Scoop with a 1-cup measure deeply into the batter and put a scant 1½ cups into the center of the pan.

BATTER

1 cup plus 1 tablespoon (120 g) whole grain spelt or Kamut flour

3 large eggs, yolks and whites separated

½ cup whole milk

½ cup water

½ teaspoon fine sea salt

¼ teaspoon freshly ground black pepper

TO FINISH

16 squash blossoms

1 cup loosely packed chopped mixed herbs such as mint, parsley, and dill

1 cup finely grated Manchego cheese or Parmesan, plus extra for serving

4 teaspoons extra-virgin olive oil

Flaked sea salt, for sprinkling

Good-quality balsamic vinegar, for drizzling

MAKES 2 LARGE PANCAKES, TO SERVE 4 TO 6

continued >

Quickly but gently spread the batter outward, using the back of the measuring cup, until it almost reaches the sides. Cook for 1 minute, until slightly puffy. Gently press 8 squash blossoms in a star pattern into the center of the pancake, with the stem facing inward. Continue cooking until a few small bubbles appear on top, the edges just start to brown, and the bottom turns golden brown (lift with a spatula), about 2 minutes more.

Sprinkle with ¼ cup of the remaining cheese and place the skillet under the broiler. Cook, watching closely, until puffy and golden brown, about 3 minutes, or 1 to 2 minutes more for a crisper pancake. Remove the pancake and slide it onto the platter. Cover loosely with foil to keep warm. Wipe the pan clean with paper towels and repeat with the second pancake.

To serve, sprinkle each pancake with a bit more cheese and some of the remaining herbs. Crush some sea salt flakes on top, cut into quarters or halves, and serve at once, passing balsamic vinegar around for drizzling.

fine points

Look for squash blossoms at farmers' markets during the summer months.

Whole grain Kamut flour makes a sturdier pancake with a golden hue and a subtle sweetness. White whole wheat flour can be substituted.

VARIATIONS You can top the pancakes with halved grape or cherry tomatoes—a scant 1 cup per pancake. Toss a few olives on too if you like.

In the winter, make use of the dark green parts of leeks, so often discarded. Slice thinly to amount to 3 cups and sauté in 1 tablespoon olive oil over medium heat, with a bit of salt, stirring often, 4 to 5 minutes.

HOW TO STORE SQUASH BLOSSOMS AND FRESH HERBS

Ideally you should cook squash blossoms the day you buy them. But life happens. I had good success storing the delicate blossoms for a day or two in the fridge, upright, in a glass of water like flowers, and loosely covered—a plastic bag works. But I much prefer perforated and reusable produce bags I found at Crate and Barrel.

I use the same method to store bunches of fresh parsley, dill, and mint—they will last for many days. No need to buy special contraptions. I also take these washable bags with me to go shopping for fruit and vegetables. I leave most produce right in the bags when I return and store them in the crisper drawer of my refrigerator.

savory seed and nut granola with nigella seeds

While I have a weakness for sweets, sometimes I crave a savory power snack. This olive oil granola, scented with aromatics from the Mediterranean, is packed with nuts and seeds and infused with the deep umami of soy sauce—perfect for a weekend hike or when your brain needs nourishing fuel. It will boost your energy level without giving you a sugar high.

The method I use here gives you beautiful chunks with a delicate snap. This is a challenge in savory granola, believe me, because of the lack of sweeteners. After endless testing and research, I learned the crucial missing piece on the fabulous community cooking site Food52: just turn the oven off and allow the granola to completely cool inside.

This granola is endlessly versatile. It is delicious sprinkled on roasted sweet potatoes or carrots when they emerge from the oven, and on creamy soups.

⋙ gluten-free

Position a rack in the center of the oven and preheat to 300°F. Line a large rimmed baking sheet with parchment paper.

Add the oats, almonds, peanuts, sunflower seeds, flax seeds, sesame seeds, and nigella seeds to a large bowl and stir to combine. Sprinkle with the herbes de Provence, paprika, and pepper and stir again until the spices are well distributed.

Beat the olive oil and the soy sauce with a fork in a small bowl until amalgamated. Drizzle over the oat mixture and stir until no dry spots remain. Beat the egg whites in a medium bowl with the same fork or a small whisk, until very foamy, about 1 minute. Pour across the oat mixture and stir with a spatula until the egg whites are well distributed throughout.

Spread the cereal evenly onto the baking sheet and press down firmly, moistening your spatula with water as needed to avoid sticking.

Bake until firm and golden brown, 20 to 25 minutes, then rotate the sheet and turn the oven off, leaving the baking sheet with the granola inside until the oven has completely cooled, about 4 hours (or overnight).

3 cups old-fashioned rolled oats (use gluten-free if desired)

¾ cup whole almonds

½ cup unsalted roasted peanuts

½ cup sunflower seeds

¼ cup flaxseeds, preferably golden

¼ cup unhulled or hulled sesame seeds

2 tablespoons nigella seeds (optional; see page 248)

2 tablespoons dried herbes de Provence (see page 249)

1½ teaspoons ground sweet paprika

½ teaspoon freshly ground black pepper

¼ cup plus 2 tablespoons extra-virgin olive oil

3 tablespoons low-sodium soy sauce

2 large egg whites

MAKES ABOUT 7 CUPS, TO SERVE 14

fine points

Reduce the amount of soy sauce from 3 to 2 tablespoons if salt is of concern and use 1 tablespoon water instead.

VARIATION If you like salty-sweet, omit the nigella seeds and stir in 1 to 1½ cups dried cranberries after the granola has cooled. Addictive!

The granola will keep for 2 weeks in an airtight container at room temperature. Or squirrel some away in the freezer, tightly wrapped, for 1 month.

olive oil popcorn with aleppo pepper and flaked sea salt

2 tablespoons extra-virgin olive oil

⅓ cup plus 1 tablespoon popcorn kernels, preferably organic

½ teaspoon Aleppo pepper, or more as needed

¼ teaspoon flaked sea salt

SERVES 4 AS A SNACK

What is all the fuss about popcorn? So were my thoughts when I arrived in America as a young adult from Germany. It is fair to say I didn't appreciate popped corn at all, let alone ever made it. I only remember eating some boring bagged dried-out kernels in my teens. Suddenly, I found myself surrounded by people who seemed to be eating popcorn all the time. And who sprinkled the aisles in movie theaters with kernels as if they were trying to find their way home in a forest.

Only much later, when working as a food writer, did I learn that you can make excellent popcorn at home, in minutes, and without special equipment. Along the way I studied two dozen recipes and tried different techniques. And I struggled. The biggest problem: lots of unpopped kernels in each batch, hard enough to break your teeth. The most valuable advice came from the tireless tinkerers at *Cook's Illustrated*. They taught me the use of 3 "test" kernels to indicate the optimal temperature of 380°F, and an even more important 30-second wait to heat all kernels to the same temperature, which means they will pop at about the same time. The result: not a single unpopped kernel in batch after batch.

My popcorn is inspired by the Mediterranean. It is flavored with olive oil, a sprinkle of Aleppo pepper (see page 247) to add intense fruitiness and a touch of heat, and a few precious flakes of Maldon sea salt. gluten-free

Add the olive oil and 3 of the popcorn kernels to a heavy 4-quart saucepan. Cover and heat over medium heat until the kernels pop, 3 to 4 minutes.

Remove the pot from the heat, add the remaining popcorn, cover, and wait for 30 seconds. Return the pot to medium heat. Once you hear the first kernels pop, start shaking the pot—be sure to keep the lid slightly ajar to allow steam to escape but not so much that the kernels fly out. Shake the pot constantly until the popping slows down noticeably, to 1 or 2 seconds between pops, about 1 minute.

Immediately tip the popcorn into a large bowl and sprinkle with the Aleppo pepper. Crush the salt flakes between your fingers and sprinkle on top as well. Taste and season with more pepper or salt if needed. Eat warm or store in a container with a tight-fitting lid if you can restrain yourself.

mussels, fast and furious

Sometimes the best you can do is cook—regardless of what life hands you. Case in point: My husband had just recovered from a severe cold, and I had been stirring up pot after pot of soup for days on end. I was so *done* with cooking. But I had just returned from shopping to stock our cleaned-out fridge and came home with two bags of glistening fresh mussels. I simply couldn't imagine *not* eating them that night. Given how wiped out I felt, I ended up using only the most basic aromatics—but we were rewarded with a feast of flavors in the concentrated juices, released by the bivalves. We have since cooked this simple one-pot meal countless times. In fact, it has become one of our favorite fast foods. ⬧ gluten-free

Heat a large Dutch oven or other heavy saucepan over medium heat. Have the clean mussels at the ready. Swirl in the olive oil and, when it shimmers, toss in the garlic and cook, stirring, until lightly golden, about 30 seconds. Increase the heat to high, add the chile flakes, and stir for 15 seconds, then gently tip in the mussels (they will hiss and crackle).

Gently stir along the bottom of the pot once, cover, and cook until the mussels open, 5 to 7 minutes, shaking the pan vigorously a few times in between. Remove from the heat and discard any unopened mussels.

Season with salt and a good dose of black pepper and garnish with the parsley. Serve at once in shallow soup plates, spooning on some of the concentrated juices and drizzling with a bit more olive oil. Eat, with baguette, and passing the lemon wedges around. Don't forget to mop up the last drop of juices in the pan!

CLEANING MUSSELS: EFFORTLESS AND EASY

Despite what so many people think, mussels are supereasy to prepare. I consider them the perfect lazy dinner because they cook up in minutes yet bring such luxurious succulence to your table. So don't hesitate to give them a try. Most mussels today are farmed and typically don't require any labor-intensive scrubbing or beard removal. I just rinse them under cold running water, sorting them as I go.

If you find a lone beard, remove it with a sharp paring knife. Discard any mussels that have cracked or broken shells. And be sure to check on any open mussels: If they don't close when you knock their shells together or tap them on the counter, discard them as well. I then place the mussels in a large sieve set on a plate next to the stove so they are ready to go.

---

4 pounds mussels, cleaned (see sidebar)

2 tablespoons extra-virgin olive oil, plus extra for drizzling

2 to 4 cloves garlic, thinly sliced

¼ teaspoon dried red chile flakes (optional)

Fine sea salt and freshly ground pepper

½ cup loosely packed chopped fresh flat-leaf parsley

2 whole grain baguettes, for serving (gluten-free if needed)

1 to 2 lemons, cut into wedges, for serving

SERVES 4

fine points

For smaller wild mussels, check earlier, as they might take only 3 minutes or so to open.

You can easily halve this recipe for two people.

VARIATION This is just as mouthwatering if you can get your hands on fresh littleneck clams. After eating a few too many sandy clams, I learned from Boston chef Jasper White to first place the bivalves in a large bowl of cold water for about 20 minutes. This allows them to cycle the water, releasing any sand, which sinks to the bottom. After the soaking, lift the clams out one by one—to leave the sand behind—and scrub off any remaining residue under cold running water.

baked feta fingers in saffron quinoa with tomatoes

1¼ cups water

⅔ cup quinoa, rinsed well and drained, or 2 cups cooked

3 cups (½ recipe) Saffron-Infused Tomato Sauce with Shallots and Vermouth (page 172)

2 slices mild feta, preferably sheep's milk (about 5 ounces each)

1 tablespoon extra-virgin olive oil

⅛ teaspoon loosely packed saffron threads

1 fresh hot Thai chile, thinly sliced crosswise into rings, seeds removed for less heat (optional)

Baguette, for serving

SERVES 4 AS A LIGHT MAIN OR 6 TO 8 AS A LIGHT APPETIZER

Pristine white feta, softening into hot bubbling tomatoes in the oven, always makes the Greek half of my heart sing. Add a few strands of royal saffron and the feeble crunch of quinoa, and you might kiss your fork.

This simple supper can be a light meal on a warm summer night. I often serve it as a starter because it can be practically made ahead. Who wants to fret over a dish while everyone is having fun at the table? Just put it in the oven shortly before your guests arrive, then offer them a glass of Prosecco and roasted Marcona almonds, and relax. In the last 10 minutes, crisp thin slices of whole grain or plain baguette in the oven to serve alongside. ➤ gluten-free

Place a rack in the center of the oven and preheat to 375°F. Oil a 9 by 9-inch glass baking dish or other 2-quart ovenproof pan with a 2-inch rim.

Meanwhile, bring the water and the quinoa to a boil in a small heavy saucepan. Decrease the heat to maintain a simmer, cover, and cook until the water is absorbed, 12 to 15 minutes. Remove from the heat and let sit, covered, for 5 minutes.

Stir the tomato sauce into the cooked quinoa and transfer the mixture into the baking dish. Cut each slice of feta crosswise into 4 "fingers" for a total of 8 pieces. Place the feta fingers into the sauce, leaving about ¾ inch in between. Combine the olive oil and saffron in a small bowl and drizzle on the feta fingers, placing a few strands on each piece for visual appeal and garnishing each with a couple of chile rings.

Bake until the quinoa is bubbly around the edges and the feta has softened, 20 to 25 minutes. Spoon some of the quinoa onto each plate and top each serving with 1 or 2 feta fingers. Serve warm, accompanied by baguette slices.

fine points

VARIATION You can replace the quinoa with 2 cups cooked millet or medium-coarse bulgur (see page 22).

MAKE AHEAD You can prepare this partway without the saffron oil and the chile, up to 1 day ahead. Chill, covered. Combine the oil and the saffron in a separate container and chill as well. Remove when you preheat the oven. Drizzle the feta with the saffron oil and garnish with chile when ready to bake.

red rice and beet cakes with honey mustard

Crispy on the outside and moist on the inside, these vegetarian cakes get their intense burgundy hue from a combination of chewy shredded beets and comforting red rice. Salty feta enhances the earthy sweetness of the beets. If someone in your family is not too fond of the root vegetable, just serve them this *new* red rice burger without divulging anything more—you might be surprised to find a beet convert at your table.

Pair the rice cakes with grilled salmon, lamb chops, or chicken breast. For vegetarians, serve the cakes topped with Greek yogurt and a simple spinach salad. Last but not least, these are terrific inside a soft whole wheat burger bun with sliced tomatoes and lettuce leaves. gluten-free

To prepare the red rice, bring the water and rice to a boil in a heavy 2-quart saucepan with a tight-fitting lid. Decrease the heat to maintain a simmer, cover, and cook until the rice is tender and the water is absorbed, about 25 minutes. Remove from the heat, cover, and let sit for 10 minutes. Drain if needed, transfer to a large shallow bowl, and spread to cool for about 20 minutes.

Meanwhile, prepare the honey mustard: Add the mustard and the honey to a small bowl and beat with a fork to combine. Stir in the gherkins and squeeze in a bit of Sriracha. Set aside for flavors to mingle, then season with Sriracha to taste. Have a small baking sheet or a large plate on hand.

To make the cakes, add the beet, feta, oats, green onions, dill, eggs, chiles, salt, and pepper to the bowl with the rice. Using your hands, thoroughly combine the mixture until the ingredients come together. No need to be gentle. If the mixture won't hold together, add oats by the tablespoon until it does.

Level the mixture inside the bowl and divide into 8 equal portions using a butter knife (cut in half like a cake, and then each half into quarters). Or use a ⅓-cup measuring cup per cake. Moisten your hands with water and form cakes about 2½ inches in diameter. Place on the baking sheet. Cover with plastic wrap and chill for 30 minutes.

To finish, heat 1 tablespoon of the olive oil in a large skillet over medium heat until it shimmers. Add 4 cakes and cook until golden brown, about 6 minutes, carefully flipping over once halfway with a metal spatula. Repeat with the remaining batch. Serve warm or at room temperature, squeezing a bit of lemon juice on each cake, and with honey mustard on the side.

RED RICE

1½ cups water

⅔ cup red rice, or about 2 cups lightly packed cooked red rice

HONEY MUSTARD

3 tablespoons Dijon mustard

1 tablespoon honey

1½ tablespoons minced gherkins

¼ to ½ teaspoon Sriracha sauce, or more as needed (optional)

CAKES

1 cup shredded raw red beet (about 1), using the large holes of a box grater

1 cup crumbled mild feta, preferably sheep's milk

¼ cup quick-cooking rolled oats, plus a couple of tablespoons more as needed

½ cup finely chopped green onions (about 3)

½ cup lightly packed finely chopped dill

2 large eggs, lightly beaten

1 to 2 teaspoons minced hot green chiles, such as serrano (optional)

¼ teaspoon fine sea salt

¼ teaspoon freshly ground black pepper

2 tablespoons extra-virgin olive oil

1 lemon, cut into wedges, for garnish

MAKES 8 CAKES, TO SERVE 4

continued >

grain burger 101

Grain burgers are an ingenious creation of our forefathers, or rather foremothers, to make use of leftovers. They are as easy as they are mouthwatering, and once you get the hang of it, you can get creative and use any forgotten tidbits in your kitchen for a quick and easy meal. Don't get discouraged if your first try is not a success. Just try again, and get your kids involved too. It's easy and it's fun!

Here are a few tricks for success if you are new to grain burgers:

SHAPING

Cook your grains the night before (or use leftovers). Chilling hardens the starches, which helps in shaping grain burgers. The grains will soften again during cooking.

Chop add-ons like onions, herbs, and carrots *finely* (about ⅛-inch dice). The mixture will adhere better.

Unlike with meat, there is no need to be gentle when shaping grain burgers. Go ahead and squish the ingredients together if needed!

Shape the burgers into evenly flat cakes, not roundish mounds. They hold up better.

Chill after shaping for at least 30 minutes. This helps the grain cakes keep their shape during frying or baking later.

Make smaller 2-inch burgers; they are easier to turn.

Always turn the burgers gently.

FRYING OR BAKING?

Panfrying grain burgers in a little olive oil in a cast-iron skillet is undeniably most flavorful.

But by all means, bake your grain patties in a preheated 425°F oven. Be sure to oil the baking sheet well before you place the cakes on it, then brush the tops with olive oil or spray with cooking spray. Bake for 10 to 14 minutes on each side, or until the grain burgers are nicely browned, turning them gently and brushing or spraying in between.

fine points

Bhutanese red rice, a Himalayan heirloom variety, has become more widely available (see "Sources," page 251).

VARIATION For children, 1 cup shredded carrots can be used instead of beets, for a more pleasing natural sweetness.

MAKE AHEAD Prepare the red rice, up to 5 days ahead. The cakes can be shaped up to 1 day ahead. Chill, covered.

Bake the burgers instead of panfrying them (see sidebar "Grain Burger 101").

minted lamb sliders with pine nuts and currants

These small succulent sliders, studded with currants and pine nuts and flavored with lots of fresh herbs and spices, are a play on *kofta*, the highly aromatic Middle Eastern meatballs. I always add a nice amount of textured bulgur, which makes for dinner on the fly because your sliders already combine a protein and a nourishing grain. Just add a vegetable or a salad, and you are done!

On hot summer days, place the sliders on the grill and serve them with a plate of sliced juicy tomatoes, drizzled with olive oil, or—for a feast—make the Minted Summer Couscous with Watermelon and Feta (page 100). Garnish the sliders with the Sriracha-spiked version of the Tart Barberry Chutney (page 88).

gluten-free option

To prepare the bulgur, place the grain in a large bowl and cover with the hot water. Let sit at room temperature until much of the water is absorbed and the kernels are tender with a bit of chew, 20 to 30 minutes. Drain the bulgur in a fine-mesh sieve, pressing on the kernels with your hands to squeeze out as much water as you can.

Meanwhile, to make the sliders, place the lamb in a large bowl. Add the mint, parsley, and garlic to the bowl of a food processor, fitted with a steel blade. Pulse until coarsely chopped, about five 1-second pulses. Add the pine nuts and pulse again until finely chopped, about five more 1-second pulses. Transfer to the bowl with the lamb. Switch to a grating disc and process the onion in the food processor. Add to the bowl as well. (Or finely chop all ingredients by hand and grate the onion on the large holes of a box grater.) Add the bulgur, currants, cumin, Aleppo pepper, cinnamon, salt, and black pepper.

Combine the mixture thoroughly but gently with your hands until it just holds together. Using portions of ⅓ cup, shape into sliders about 2½ inches wide and about 1 inch thick, and place them on a large platter or baking sheet.

To finish, heat a large grill pan over medium heat and brush lightly with olive oil. Brush half of the sliders with oil as well and add them to the pan, leaving enough space in between so you can flip them. Cook, brushing and flipping them once (or twice for nice grill marks), until almost no pink remains when you cut one in half, 6 to 7 minutes total. Allow to sit for a few minutes—as the sliders cool, their flavors shine. Repeat with the remaining 8 sliders.

BULGUR
¾ cup medium-coarse
or coarse bulgur

1½ cups hot water

SLIDERS
1 pound ground lamb

1 cup loosely packed fresh mint

½ cup loosely packed fresh
flat-leaf parsley

2 to 3 cloves garlic

½ cup pine nuts

1 medium yellow onion

½ cup currants

1 tablespoon ground cumin

1 teaspoon Aleppo pepper
(see page 247), or ⅛ teaspoon
cayenne

½ teaspoon ground cinnamon

1 teaspoon fine sea salt

¼ teaspoon freshly ground
black pepper

Extra-virgin olive oil,
for brushing

MAKES 16 SLIDERS,
TO SERVE 4 TO 6

fine points

Use golden raisins, chopped up a bit, if you can't find currants.

GLUTEN-FREE Instead of bulgur, use cooked medium- or short-grain brown rice or quinoa (1¾ lightly packed cups)

VARIATION If lamb is not your thing, use ground beef or bison.

MAKE AHEAD Prepare the bulgur 1 day ahead; chill, covered. The sliders can be shaped up to 1 day ahead. Cover with plastic wrap; chill.

tart barberry chutney

1 cup dried barberries or cranberries (preferably unsweetened)

½ cup golden raisins

¾ cup dry white wine or apple juice

2 tablespoons pomegranate molasses or honey, or more as needed

1 (2-inch) strip orange zest, preferably organic

1 (3-inch) sprig rosemary

1 tablespoon Grand Marnier or other good-quality citrus-scented liqueur

MAKES GENEROUS 1 CUP

I created this intensely tangy condiment to make use of an overflow of delicate dried barberries my sister-in-law gave me from her home country, Iran. The tiny ruby-red fruit with their almost petal-like lightness are used in many traditional recipes, the most famous being festive jeweled rice. Unlike cranberries, which are similarly tart, barberries are typically sold in their natural state—no oil or sugar added (see "Sources," page 251).

The chutney pairs beautifully with the Minted Lamb Sliders with Pine Nuts and Currants (page 87), or serve it next to turkey or pork. It also works well next to salmon or a firm white-fleshed fish such as haddock, cod, or halibut. Or spoon it over Greek yogurt or vanilla ice cream. My husband spreads it on dark whole grain rye bread drizzled with olive oil. 🌾 gluten-free

Add the barberries, raisins, wine, molasses, zest, and rosemary to a small heavy saucepan. Bring to a boil over medium-high heat, stirring occasionally. Decrease the heat to maintain a lively bubble and cook, uncovered and stirring a few times, until the dried fruit have plumped and a bit more than ¼ inch of liquid (just eyeball it) remains at the bottom, 9 to 12 minutes. (If you have a sweet tooth, test the berries after 5 minutes of cooking time and add more molasses to taste.) Stir in the limoncello, cook for 30 seconds more, and remove from the heat. Remove the zest and the sprig and allow to cool—the chutney will thicken a bit more, and the flavors will intensify.

fine points

Pomegranate molasses is worth seeking out—it adds an intense sour-sweet complexity (see page 249, and "Sources," page 251).

If I make this for the holidays, I splurge on golden Hunza raisins from the Himalayas, as they add a deep fruitiness.

To serve next to grilled steak or salmon, I make a spicy version, adding about 1 teaspoon Sriracha sauce to ½ cup of chutney, or to taste.

sweet potato and oat cakes with blue cheese and sage

STEEL-CUT OATS

1½ cups water

¾ cup steel-cut oats
(gluten-free if desired)

CAKES

3 tablespoons extra-virgin
olive oil

2 shallots, thinly sliced
crosswise (about ¾ cup)

½ teaspoon fine sea salt

1 cup shredded uncooked sweet
potato (about ½ small, peeled if
you like), using the large holes
of a box grater

2 tablespoons minced fresh
sage, or 2 teaspoons dried

1½ teaspoons smoked paprika
or sweet paprika

¼ cup dry white wine

½ cup crumbled blue cheese

⅓ cup toasted slivered
almonds, chopped up a bit

1 cup quick-cooking rolled
oats, or more as needed
(gluten-free if desired)

½ cup dried tart cherries,
roughly chopped

2 large eggs, lightly beaten

¼ teaspoon freshly ground
black pepper

MAKES 8 CAKES, TO SERVE 4

Sweet and sour, salty and savory all rolled into one bite, plus pockets of oozing cheese and the crunch of nuts—this is what you get in these delectable vegetarian cakes. They are perfect on their own, with a dollop of ketchup and Sriracha, or next to a simple green salad. Or make 16 smaller cakes as finger food for your next party buffet. But my favorite way of serving them is next to pan-seared steak. While the meat rests, cook the cakes in the same pan to further boost their flavor. Irresistible. ⌒⌒ gluten-free

step one

Prepare the steel-cut oats the night before, or about 75 minutes ahead: Bring the water and the oats to a boil in a 2-quart saucepan. Cook, uncovered, for 2 minutes over medium to medium-low heat, stirring a few times. Remove from the heat, cover, and let sit at room temperature until the liquid is absorbed, about 1 hour. Transfer the oats to a large bowl and spread to cool for about 10 minutes (or cover and chill overnight or for up to 2 days).

step two

When you are ready to make the cakes, heat 1 tablespoon of the olive oil in a 10-inch skillet over medium heat and wait until it shimmers. Add the shallots and ¼ teaspoon of the salt and cook, stirring, until they just start to brown, 1 to 2 minutes. Add the sweet potato, sage, and paprika and cook, stirring all the while, until the sweet potatoes soften, 1 to 2 minutes. Add the wine, stir to loosen any browned bits, and cook until it evaporates, about 1 minute. Take the pan off the heat and allow the vegetables to cool for about 10 minutes.

Add the vegetables, cheese, almonds, rolled oats, cherries, and the eggs to the bowl with the steel-cut oats. Season with the remaining ¼ teaspoon salt and the pepper. Using your hands, thoroughly combine the mixture until the ingredients come together. The mixture will be moist but should hold up. Otherwise add a tablespoon or two more quick-cooking oats.

Level the mixture inside the bowl and divide it into 8 equal portions using a butter knife (cut in half like a cake, and then each half into quarters). Or use a scant ½ cup per cake. Moisten your hands with water and form cakes about 3 inches in diameter. Place the cakes on a small baking sheet or large plate. If you have time, cover with plastic wrap and chill for 30 minutes.

To finish, heat 1 tablespoon of the remaining olive oil in a large skillet over medium heat until it shimmers. Add 4 cakes and cook until golden brown, about 4 minutes on each side, carefully flipping once with a metal spatula. Add the remaining 1 tablespoon olive oil and repeat with the second batch. Serve warm or at room temperature.

fine points

I like mine just as much without the crunchy almonds, but my tester's preference was with—so it's your choice!

Leftover cakes are a satisfying box lunch the next day. Eat at room temperature or reheat in a 325°F oven for 15 to 20 minutes.

MAKE AHEAD The cakes can be prepared and shaped up to 1 day ahead. Chill, covered.

Bake the cakes instead of panfrying them (see "Grain Burger 101," page 86).

one good plate of greens

The more I cook, the simpler my ways around the stove have become. Sometimes this is because I have learned to work more efficiently in my kitchen, and sometimes it's because I have learned to break down steps and plan ahead. But what has been hardest to learn was simply to allow fresh ingredients to shine—without much fuss.

There was a time when I used to experiment *a lot* in my kitchen. In fact, I was exploring so many flavors from so many cultures and merging them all into one dinner dish—the fusion of fusions so to speak—that I'm surprised my husband never got up from the table and went for takeout. He is one patient man. I have since learned that there is a reason why Italian flavors are typically best when combined with ingredients native to Italy. Or why some of the Indian spices I revere in my husband's family dishes should never be tossed into my own Mediterranean-inspired meals.

Still, some tweaking of tradition can result in divine creations, but only when done with great restraint. I still have to remind myself not to fall into my very own fusion trap—between my new fascination with the umami-rich cuisine of Korea, my adoration for the bright aromas and earthbound roots of Mexican cooking, and my endless curiosity for the skillful layering of Indian spicing.

In this chapter, I would like to introduce you to the one recipe that brought home this message of simplicity to me. I hope it will simplify your life as well. It is a recipe for greens (page 96). You will see its spirit reflected in many recipes in this chapter, especially in the Teff Polenta Verde (page 115), the Warm Wild Rice Salad with Herb-Roasted Mushrooms and Parmesan (page 112), the simple Saffron Millet (page 135), and the Citrus Boost Dressing for Any Grain (page 105).

Here is this recipe's story: Until a few years ago, I was no leafy greens enthusiast—despite all of the well-meaning advice to eat more of them. Of course I enjoyed the occasional sautéed spinach, or chard, tossed into a pot of soup at the end, but eating loads of greens on their own? Not me. It seemed like too much of a good thing. As a result, leafy green vegetables were largely an afterthought on my table. I hardly bought them nor did I cook them much.

A matrimonial challenge, however, loomed ahead. It turns out that my omnivore husband, for reasons I have not understood to this day, evolved into a passionate greens lover over the years. Left to his own devices he would forget to eat fish, meat, dairy, grains, and pasta, even dessert. Not so, greens.

Whenever it was his turn to go grocery shopping, he would return with more greens than I ever imagined could fit into our fridge. May I add, the greens were *not* on the shopping list. Week after week we had this, and more: humongous bunches of chard, kale, beet greens, spinach, dandelion greens, carrot tops, you name it. As long as something had giant leaves, fresh and dark green, he would bring it home. And stoically fill the whole bottom shelf of our fridge, despite my protests. Week after week. And I grew more exasperated each time I opened the door.

For a long time, I kept sighing at the overflow for which there are no roots in his Indian family. And I wondered, jokingly, whether he was related to my Greek grandfather. Because, according to my mom, greens were his first food group too.

The fast-wilting fresh leaves caused problems—of space, of the occasional decay, of boring sides, cooked up last minute, and, in desperation, heaping portions on our plates only a greens maniac could embrace. Finally the cook in me stepped in. And my frugal self. Because I couldn't take letting this bounty go to waste or eating so-so greens any longer.

One day I decided I had to figure out a way to make greens work for me: I needed a good recipe. And it had to be endlessly adaptable, to accommodate whatever my husband happened to pick up. So I started cooking greens. Still puzzled but with curiosity. I was trying to understand why someone would fall for them. Even long for them. After mountains of chopped leaves and much trial and error, I report back: I can't stop eating greens. In fact, we now—to the dismay of my husband—compete for them at the dinner table. In the end, my endlessly adaptable recipe became a simple plate of greens. I could eat them every day.

my go-to greens

2 tablespoons extra-virgin olive oil, plus extra for drizzling

1 cup chopped green onions, light and dark parts (about 6)

2 large bunches of chard or beet greens, stems chopped into ¼-inch pieces and kept separately (3 to 4 cups) and leaves cut into ½-inch ribbons (5 to 10 cups)

2 or 3 cloves garlic, thinly sliced

½ teaspoon Aleppo pepper, or ⅛ to ¼ teaspoon dried red chile flakes (optional)

¼ teaspoon fine sea salt

½ cup white wine or low-sodium chicken or vegetable broth

½ cup loosely packed fresh mint leaves, plus 2 tablespoons torn leaves for garnish, or 1 tablespoon dried mint and 1 teaspoon for garnish (see page 247)

1 tablespoon low-sodium soy sauce (plus more as needed)

2 to 3 teaspoons red wine vinegar

Freshly ground black pepper

SERVES 4 TO 6 OR MORE, DEPENDING ON ADD-ONS

My greens recipe makes a simple, tangy, yet satisfying side dish with enough umami to make you long for more. And the preparation is as easy as it is adaptable. I make a large pot almost every week, usually on the day after I return from my weekly shopping trip as to make best use of their freshness. Sometimes I add other vegetables as well before they become lifeless in the crisper drawer. Of course, now that I think about it, my mom does that too. It just took me a while to understand how useful this is.

Serve the greens with meat, fish, or pasta, and use leftovers to make Frittata Muffins for Any Grain (page 74). Or top them with a fried egg for a quick bite. Or stir them into leftover grains, add a few olives, a drizzle of olive oil, and a slice of feta, and you have a superfast meal! The possibilities are endless.

🌿 gluten-free

Heat a large Dutch oven or heavy saucepan over medium heat. Swirl in the oil and wait until it is shimmering. Add the green onions, chard stems, garlic, Aleppo pepper, and salt. Cook, stirring often, until the vegetables wilt and the stems soften, 4 to 6 minutes. Add the wine and cook until it is syrupy and almost evaporated, 4 to 5 minutes.

Stir in the chard leaves, in two to three stages, allowing them to wilt each time in between, 3 to 5 minutes. Stir in the mint with the last batch of leaves. Stir in the soy sauce and cook until it evaporates, about 30 seconds. Drizzle with 2 teaspoons of the vinegar and remove the saucepan from the heat. Grind on a good dose of pepper. Season with a bit more soy sauce, and salt and pepper to taste, and perhaps a bit more vinegar.

Serve warm or at room temperature, sprinkled with the remaining 2 tablespoons mint and drizzled with a bit more olive oil.

fine points

The amount of stems and leaves can vary quite a bit, depending on the size of your bunches, the thickness of stems, and so on. But it doesn't matter in this recipe; just toss everything in.

Sturdy leaves such as collards and kale need a bit more cooking time, as do, for example, the stems of beets. You'll get the hang of it.

Don't pat your leaves dry after rinsing. The water that still clings to them adds just the right amount of moisture to help them cook to perfection. In the rare case that your pan does go dry, just add a tablespoon or two of water.

Do try the recipe once or twice as is and then adapt it to the greens in your fridge

how to prepare large leafy greens and their sweet stems

A mountain of leafy greens will melt into a fistful of vegetables on your plate. But at first, the large unwieldy leaves take up a good amount of counter space. How do you get them ready for cooking? And how do you remove the leaves from their stems?

It's easy: First, give the leaves a good rinse under cold running water and place them in a colander to allow the water to drip off. Work with one leaf at a time. You can either fold the leaf over lengthwise and cut out the stem, or, with sturdy greens such as collards or kale, you can simply strip the leaf off the stem with your hands using a quick pulling motion. With a little practice you will get the hang of it. This easy step allows you to chop and use the stems and leaves separately. Now simply line up all of your stems and slice them crosswise. Pile the leaves on top of each other and slice them crosswise into ribbons. If they are very large, I cut the ribbons a few times to make them more manageable.

Please don't toss out the stems. Be it kale, chard, spinach, or mustard greens, stems have a delicate sweetness you will not want to miss. And even if you don't use them with their leaves, sauté them on another day together with onions and other vegetables for a richly aromatic base in many recipes—from soups to stews and stir-fries.

GREEN VARIATIONS

Here are a few ideas and seasonal variations I enjoy. You might have to increase flavorings such as salt, Aleppo pepper, and soy sauce depending on the amount of vegetables you use.

- Instead of green onions, you can use the same amount of spring onions or 1 chopped yellow or red onion (about 1½ cups). Or use 2 leeks instead, tough outer leaves and dark green parts removed, cut in half lengthwise, and cut into ¼-inch-wide slices (about 4 cups).

- Add 1 large bell pepper, cut into ¾-inch pieces (about 2½ cups) together with the green onions.

- Cut 1 or 2 carrots, crosswise, into ¼-inch-wide slices and add for color with the green onions.

- Add 2 cups sugar snap peas just before you add the wine.

- Carrot tops: Chop 1 cup quite finely; add half the amount with the green onions at the start and half at the end with the last heaping of leafy greens.

- One bunch each of mustard greens and dandelion greens makes a delicious bittersweet side for four. The leaves wilt a bit faster. Allow to sit for a few minutes, covered, for best flavor.

farro salad with roasted eggplant, caramelized onion, and pine nuts

FARRO

2 cups water

1 cup semipearled farro, or about 3 cups cooked

1 bay leaf

1 dried red chile pepper (optional)

1 teaspoon minced hot green chile such as serrano (optional)

¾ teaspoon Aleppo pepper, or more as needed

¾ teaspoon dried mint, preferably spearmint (optional)

SALAD

1½ pounds eggplant, cut into 1-inch cubes (about 8 cups)

½ red onion, thinly sliced (less than ¼ inch)

4 tablespoons extra-virgin olive oil

½ teaspoon fine sea salt

½ cup loosely packed torn fresh mint leaves

2 tablespoons white balsamic vinegar or red wine vinegar

¼ cup lightly toasted pine nuts

SERVES 4 TO 6

During the summer months, roasted eggplant has a lush silkiness and rich natural sweetness that is unsurpassed. This is the time to make this aromatic farro salad. Two types of mint, fresh and dried, work their magic in tandem: dried spearmint (see page 247), commonly used in Greece and across the Middle East, adds warm notes in the background, while fresh mint bursts on your fork to brighten every bite.

This salad pairs beautifully with grilled steaks, chicken, or lamb. Vegetarians can top it with crumbled ricotta salata or feta for more substance.

Place a rack in the center of the oven and preheat to 425°F.

To prepare the farro, add the water, farro, bay leaf, and dried chile to a 2-quart heavy saucepan and bring to a boil. Decrease the heat to maintain a simmer, cover, and cook until the grain is tender with a slight chew, 20 to 25 minutes. Remove the bay leaf and chile, drain if needed, and transfer to a large serving bowl. Sprinkle with the minced chile, Aleppo pepper, and dried mint and toss to combine.

Meanwhile, to make the salad, place the eggplant and the onion on a large rimmed baking sheet. Drizzle with 2 tablespoons of the olive oil, sprinkle with the salt, and combine well, using your hands. If you don't mind the extra dish, it's a bit easier to toss everything in a large bowl.

Roast the mixture until the eggplant pieces have softened and are browned in spots, and the onion slices have caramelized, turning them once with a spatula in between, 30 to 35 minutes. Remove the baking sheet from the oven and immediately sprinkle the vegetables with ¼ cup of the fresh mint and drizzle with 1 tablespoon of the vinegar. Toss well with a spatula—this will soften the mint leaves and take the sting out of the vinegar.

To finish, add the warm eggplant mixture to the farro. Drizzle with the remaining 2 tablespoons olive oil and 1 tablespoon vinegar and toss to combine. Season with salt and vinegar to taste. Top with the remaining ¼ cup mint and the pine nuts and serve.

fine points

To speed things up, I use semipearled farro here, but feel free to use whole grain farro or farro piccolo (also known as einkorn, see page 12).

MAKE AHEAD The vegetables can be roasted 1 day ahead. Chill, covered. Bring to room temperature before serving. The salad can be made completely ahead, up to 4 hours, reserving the remaining ¼ cup mint and the pine nuts. Chill, covered, and bring to room temperature before serving, about 1 hour. Refresh with a bit of oil and vinegar if needed, top with the mint and the nuts, and serve.

minted summer couscous with watermelon and feta

1¼ cups water

1 cup whole wheat couscous

½ teaspoon fine sea salt

Pinch of saffron (optional)

2 or 3 limes, preferably organic

2 tablespoons extra-virgin
olive oil, plus extra for drizzling

1 to 2 teaspoons honey,
depending on your preference

¼ teaspoon freshly ground
black pepper

1½ cups seedless watermelon,
cut into ¾-inch cubes

½ cup celery, cut into ¼-inch-
wide slices (about 1 stalk)

½ cup loosely packed torn fresh
mint leaves, plus a few leaves
for garnish

½ cup crumbled mild feta,
preferably sheep's milk

SERVES 4 TO 6

Serve this easy one-bowl meal on a sweltering summer night when doing anything more than pouring yourself a glass of ice water seems prohibitive. Speedy whole wheat couscous is my go-to grain on such evenings, as it needs just a brief steaming and no cooking.

In Greece, we love pairing sweet, juicy watermelon with briny, salty feta. Crunchy celery, lots of fresh mint, and lime make this a refreshing cross between a fruit and a savory salad. Pair it with grilled chicken, fish, or shrimp. Or simply add a bowl of olives and a plate of dry-cured serrano ham or prosciutto and call it a day. ⋙ gluten-free option

Add the water to a small heavy saucepan and bring to a boil. Remove from the heat. Stir in the couscous, ¼ teaspoon of the salt, and the saffron, cover, and set aside until the liquid is absorbed, about 10 minutes. Fluff the couscous with a fork and transfer to a large serving bowl, spreading and fluffing the grains again. Set aside to cool for about 15 minutes.

Meanwhile, zest the limes until you have 2 teaspoons zest. Squeeze the fruit until you have 3 tablespoons juice. Place the zest and juice in a small screw-top jar and add the olive oil, honey, the remaining ¼ teaspoon salt, and the pepper. Shake vigorously until the dressing is amalgamated.

Once the couscous has cooled, distribute the watermelon, celery, and mint across. Drizzle the dressing across and gently toss to combine. Season with salt and pepper to taste (keeping in mind that feta can be quite salty). If you have time, allow to sit for 30 minutes for flavors to meld.

To finish, toss again, top with the crumbled feta and the mint leaves for garnish, and drizzle with a touch more olive oil.

fine points

A bit of saffron adds glamour to this lazy preparation, coloring your couscous with enticing golden flecks.

GLUTEN-FREE About 2½ cups cooked white quinoa is a fine replacement for the couscous.

MAKE AHEAD This is lovely when made up to 4 hours ahead—the citrus aroma will only intensify. Just leave out the feta and the mint leaves for garnish. Chill, covered. Remove a few minutes before serving to take the chill out before finishing.

spring salad with asparagus coins, kamut, and lemon vinaigrette

This lemony salad wakes you up after a long cold winter. Lots of crisp fresh asparagus and radishes are tossed with a brazen dressing that packs a tangy punch but also miraculously mellows and marries the ingredients.

Add the water and the Kamut to a small heavy saucepan and bring to a boil. Decrease the heat to maintain a simmer, cover, and cook until tender with a slight chewiness, 50 to 60 minutes. Remove from the heat and let sit, covered, 10 to 15 minutes. Drain any remaining liquid and transfer the Kamut to a large serving bowl to cool.

Finely grate the lemon until you have 2 teaspoons zest, then squeeze it until you have ¼ cup juice. Add the lemon juice, zest, mustard, salt, and pepper to a medium bowl and combine with a fork. Stir in the shallots and set aside.

Meanwhile, cut off the asparagus tips, slice the tips in half lengthwise, and set aside for garnish. Equip your food processor with the slicing disc. Cut the stalks in half crosswise. Add 8 to 10 pieces at a time to the feeding tube, depending on thickness, and process until you have 2½ cups asparagus coins (reserve the rest for another use). Transfer to the bowl with the Kamut. Add the radishes. Set aside 2 tablespoons of the dill for garnish and add the remaining dill to the bowl.

To finish, using a small whisk, slowly add the olive oil to the dressing, whisking until it is emulsified. Drizzle ½ cup of the dressing over the salad and toss to combine well. Season with salt, pepper, and perhaps a bit more lemon juice to taste. Allow to sit for about 10 minutes for the flavors to mingle.

Toss again, top with the Parmesan, and garnish with the asparagus tips and the remaining radishes. Sprinkle with the remaining 2 tablespoons dill and serve.

fine points

Make this salad only if you can find really fresh asparagus stalks—otherwise it just won't taste good. The stems should be firm, not wobbly, with equally firm tips. There will be a bit of vinaigrette left, which you need if you add other ingredients.

VARIATIONS Add 1 cup cooked shredded chicken or 1 cup packed fresh baby spinach. Instead of Parmesan top with ½ cup crumbled feta.

Try using spelt, emmer, einkorn, and whole wheat berries, preferably the soft type, in place of Kamut.

KAMUT

1¾ cups water

1 cup Kamut berries, soaked overnight and drained, or 2½ cups cooked

SALAD

1 or 2 lemons, preferably organic

2 teaspoons Dijon mustard

¼ teaspoon fine sea salt

¼ teaspoon freshly ground black pepper

¼ cup minced shallots (about 1 medium)

1 small bunch asparagus, rinsed and trimmed (scant 1 pound)

1 cup thinly sliced radishes (about 8), plus a few small ones for garnish, preferably with a bit of their green stems attached

½ cup loosely packed chopped fresh dill

¼ cup plus 2 tablespoons extra-virgin olive oil

½ to ¾ cup thinly shaved Parmesan, using a box grater, for serving

SERVES 4 TO 6

quinoa tabbouleh with purslane and mustard dressing

QUINOA

1¼ cups water

¾ cup quinoa, well rinsed and drained, or about 3 cups cooked quinoa

SALAD

½ cup finely chopped red onion (about ½ medium)

2 to 3 tablespoons red wine vinegar

¾ teaspoon fine sea salt

3 cups (about 8 ounces) fresh purslane leaves and small twigs, coarsely chopped, stems discarded

1½ cups coarsely chopped ripe tomatoes (about 2)

1 teaspoon minced serrano chile (optional)

1 teaspoon Dijon mustard

¼ teaspoon freshly ground black pepper

¼ cup extra-virgin olive oil

SERVES 4 TO 6

fine points

VARIATION If you can't get your hands on purslane, replace it with 2 cups packed chopped arugula—to mimic the interesting pepperiness of the wild green—and 1 cup loosely packed chopped flat-leaf parsley.

MAKE AHEAD The salad can be made up to 4 hours ahead. Chill, covered. Bring to room temperature before serving, about 1 hour. Leftovers hold up well for your lunch box the next day.

Every summer my mom studiously cultivates purslane in large clay pots, at the feet of other plants. She carefully guards the plants and plucks only the top leaves for her lunch during long Greek summers. Most often, she tosses the crunchy succulent greens with a superb tangy dressing and serves them on their own or together with juicy tomatoes. When I discovered purslane at my farmers' market, I decided it was high time to create a grain dish to honor this sturdy weed that grows wild in many gardens.

For this refreshing salad, inspired by tabbouleh, traditional bulgur has been replaced with quinoa, and parsley with coarsely chopped purslane. Together, they are magnificent: the crunchy seeds of the grain enhance the mouth-watering crunch of the greens, with sweet, soft tomatoes to balance the lot. To spice up the natural pepperiness of the greens, I added mustard to my mother's ultrasimple olive oil dressing.

This is a versatile salad that pairs well with grilled fish and meat. We enjoy it with grilled chicken breasts rubbed with mustard and olive oil. Vegetarians can top it with feta for an easy meal. gluten-free

To prepare the quinoa, bring the water and quinoa to a boil in a small heavy saucepan. Decrease the heat to maintain a simmer, cover, and cook until the water is absorbed, 14 to 17 minutes. Remove from the heat and let sit, covered, for 5 to 10 minutes. Transfer the quinoa to a large serving bowl and spread to cool for about 20 minutes.

Meanwhile, to make the salad, combine the onion, 2 tablespoons of the vinegar, and the salt for the dressing in a small bowl and set aside (the rest will take the sting from the onion).

Once the quinoa has cooled, add the purslane, tomatoes, and chile to the quinoa and gently toss to combine. Whisk the mustard and pepper into the dressing and slowly drizzle in the olive oil, whisking all the while, until amalgamated.

To finish, drizzle the dressing over the tabbouleh and toss to combine. Set aside for 10 minutes, if you can, for the flavors to meld. Gently toss once more. Season with salt and pepper to taste, drizzle on the remaining 1 tablespoon vinegar if you like (I enjoy the zing!), and serve.

citrus boost dressing for any grain

I will never forget the intense swell of scent the first time I tossed a whole orange into a food processor, peel, seeds, and all. Together with dark, sweet maple syrup, and fresh cranberries, the chunky sauce that emerged had a brazenness amplified by the complex aromas of the orange—its sweet juice, its bitter pith, and the essential oils in the peel. This was the first cranberry sauce I ever made, inspired by a recipe from Patrick O'Connell, chef of the Inn at Little Washington in Virginia. A variation of it has been on my Thanksgiving table ever since.

A few years ago, I noticed blender dressings using whole citrus and olive oil in Greece for the first time, so I decided to create my own. This dressing has a beguiling chunkiness, almost puddinglike.

Try it in the Artichoke and Spelt Salad with Cara Cara Citrus Boost (page 106) or any other whole grain salad, or toss it with a chickpea or lentil salad. I also enjoy it stirred into warm millet and quinoa. gluten-free

1 large whole lemon or ½ orange (about 5 ounces), preferably organic, cut into a few chunks, skin and all

½ shallot cut into chunks

2 tablespoons white balsamic vinegar or white wine vinegar

2 to 3 teaspoons honey, or more as needed

½ teaspoon Aleppo pepper, or ⅛ teaspoon dried red chile flakes (optional)

½ teaspoon fine sea salt

¼ cup extra-virgin olive oil

MAKES 1 GENEROUS CUP, ENOUGH TO DRESS ABOUT 4 CUPS OF GRAINS

In a food processor: Add the lemon, shallot, vinegar, and 2 teaspoons of the honey to the bowl of the processor, fitted with a steel blade. Process until you have a chunky puree, about 10 seconds. Scrape down the sides and sprinkle on the pepper and salt. Drizzle with the olive oil and process until you have a nicely creamy but still slightly chunky dressing, about 20 seconds more (do not over-process as the dressing will solidify). Season with salt and honey to taste and pulse a few more times to combine.

In a blender: Toss in all of the ingredients and blitz until creamy with small chunks, about 30 seconds.

fine points

The olive oil in this dressing can firm up when chilled; it will soften again when returned to room temperature.

This recipe is infinitely adaptable, using any citrus you can get your hands on, including Cara Cara, blood oranges, or tangerines, as long as you weigh or eyeball the amount of fruit to get a similar ratio.

The dressing will keep for up to 7 days in the fridge, so start dressing up your grains and more.

artichoke and spelt salad with cara cara citrus boost

2 cups cooked spelt berries (see page 23)

1 cup cooked chickpeas (see page 152), or about ½ (14-ounce) can, rinsed and drained

About ⅔ cup Citrus Boost Dressing (page 105)

1 (12- to 14-ounce) jar or can marinated artichoke hearts, drained and cut into quarters or halves, depending on size

½ Cara Cara or regular orange, peeled and cut into ½-inch chunks (about 1 cup)

⅓ cup Moroccan salt-cured olives, pitted if you like

Fine sea salt and freshly ground black pepper

½ cup crumbled feta, preferably sheep's milk

¼ cup loosely packed chopped fresh herbs such as dill or parsley, for garnish

Extra-virgin olive oil, for drizzling

SERVES 4 TO 6

First, pick your whole grain berries. Spelt and rye are splendid here, but oat berries, Kamut, or wheat berries, preferably soft, are lovely as well—any leftovers will do. Second, add a few ingredients you likely have in your pantry. Third, whirl up a magnificent citrus dressing in the food processor. Dinner!

gluten-free option

Place the spelt berries and the chickpeas in a large serving bowl. Add the dressing and stir to combine well. Add the artichoke hearts, orange, and olives and gently toss to combine. Season with a bit of salt and pepper to taste (keeping in mind that feta can be salty). If you have time, allow to sit for 10 minutes for flavors to meld.

Toss again. Sprinkle with the feta and garnish with the fresh herbs. Drizzle on a nice pour of olive oil and serve.

fine points

Delicious red-fleshed Cara Cara oranges are becoming more widely available. Cara Cara is a type of navel orange, sweet but not one-dimensional, with a more interesting complexity than regular oranges.

Use half of the orange for the dressing and cut the other half into chunks for the salad.

For best flavor, buy simple oil-marinated artichokes. Otherwise, drizzle on a bit more oil.

Leftover cooked chicken or grilled salmon can be tossed in as well—just use a bit more dressing. Or garnish with a 5-ounce can of olive oil–packed tuna, drained.

GLUTEN-FREE Cooked sorghum has a fabulous chew and works well here instead of the spelt.

last-minute broiled asparagus with citrus boost dressing

Green asparagus was completely foreign to me until I arrived in the United States many years ago. I spent my formative years in a country where the arrival of white asparagus is treated like a king's homecoming. *Spargelzeit*, or asparagus season, in Germany lasts only a few weeks. During this time, *spargel* fans eat the pristine white stalks, grown without sunlight to prevent photosynthesis, as often and in as many ways as possible. My favorite is the most austere, simply boiled, next to steaming boiled potatoes, drizzled with melted butter and sprinkled with parsley.

Today, in spring, I greet the arrival of green asparagus almost with the same reverence. This is my number one weeknight preparation. Yet you can also feed it to a crowd. ⸎ gluten-free

2 bunches asparagus (about 2 pounds), stalks about ½ inch thick, trimmed at the bottom (see Fine Points)

½ teaspoon fine sea salt

¼ teaspoon freshly ground black pepper

½ cup Citrus Boost Dressing (page 105)

2 shallots, thinly sliced crosswise

SERVES 4 TO 6

Place a rack 4 inches away from the broiler and preheat on high for 5 minutes.

Meanwhile, add the asparagus to a large rimmed baking sheet (it will be full). Sprinkle with the salt and pepper, then toss with the dressing, using your hands.

Broil until the asparagus just starts to brown, about 10 minutes Remove the baking sheet, add the shallots and toss with tongs. Continue broiling until the asparagus is blackened in spots and the shallots start to caramelize, 6 to 8 minutes more, depending on the thickness of the stalks. Season with salt and pepper to taste and serve warm or at room temperature.

fine points

Use whatever Citrus Boost Dressing you have, made with lemon or orange (or mix it!).

How do you trim green asparagus? By bending the stems near the fibrous bottom until they break naturally.

kamut salad with oranges, leeks, and blue cheese

If there is one vegetable I would love to go sky-high on the trend barometer, it is the sturdy leek. To me, its elegant slender stalks are vegetable candy. My own appreciation for this humble vegetable started when I was growing up in Germany, where leeks, potatoes, and carrots were the trinity of cold long winter months when not much else was available. Even when just allowed to soften, leeks add an alluring sweetness to every dish that features them.

In this colorful winter salad, Kamut, an ancient wheat variety, provides superb chew—each bite interspersed with juicy oranges, crunchy walnuts, and pungent blue cheese. Use farro, wheat berries, or gluten-free sorghum to vary. This salad makes for a satisfying yet light lunch, or serve it next to grilled chicken or steak. gluten-free option

Add the water, Kamut, bay leaf, and chile to a small heavy saucepan and bring to a boil. Decrease the heat to maintain a simmer, cover, and cook until tender but slightly chewy, 50 to 60 minutes. Remove from the heat and set aside to steam for 10 to 15 minutes. Drain, if needed. Transfer to a large serving bowl, remove the spices, and spread to cool.

Add the raisins to a small bowl and cover with hot water. Cut off a 2 by 1-inch strip of zest from the orange, removing any white pith, and set aside. Finely grate the remaining skin until you have 1 teaspoon zest and set aside. Peel the fruit, removing any pith, and cut into ½-inch pieces to make about ¾ cup (reserve the rest for another use).

Add the leeks, broth, wine, and the zest strip to a large skillet and bring to a boil. Decrease the heat to maintain a simmer, cover, and cook until the leeks are soft, 5 to 7 minutes. Drain, remove the zest strip, and add the leeks to the bowl with the Kamut. Drain the raisins and add them to the bowl along with the orange pieces.

In a small bowl, beat the lemon juice, grated orange zest, honey, salt, and pepper with a fork until smooth. Slowly beat in the olive oil in a thin stream until emulsified.

To finish, pour the dressing over the salad, gently toss, and season with salt and pepper to taste. Let sit at room temperature for 10 to 15 minutes, gently toss again, and sprinkle with the walnuts and blue cheese. Garnish with parsley and serve.

KAMUT

1½ cups water

¾ cup Kamut berries, soaked overnight and drained, or about 2 cups cooked

1 bay leaf (optional)

1 small dried red chile (optional)

SALAD

¼ cup golden raisins

1 large orange, preferably organic

2 leeks, cut in half lengthwise, rinsed well, and cut into ¾-inch segments (about 4 cups; see page 247)

½ cup low-sodium chicken or vegetable broth

½ cup dry white wine

1 tablespoon freshly squeezed lemon juice

1 teaspoon honey

½ teaspoon fine sea salt

¼ teaspoon freshly ground black pepper

2 tablespoons extra-virgin olive oil

⅓ cup coarsely chopped toasted walnuts

⅓ to ½ cup mild crumbled blue cheese such as Stilton

3 tablespoons finely chopped fresh flat-leaf parsley, for garnish

SERVES 4 TO 6

freekeh salad with caramelized cauliflower and tuna

FREEKEH

1½ cups low-sodium vegetable broth

1 cup water

1 cup cracked freekeh or about 3 cups cooked

3 whole peppercorns (optional)

SALAD

6 cups cauliflower florets, cut into 1-inch pieces (from one 2-pound head)

5 tablespoons extra-virgin olive oil

¾ teaspoon fine sea salt

½ teaspoon freshly ground black pepper

5 green onions, white and light green parts chopped (about ¾ cup), dark tops finely chopped (about ½ cup) and reserved for finishing

2 tablespoons freshly squeezed lemon juice, plus more for serving

1 teaspoon Dijon mustard

1 teaspoon finely grated lemon zest

½ cup pitted Castelvetrano olives (about 13) or other good-quality mixed olives

2 tablespoons capers, rinsed

½ cup loosely packed chopped fresh flat-leaf parsley

3 to 4 tablespoons lightly toasted pine nuts

2 (5-ounce) cans tuna, preferably in olive oil, drained and separated into chunks

SERVES 4 TO 6

Germany has a centuries-old tradition of using green wheat, better known in this country by its Middle Eastern name *freekeh*. Germans call it *Grünkern*, which literally means "green seed," traditionally made from spelt. I like it best in savory dishes such as burgers or soups to highlight its distinct smokiness (see also "Freekeh Soup with Spicy Harissa Shrimp and Dates," page 147).

This lemony grain salad is loaded with caramelized cauliflower and green onions, which I prepare in two ways: I roast much of them for sweet flavor and finely chop the dark tops together with ample parsley to brighten the salad.

Position a rack in the center of the oven and preheat to 425°F.

To prepare the freekeh, add the broth, water, freekeh, and peppercorns to a heavy 2-quart saucepan and bring to a boil. Decrease the heat to maintain a simmer, cover, and cook until the freekeh is tender with a bit of chewiness, 18 to 20 minutes. Drain, return the grains to the pot, cover, and allow to steam for 5 minutes. Transfer to a large serving bowl and spread to cool.

Meanwhile, to make the salad, add the cauliflower florets to a large rimmed baking sheet and drizzle with 2 tablespoons of the olive oil. Season with ½ teaspoon of the salt and ¼ teaspoon of the pepper and toss to coat well with your hands. Roast for 12 minutes, then add the chopped green onions (white and light green parts) and turn with a spatula. Continue roasting until the cauliflower is soft (the tip of a knife should slide in easily) and the green onions start to caramelize, 11 to 15 minutes more.

While the vegetables are roasting, prepare the dressing: add the lemon juice, the remaining 3 tablespoons olive oil, the mustard, zest, and the remaining ¼ teaspoon salt and ¼ teaspoon pepper to a small lidded jar and shake vigorously until emulsified.

To finish, add the roasted vegetables, the reserved green onion tops, the olives, and capers to the bowl with the freekeh. Set aside 2 tablespoons of the chopped parsley for garnish and add the remaining parsley to the bowl. Drizzle with the dressing and toss to combine. Season with salt and pepper to taste. If you have time, allow to sit for 10 minutes for flavors to mingle.

Top the salad with the tuna and garnish with the remaining parsley. Serve, passing more lemon juice around.

fine points

Be sure to zest your lemon before you squeeze it. It makes life easier.

Vegetarians omit the tuna and top the salad with ½ to ¾ cup crumbled mild goat cheese.

For a more substantial meal, garnish the salad with 3 hard- or medium-boiled eggs, cut in half.

VARIATION If you can't find freekeh (see "Sources," page 251), replace it with 3 cups cooked medium-coarse bulgur (see page 22).

MAKE AHEAD The salad, before adding the tuna, can be made 4 hours ahead. It holds up very well, so you can enjoy leftovers in your lunch box.

warm wild rice salad with herb-roasted mushrooms and parmesan

Wild rice with its stunning elongated shape is often resered for the holiday table—here it becomes a deeply aromatic side you can serve anytime. It pairs well with fish and meat alike, or serve it on its own as a light supper.

⁂ gluten-free

WILD RICE

2 cups water

1 cup wild rice, or about 2½ cups cooked

1 (3-inch) sprig fresh rosemary, or ½ teaspoon dried (optional)

SALAD

1 pound (about 7 cups) cremini or mixed mushrooms, halved if large and sliced ¼ inch thick

2 shallots, thinly sliced crosswise (about ¾ cup)

2 tablespoons finely chopped fresh sage leaves

2 teaspoons minced fresh rosemary

½ teaspoon fine sea salt

¼ teaspoon freshly ground black pepper

3 to 4 tablespoons extra-virgin olive oil, plus more as needed

1 tablespoon plus 2 teaspoons good-quality balsamic vinegar, or more as needed

2 teaspoons low-sodium soy sauce

4 ounces Parmesan, half of it coarsely shredded (about ⅔ cup) and half of it shaved (about ¾ cup)

SERVES 6

Position a rack in the center of the oven and preheat to 425°F.

Add the water, rice, and rosemary to a small heavy saucepan and bring to a boil. Decrease the heat to maintain a simmer, cover, and cook until the kernels split and are tender with a slight bite, 40 to 50 minutes. Drain, return to the pot, cover, and set aside.

Meanwhile, add the mushrooms, shallots, 1 tablespoon of the sage, and 1 teaspoon of the rosemary to a large rimmed baking sheet. Sprinkle with the salt and pepper and drizzle with 2 tablespoons of the olive oil. Toss with your hands to coat well.

Roast until the mushrooms have released their liquid and start to brown and the shallots caramelize, 18 to 20 minutes, turning once or twice with a spatula. Remove, drizzle with the 2 teaspoons balsamic vinegar, and toss to combine well. If the rice is not ready, push the mushrooms into a pile, loosely cover with aluminum foil, and leave them in the oven with the door ajar.

To finish, transfer the wild rice to a large salad bowl. Add the mushroom mixture, drizzle with the remaining 1 to 2 tablespoons olive oil, the remaining 1 tablespoon vinegar, and the soy sauce. Add the remaining 1 tablespoon sage and 1 teaspoon rosemary and toss to combine. Stir in the shredded Parmesan and allow to sit for a few minutes, loosely covered with foil. Season with salt and pepper to taste, drizzling on a bit more vinegar or olive oil if you like.

Top with the shaved Parmesan and serve at once, grating more pepper on top.

fine points

If you're in a hurry, you can used presliced mushrooms and look for quick-cooking wild rice varieties (see "Sources," page 251).

Briefly reheat cooked wild rice (see page 17) before combining with the other ingredients.

teff polenta verde with dandelions and parmesan

Teff, the smallest of all of the grains, has an intriguing meatiness. This gluten-free Ethiopian staple also develops a soul-warming creaminess, similar to polenta, which I love. It is this quality that inspired me to pair it with bittersweet dandelion greens. In this recipe, I stir half the greens into the soft teff polenta and serve the rest of the vegetables on top. But you could also keep the greens and the polenta separate to make it a light vegetarian meal. As a side dish, it is versatile: try it next to simple sautéed chicken or grilled salmon.

gluten-free

Add the broth, water, teff, and ¼ teaspoon of the salt to a large heavy saucepan and bring to a boil. Decrease the heat to maintain a simmer, cover, and cook until the liquid is absorbed and the grains are tender, 15 to 20 minutes. You have to stir a few times with a wooden spoon, vigorously and scraping the bottom, especially after 8 minutes or so, because teff has a tendency to become sticky. Any lumps will dissolve with good stirring. If the pan runs dry, just add a few tablespoons of water and stir well.

Meanwhile, cut off the dandelion stems and slice them crosswise into ¼-inch pieces. You will have 2 to 3 cups. Cut the leaves crosswise into ½-inch ribbons. You will have 3 to 6 loosely packed cups; use whatever you have.

Add the olive oil to a large skillet over medium heat until shimmering. Add the green onions, dandelion stems, garlic, chile flakes, and the remaining ¼ teaspoon salt, and cook, stirring all the while, until the onions wilt and the stems soften, 2 to 3 minutes. Add the dandelion leaves, in stages if needed, and cook until they just wilt, about 2 minutes. Remove from the heat, stir in ½ cup of the cheese, and set aside, covered, until the teff is ready.

To finish, add the remaining ½ cup of the cheese, the soy sauce, butter, and the pepper and stir to blend well. Stir in about half of the greens and season with salt and pepper to taste.

Place some teff polenta on a plate and top with a portion of the remaining greens. Grind on a few turns of pepper and serve at once, passing more cheese around.

2 cups low-sodium vegetable, chicken, or beef broth

1 cup water, or a bit more as needed

1 cup whole grain teff

½ teaspoon fine sea salt

1 large bunch dandelion greens (about 12 ounces)

1 tablespoon extra-virgin olive oil

2 cups chopped green onions (about 12)

2 cloves garlic, peeled and thinly sliced

⅛ teaspoon dried red chile flakes

1 cup (2 ounces) finely grated Parmesan, plus more for serving

1 tablespoon low-sodium soy sauce

1 tablespoon unsalted butter or extra-virgin olive oil

¼ teaspoon freshly ground black pepper

SERVES 4 TO 6

fine points

Peppery arugula is a good substitute for the dandelion greens, as are chard or beet greens.

Many options for leftovers: Teff behaves like Italian polenta after it is cooked—it stiffens fast. But don't despair because this gives you an opportunity for terrific leftover meals. So be sure to make double and follow the leftover tips for polenta (see page 122).

oven-roasted tofu with mediterranean herbs

1 (14- or 15-ounce) package extra-firm or firm tofu, drained (see page 118)

2 tablespoons low-sodium soy sauce (use gluten-free if needed)

½ tablespoon red wine vinegar

1½ teaspoons dried herbes de Provence (see page 249), dried thyme, or dried oregano

⅛ teaspoon dried chile flakes (optional)

2 tablespoons extra-virgin olive oil

6 (2-inch) sprigs fresh oregano, thyme, or rosemary (optional)

SERVES 4 TO 6

For reasons I cannot explain, I am an unabashed lover of tofu. If you still can't wrap your taste buds around tofu, I invite you to try this recipe. But first I have to apologize to all my Asian readers who grew up eating tofu. Because mine, of course, is not a traditional preparation. It is a recipe I often turn to, and it is the one that turned even my Greek mom into a tofu fan. Believe me, this is no small feat, as she belongs to the group of people who don't easily swerve into foreign-food territory. Which means, if it's not Greek (or maybe Italian), it's not edible in her mind. Period.

I almost always marinate tofu. I have done this for as long as I can remember, largely because I used to think that tofu was a bland block of soy waiting to be dressed. I am referring, of course, to widely available mass-produced tofu. I have since been introduced to fresh local tofu with amazing nuance in texture and flavor.

Since fresh local tofu is still no easy find, allow me to introduce you to my nontraditional preparation. My tofu is dressed in Mediterranean herbs, but I'm very casual about its composition. I typically use any dried and/or fresh herbs I have at home and marinate it a few hours ahead or the day before to allow the flavors to seep in. But in a pinch, 15 minutes will do.

Use these aromatic slices on a meatless Monday to replace the protein on your plate or pack them into a whole wheat roll with salad leaves and tomatoes like a burger with all the trimmings. Leftovers can top off a fresh salad or make a terrific sandwich for your lunch box. ⁓ gluten-free

....

Place a rack in the center of the oven and preheat to 425°F.

Slice the block of tofu crosswise into 6 equally thick slices. Lay the slices next to each other in a glass or other nonreactive container so they fit snuggly. Combine the soy sauce and the vinegar in a small bowl and drizzle across. Sprinkle with herbes de Provence and chile flakes, then drizzle the olive oil across and gently rub it in. Allow to marinate for at least 15 minutes or up to 2 hours at room temperature, turning once. (Or cover and chill for up to 1 day.)

Brush a rimmed baking sheet with olive oil. Remove the tofu from the marinade, reserving the liquid (it will last in the fridge for at least 5 days; use it to add rich umami to soups or cooked grains). Place the slices on the baking sheet. Using your fingers or a small spoon, scoop up any dried herbs from the marinade and spread

continued >

them across the top. Dip the fresh herb sprigs into the marinade to thoroughly coat them with any remaining oil, then firmly press one on top of each tofu slice.

Roast until the slices are nicely browned, about 20 minutes. Carefully flip with a thin spatula so the herb sprigs are underneath and continue roasting until the slices have crisped and are beautifully browned, a scant 15 minutes more (don't leave them in too long, as they can become rubbery). Gently slide the spatula underneath the slices to flip again so the herb sprigs are on top before serving. Eat right away or at room temperature.

fine points

The oven-roasting method makes the most appealing slices with a nice chewiness. But in a hurry, I broil the tofu, 4 inches away from the heat, in about 15 minutes, turning once halfway. They taste almost as good and that's good enough for me on a busy night.

VARIATION Replace the dried herbs with 1½ teaspoons dried spearmint combined with 6 sprigs of fresh mint and ½ teaspoon Aleppo pepper (instead of dried chile) for a Middle Eastern take.

HOW TO DRAIN TOFU

Draining tofu is worth the little extra time it adds to dinner prep, as it results in a more appealing texture, and it intensifies the flavors of any marinade you use. There are a number of ways to drain tofu. You can even buy kitchen contraptions to make the job easier, but you don't need one. I like to wrap a block of tofu in a clean dish towel or use a few layers of paper towels and set the package on a plate. Alternately, you can place a block of tofu into a colander that you set on a plate or put into the sink. Place a smaller plate right on top of the tofu and weigh it down with a large can. Allow the tofu to drain for 10 to 20 minutes. How much liquid it releases depends on the type (soft, firm, extra-firm) and the brand. In any case, be sure to taste different brands to find the one you like.

creamy millet with yogurt, avocado, and basil

⅔ cup millet, or 2½ cups cooked

1 small bay leaf, broken in half

1½ cups water

¾ teaspoon fine sea salt

2 limes

1½ cups coarsely mashed avocados, using a fork or potato masher (about 3 Hass avocados, or about 1 Choquette if you can get your hands on them)

1¼ cups whole milk, 2%, or nonfat Greek yogurt

1 clove garlic, minced or pressed

¼ cup loosely packed torn fresh basil leaves, preferably Thai

SERVES 4

fine points

Depending on the size of your avocados, you might have some left. Use as garnish, cut into cubes, or if you have an extra half, cut it into thin slices lengthwise and fan it on top of the bowl.

I prefer to beat the avocado yogurt cream with a fork for a nice chunky texture. You can use a food processor, fitted with the steel blade, instead.

VARIATION 2½ cups cooked quinoa can be used as well (see page 22).

MAKE AHEAD Briefly rewarm the millet if using previously cooked grains. This recipe can easily be doubled for a crowd.

At least once a year, a heavy, often dented cardboard box arrives at our doorstep with the most beautiful avocados I've ever known: Choquettes. These huge fruit, common in Florida but rarely available in supermarkets elsewhere, have an intense golden-green hue and a light butteriness that I have come to relish. They arrive courtesy of my sister-in-law, who has cultivated a huge tree in her backyard.

While I love these generous shipments, they create a challenge: what to do with all the avocados, ripening more or less all at once while we watch. Ice cream? Check. Guacamole? Of course! But it is this lush creamy millet I'm especially proud of. It uses my well-tested "stealth serving technique" for all of the people who don't know yet how much they love millet—just be sure to not reveal the mystery grain until their plates are empty.

Enjoy this side in the summer months, paired with pan-seared salmon or shrimp. ◁◁ gluten-free

Heat a small heavy saucepan over medium heat for 2 minutes. Add the millet and the bay leaf pieces and toast the grains, stirring occasionally and watching closely, until they start to crackle, turn golden brown, and smell intensely nutty, about 2 minutes. Add the water (it will hiss and bubble up!) and ¼ teaspoon of the salt and bring to a boil. Decrease the heat to maintain a simmer, cover, and cook until the water is absorbed and the grains have plumped but still retain their shape, about 20 minutes. Remove from the heat and, if you have time, allow to steam, covered, for 5 minutes.

Meanwhile, finely grate the limes until you have 2 teaspoons zest. Squeeze both fruits. You will need 2 tablespoons juice—reserve the rest for seasoning at the end. Add the avocado, yogurt, garlic, lime juice, zest, and the remaining ½ teaspoon salt to a medium bowl and beat vigorously with a fork until the mixture turns silky, light, and creamy, almost fluffy. Stir in about half the basil leaves.

Remove the bay leaf pieces from the millet and transfer the grains to a large serving bowl. Add the avocado yogurt and stir to combine. Season with more salt and lime juice to taste. Allow to sit for 5 minutes for the flavors to meld. Garnish with the remaining half of the basil leaves and serve warm.

my basic stove top polenta

2 cups water

2 cups low-sodium chicken or vegetable broth

½ teaspoon fine sea salt

1 cup (5½ ounces) polenta or stone-ground coarse cornmeal

1 to 2 tablespoons unsalted butter

¼ teaspoon freshly ground black pepper

About ½ cup (1 ounce) finely grated Parmesan, plus more for serving

SERVES 4 TO 6

This is the no-nonsense way I've cooked polenta all my life. Use it for the days when you forget to soak the grains in advance (see Shortcut Polenta, opposite).

🍃 gluten-free

Add the water and the broth to a large heavy saucepan and bring to a boil over medium-high heat. Add the salt. Using a large whisk, slowly add the polenta in a thin stream and continue whisking for 1 minute more. Decrease the heat to maintain a gentle bubble. Cover and cook until the polenta grains swell and become tender, about 25 minutes (30 minutes for coarse cornmeal), stirring vigorously every few minutes with a wooden spoon to keep the polenta from sticking to the bottom.

To finish, stir the butter, pepper, and Parmesan into the polenta. Season with salt and pepper to taste. Serve right away, passing more Parmesan along.

LOCAL CORNMEAL

At farmers' markets and in specialty stores, locally grown and freshly milled cornmeal has become a national trend. If you can get your hands on it, try it! You will most likely be smitten by its rich texture, often colorful speckles, and distinct character. However, when you prepare these new offerings, you have to keep their character in mind: local cornmeal is less uniform than widely available store-bought brands. Each batch, even from the same mill, might cook up slightly differently. And because of some finer particles, you will most likely have to stir more vigorously and scrape the bottom of your pot on occasion to avoid sticking. But really, that's it!

The most important rule is, don't despair—cornmeal and polenta are forgiving. You can always add a bit more water or broth for a softer outcome or—if the mixture is too liquid—uncover and cook for a bit longer, stirring often, to thicken it. Sometimes just removing the pot from the heat and waiting a few minutes will thicken cornmeal. Delicious? Always!

shortcut polenta

Restaurant chefs have elevated humble Italian polenta, golden cornmeal, to star status in recent years. And a revival of freshly milled corn has brought colorful textured heirloom varieties back to our tables. Yet this simple peasant dish stirs fears in many people. How do I add the golden meal without clumping? Will I need to stir endlessly? Will the polenta stick to the pot? Why even try?

Here's why: Because polenta, cooked right, can be a feast in its simplicity, perfect for cold mornings or chilly winter nights. Not a week goes by in the cooler months of the year when I don't simmer a large pot on the stove, even on busy weeknights. Be sure to always make extra for another day. Polenta firms up beautifully so you can grill, bake, or panfry it later. Your kids will love panfried cornmeal fingers, grilled triangles, or baked squares.

Of course, you can grab a box of precooked instant polenta, but it has little texture and even less flavor. All my life, I have used a no-nonsense method I learned in Germany. It requires little stirring and a much shorter cooking time than classic Italian recipes say is needed (see page 120).

But one day it hit me. Why not try the Two-Step Method I had successfully used on chewy steel-cut oats before? Dozens of tests later, I report back: it does work, and very well indeed. Soaking the cornmeal in boiling water the night before mellows the granules to bring you a flavorful, satisfying polenta with just 10 minutes of cooking time the next day. Here's to a bowl of no-stress polenta. *Buon appetito!* gluten-free

2 cups (11 ounces) polenta, preferably medium grind

3 cups boiling water

3 cups low-sodium chicken broth or water, or more as needed

1 teaspoon fine sea salt

3 tablespoons unsalted butter

1 cup (2 ounces) finely grated Parmesan, plus more for serving

½ teaspoon freshly ground black pepper

SERVES 8

....

step one
Start the polenta at least 8 hours ahead: Add the polenta to a 4-quart heavy saucepan and whisk in the boiling water. Cover and let sit at room temperature for up to 12 hours. (If not using at this point, chill, covered, for up to 2 days.)

step two
When you are ready to cook the polenta, add the broth and the salt to the saucepan and whisk well to loosen the polenta, breaking up any clumps. Bring to a boil over medium-high heat, whisking occasionally. Cook, whisking continuously and adjusting the heat to maintain a gentle bubble until the mixture thickens, about 2 minutes (beware of splatters!).

Decrease the heat to low to maintain a simmer. Cover and cook, stirring vigorously with a wooden spoon every couple of minutes, and scraping the bottom until the

continued >

polenta becomes creamy and thick, 10 to 12 minutes. The polenta granules will swell and become tender, and the polenta should retain an appealing toothsomeness.

Remove from the heat and stir in the butter, Parmesan, and pepper. Season to taste with salt and pepper and serve at once, passing more cheese around.

fine points

For more on types of polenta, see page 8.

This recipe makes a polenta on the firmer side. You can add a bit more broth or water before you add the butter for a softer, more billowy polenta.

Using boiling broth will further speed up the cooking. For a cheesy polenta, double the amount of Parmesan.

How thick should polenta be? As thick or thin as *you* like it. Some people enjoy a soupy polenta; I prefer mine firmer. In either case, this is easy: you can always thin it out with a bit more hot water, broth, milk, or cream (very tasty!). Or, if you find it too thin, uncover and cook for a few more minutes at a gentle bubble, stirring, until the polenta thickens to your liking. Polenta can be kept soft for 1 to 2 hours in a crockpot, using the *warm* setting.

CORNMEAL INSTEAD OF POLENTA In the Two-Step Method, stone-ground medium cornmeal works best (be sure to use weight measures, as the volume can vary widely).

In step 2, add only 2 cups (instead of 3) liquid and stir more vigorously and scrape the bottom of your pot to avoid sticking. Cornmeal will stay softer throughout and benefits from a few minutes rest.

The beauty of cornmeal: Leftovers reheat well in the microwave on high, covered, stirring once or twice. Or reheat on the stove top in a heavy pot over medium, whisking to dissolve any lumps, and adding a little water or broth as needed.

LEFTOVERS This recipe makes enough for 2 meals. Be sure to spread extra polenta, about ½ to ¾ inch thick, into an oiled casserole dish or a rimmed baking sheet *before* you start eating, as it firms up *fast*. Allow to cool at room temperature, then chill, covered with plastic wrap, for up to 2 days. If moisture develops, blot dry with paper towels before using. Then cut into triangles or elongated fingers and panfry in a little olive oil or bake on an oiled baking sheet.

four more ways with polenta, from everyday to festive

WITH GREEK YOGURT, LEMON, AND DILL

Classic polenta gets a tangy twist in this creamy yet light variation with Greek yogurt. Lots of fresh dill and bright lemon zest makes it an appealing addition to grilled fish or shrimp. Flat-leaf parsley can be used in a pinch. The rich Greek yogurt replaces the butter here as a flavor carrier, so for best results do not use low-fat or nonfat Greek yogurt.

1 cup packed finely chopped fresh dill

2 teaspoons finely grated lemon zest

1 cup whole milk Greek yogurt

Omit the butter, add the Parmesan, dill, zest, and pepper, and stir until well combined. Blend in the yogurt, leaving streaks of white for visual appeal. Season to taste with salt and pepper. Serve at once, passing extra Parmesan around.

HERB-FLECKED POLENTA

This highly aromatic polenta packs an enticing punch from marjoram—use 2 tablespoons for a mellower aroma. The flavors will vary throughout the year, depending on the vibrancy of your herbs. Enjoy it with chicken or lamb.

2 cups packed fresh basil leaves, rinsed and gently patted dry

1 cup loosely packed fresh flat-leaf parsley, rinsed and gently patted dry

4 tablespoons loosely packed fresh marjoram leaves, rinsed and gently patted dry

½ cup whole milk ricotta or low-fat ricotta

While the polenta is cooking, add the basil, parsley, and marjoram to the bowl of a food processor, fitted with a steel blade. Pulse just until the herbs are finely chopped, about seven 1-second pulses (do not process into a paste).

After removing the polenta from the heat, stir in the butter, omit the pepper, and add the Parmesan, followed by the ricotta and the herb mixture. Stir to blend well, then season to taste with salt. Serve at once, passing extra Parmesan around.

SAFFRON-POLENTA

Stellar in its simplicity, this festive polenta is a glorious addition to any holiday table. First infused with golden threads of saffron, it is topped with a sprinkle of lightly toasted pistachios for appealing crunch. Pair with fish or chicken.

½ teaspoon loosely packed saffron threads

1½ cups whole milk

¾ cup lightly toasted chopped pistachios

In step one, sprinkle the saffron threads across the polenta before adding the boiling water.

In step two, add the milk and 1½ cups (instead of 3 cups) broth together with the salt.

After removing the polenta from the heat, add the butter and the Parmesan but omit the pepper. Stir until well blended and season to taste with salt. Sprinkle with the toasted nuts and serve at once.

WITH ANCIENT WHEAT BERRIES (NOT GLUTEN-FREE)

Stir in 1 cup cooked whole grain spelt, farro, or Kamut or regular whole wheat berries with the butter, Parmesan, and pepper. Stir to blend well, then season to taste with salt and pepper. Serve at once, passing extra Parmesan around.

roasted pomegranate tomatoes with fresh mozzarella and lime

No one wants to slave at the stove in the heat of summer. This simple riff on the classic caprese appetizer has become a standby in our house. It is mouth-watering, and it does double duty: I make a large amount as a starter one day and toss the remaining pomegranate-infused tomatoes the next day with leftover grains or pasta. Sometimes, this starter is all we eat on a hot night, accompanied by a bowl of olives, a crisp whole grain baguette, and a glass of red wine. ⬧ gluten-free

Place a rack 4 inches below the heat and preheat the broiler on high for 5 minutes.

Place the tomatoes on a large rimmed baking sheet. Drizzle with 1½ tablespoons of the olive oil and the molasses and sprinkle with the salt and pepper. Gently toss with your hands until the tomatoes are well coated.

Broil, watching closely, until the tomatoes shrivel and burst and some are blackened in spots, 8 to 10 minutes, and shaking the sheet or turning them with a metal spatula once halfway. Remove the sheet from the oven and drizzle the vinegar on top. Gently toss with the spatula to combine. (If you are making an appetizer for 4, remove half the mixture, about 2½ cups, with some of the juices to a glass or nonreactive container after the tomatoes have cooled a bit to use on another day.)

Transfer the remaining tomatoes with their juices to a shallow serving platter. At this point you can set them aside at room temperature for up to 2 hours, or chill if making ahead.

Finish the salad about 10 minutes before serving: finely grate the zest of the lime until you have 1 teaspoon. Squeeze the lime; you will need at least 1 tablespoon juice, maybe a bit more. Distribute the mozzarella across the platter. Drizzle with the remaining 2 tablespoons olive oil, sprinkle with the lime zest, and drizzle with 1 tablespoon of the lime juice. Sprinkle with a good pinch of salt, grind some pepper on top, and gently combine. Season with salt, pepper, and more lime juice to taste. Allow to sit for a few minutes for the tomatoes to release their juices. Just before serving, garnish with the fresh basil leaves.

6 to 7 cups (about 2 pounds) grape or cherry tomatoes

3½ tablespoons extra-virgin olive oil

1½ tablespoons pomegranate molasses (see page 249, and "Sources," page 251)

½ teaspoon fine sea salt

¼ teaspoon freshly ground black pepper

1½ tablespoons balsamic or sherry vinegar

1 lime

About 1½ cups small mozzarella balls (ciliegini) or other fresh mozzarella, torn into ½-inch pieces

10 to 12 fresh basil leaves, torn if large

SERVES 4 AS A STARTER

fine points

This makes enough roasted tomatoes for another dish such as the Pomegranate Tomatoes for Any Grain (page 126).

In the waning days of summer, when the last tomatoes hit farmers' markets, the first pomegranates show up in stores—toss on some of the glistening seeds for a splash.

MAKE AHEAD Roasted tomatoes can be made up to 1 day ahead. Chill, covered; bring to room temperature before serving, about 1 hour.

pomegranate tomatoes for any grain

3 to 3½ cups cooked whole oat berries (see page 23; use gluten-free if desired)

About 2½ cups Roasted Pomegranate Tomatoes with their juices (½ recipe, page 125)

5 tablespoons Pomegranate Lime Dressing (½ recipe, page 127)

3 or 4 tablespoons chopped fresh tarragon or torn basil leaves or a mixture

Fine sea salt

3 cups packed fresh arugula, rinsed and patted dry

SERVES 4

Unlike my husband, I have never been able to enjoy last night's leftovers. But, no, I don't toss them out. I prefer to make a new meal out of them. This summer salad, packed with leftover lime-scented tomatoes, is a favorite. It uses up yesterday's bounty but feels like a feast by itself.

This salad is a beautiful vehicle to showcase naturally sweet whole oat berries, but many leftover grains work. It makes a versatile side, next to chicken or lamb or a piece of grilled fish. Or, get inspired by the Mediterranean table and pull out any or many of the following: prosciutto, feta, shaved Parmesan, anchovies, oil-cured black olives, hard-boiled egg halves, or a can of tuna. Vegetarians can top it with panfried or broiled feta (page 128) or tofu (page 116). ⁓ gluten-free

Add the oat berries and the roasted tomatoes to a large bowl. Drizzle on 3 tablespoons of the dressing, add about half of the tarragon, and toss to combine. Season with salt to taste. If you have time, wait 10 minutes for the flavors to meld (can be made at least 4 hours ahead; bring to room temperature before serving).

Place the arugula on a large serving platter and toss with the remaining 2 tablespoons of the dressing. Tip the grain mixture on top, sprinkle with the remaining tarragon, and serve.

fine points

Don't hesitate to use leftover grains here. Try it with freekeh, rye, farro, spelt, or einkorn.

GLUTEN-FREE Cooked quinoa is also stellar here, for its gentle crunch contrasts nicely with the juicy tomatoes. Or try it with millet and wild rice.

For best flavor, bring the grains and the tomatoes to room temperature. If your grains have hardened in the fridge, gently reheat them in the microwave or on the stove top (see page 17).

pomegranate lime dressing

Lime makes this versatile dressing pop, but lemon is a delicious replacement. You can also drizzle it on green leaf salad or add some zing to simple sautéed chard at the end of cooking. Or toss it with sweet potatoes or carrots before roasting. Double the recipe to always have some on hand. ◌◌◌ gluten-free

Add the molasses, vinegar, zest, 4 teaspoons of the lime juice, Aleppo pepper, and salt to a medium bowl and whisk to combine. Slowly whisk in the olive oil until the mixture is emulsified. Season with salt to taste, and perhaps more lime juice, depending how tangy you like things.

fine points

Honey can replace the pomegranate molasses, but it lacks the interesting complexity (see page 249).

MAKE AHEAD The dressing will keep in the fridge for up to 7 days.

2 tablespoons pomegranate molasses

2 tablespoons good-quality balsamic vinegar

1 tablespoon finely grated lime zest (from about 2 large limes, preferably organic)

4 to 6 teaspoons freshly squeezed lime juice

1 teaspoon Aleppo pepper

¾ teaspoon fine sea salt

5 tablespoons extra-virgin olive oil

MAKES ABOUT ⅔ CUP

tangy farro with honey-roasted kumquats, feta, and tomatoes

FARRO

2 cups water

1 cup semipearled farro, or 3 cups cooked

¼ teaspoon fine sea salt

SALAD

2 (4- to 5-ounce) slices feta, preferably sheep's milk

2½ cups cherry tomatoes

1⅓ cups (6 ounces) kumquats, cut in half lengthwise, large seeds removed

16 green and black pitted olives (about ⅓ heaped cup)

3 tablespoons plus 2 teaspoons extra-virgin olive oil

1 tablespoon honey

2 teaspoons finely grated orange zest

¼ teaspoon fine sea salt

¼ teaspoon freshly ground black pepper

¾ teaspoon dried herbes de Provence (see page 249) or dried thyme

½ teaspoon Aleppo pepper, or ⅛ teaspoon dried red chile flakes

2 tablespoons golden balsamic vinegar or sherry vinegar, or more as needed

SERVES 4 AS A LIGHT MEAL; 6 AS A SIDE

During long cold winters in Boston, when the snow is piled high in front of my kitchen window, I sometimes need a reminder of Greece and summer. This is when the broiler with its intense heat becomes my cooking equipment of choice. In such moments, I admit to buying out-of-season cherry tomatoes to marry them with tangy-sweet kumquats, honey, and herbed feta to crown a plate of plumped farro. It comes together even on a hurried weeknight, especially if you have leftover grains.

This makes a light supper on its own, not only for vegetarians. As a side, it is immensely versatile. Serve it next to grilled steak, burgers, or chicken breast or with grilled or pan-seared fish such as halibut or salmon.

To prepare the farro, bring the water, farro, and salt to a boil in a small heavy saucepan. Decrease the heat to maintain a simmer, cover, and cook until the farro is tender but still slightly chewy, 20 to 25 minutes. Drain and transfer the grain to an elongated rimmed platter (about 16 by 9 inches) or a large bowl and spread a bit to cool. If you are using cooked farro from the fridge, spoon it onto a serving plate when you assemble the ingredients so it can come to room temperature or warm it if you like (see page 17).

Meanwhile, place a rack 4 inches below the heat and preheat the broiler on high for 5 minutes. Place the feta in the freezer for 10 minutes.

Place the tomatoes, kumquats, and olives on a large rimmed baking sheet. Drizzle with 1 tablespoon of the olive oil, the honey, and sprinkle with the zest, salt and pepper. Using your hands, gently toss to combine well. Make space in the center of the baking sheet. Remove the 2 slices of feta from the freezer and place them into the center, leaving about 1 inch in between. Sprinkle with herbes de Provence and Aleppo pepper, and drizzle each slice with 1 teaspoon extra-virgin olive oil.

Broil until the tomatoes are shriveled and blackened in spots, the kumquats are softened and glistening, and the feta is golden brown around the edges, 6 to 8 minutes. Remove the sheet from the oven and drizzle the vinegar on top of the tomato mixture.

To finish, using oven mitts and a metal spatula, carefully transfer the tomato mixture on top of the grains. Cut each softened slice of feta in half (or into 3 pieces when serving six) and arrange on the top. Scrape any juices from the baking sheet and drizzle across as well. Drizzle with the remaining 2 tablespoons olive oil. I like it tangy, so I often add a splash more vinegar, but you can also pass the bottle around the table. Grind on a bit more pepper (there is probably no need for more salt, as olives and feta can be salty) and serve warm or at room temperature.

fine points

VARIATIONS Any whole grain from the wheat family, such as spelt, Kamut, or whole wheat, works beautifully here. So does hulled (whole grain) barley.

Stretching the leftovers with cooked cannellini beans gets you a delicious extra lunch or two.

quinoa bites with smoked salmon and dill

QUINOA
1¼ cups water

¾ cup quinoa, well rinsed and drained, or about 2½ cups cooked (see page 22)

LEMONY SOUR CREAM
1 cup low-fat sour cream

1½ teaspoons finely grated lemon zest

1 teaspoon minced serrano chile, veins and seeds removed for less heat (optional)

½ teaspoon freshly squeezed lemon juice

QUINOA BITES
8 ounces smoked salmon, torn into ½-inch pieces

½ cup finely chopped green onions (about 3)

½ cup finely chopped fresh dill, plus more for garnish

½ cup whole wheat panko or other coarse dry bread crumbs (use gluten-free if needed)

2 large eggs, lightly beaten, plus 1 egg white, lightly beaten, as needed

1 to 2 teaspoons minced serrano chile, veins and seeds removed for less heat (optional)

1 teaspoon finely grated lemon zest, preferably organic

½ teaspoon freshly ground black pepper

2 tablespoons extra-virgin olive oil, for frying

MAKES 32 TWO-INCH CAKES, TO SERVE 8

When I cook for a party, I always make sure that much of my work can be done ahead. These crunchy quinoa bites are a perfect example. Flecked with smoked salmon and accompanied by a simple lemony sour cream, they set a festive tone. You can shape them ahead and briefly panfry or bake them when your guests arrive, making them stress-free. Or cook the mini cakes ahead and serve at room temperature. gluten-free

To prepare the quinoa, add the water and quinoa to a heavy 2-quart saucepan and bring to a boil. Decrease the heat to maintain a simmer, cover, and cook until the water is absorbed, 10 to 15 minutes. Remove from the heat and let sit, covered, for 5 minutes. Transfer the quinoa to a large bowl and spread to cool for 20 minutes.

Meanwhile, prepare the lemony sour cream: In a small bowl, combine the sour cream, lemon zest, chile, and lemon juice. Chill, covered, until ready to serve.

To make the quinoa bites, add all of the ingredients (except the olive oil) to the bowl with the quinoa. Using your hands, thoroughly combine and squeeze the mixture to bring it together. If it doesn't hold up, add the additional egg white. Pat down and level the mixture inside the bowl and divide it into 8 equal portions using a butter knife (cut in half like a cake and then each half into quarters). Moisten your hands with water and form 4 small cakes from each segment, about 1¾ inches in diameter, pressing firmly to ensure they hold together and remoistening your hands as needed (or use 1 heaped tablespoon per cake). Place the cakes on a small baking sheet or a large plate. Chill, covered with plastic wrap, for at least 30 minutes.

To finish, heat 1 tablespoon of the olive oil in a 12-inch skillet over medium heat until it shimmers. Gently add 16 cakes at a time and cook until golden brown, carefully turning once with a metal spatula, 3 to 4 minutes on each side. Add the remaining 1 tablespoon olive oil and repeat with the remaining cakes.

Serve the bite-size cakes warm or at room temperature, topping each with a slightly heaped teaspoon of lemony sour cream and a sprig of dill.

fine points

For baking instructions, see page 86, reducing the time to 8 to 10 minutes per side.

MAKE AHEAD Lemony sour cream can be made 1 day ahead, which also boosts flavor. Quinoa bites, can be shaped up to 6 hours ahead.

honeyed spelt cornbread with fresh and dried cranberries

For someone who didn't really know what cranberries were when I moved to the United States as a young adult, I've really come around to them. Today, I admit to an overenthusiastic use of the ruby-red fruit, especially during the holidays. A combination of both fresh and dried cranberries in this golden cornbread works well in tandem—the dried cranberries mellow the sour burst of the fresh fruit. Serve with honey and butter, of course. *gluten-free option*

Position a rack in center of the oven and place a 10-inch cast-iron skillet on it. Preheat the oven to 450°F for at least 15 minutes. Remove 2 tablespoons of the measured cornmeal and add it to a small bowl.

Whisk together the remaining cornmeal, the spelt flour, baking powder, baking soda, and salt in a large bowl. Make a well in the center. In a medium bowl, lightly whisk the eggs to blend. Gently whisk in the buttermilk, followed by the oil, honey, and zest until smooth. Add the egg mixture to the center of the flour mixture, and stir with a rubber spatula until just combined. Do not overmix; the batter should look lumpy. Add the fresh and dried cranberries to the bowl of reserved cornmeal and toss to coat—this prevents the fruit from sinking to the bottom. Gently fold the mixture into the batter.

Using thick oven mitts, carefully remove the hot skillet from the oven. Add the butter (it will sizzle! and brown for great flavor) and tilt it carefully to coat the bottom and the sides of the pan. Scrape the batter into the hot skillet. Decrease the oven temperature to 400°F.

Bake until the edges of the cornbread turn golden brown and a toothpick inserted into the center comes out clean, about 25 minutes. Let sit for 10 minutes before cutting into wedges. Serve warm or at room temperature.

1¾ (225 g) stone-ground fine whole grain cornmeal

1 cup minus 1 tablespoon (120 g) whole grain spelt flour

1 teaspoon baking powder

1 teaspoon baking soda

¼ teaspoon fine sea salt

2 large eggs

1½ cups well-shaken low-fat buttermilk

⅓ cup extra-virgin olive oil

¼ cup honey

1 tablespoon finely grated orange zest (about 1 orange)

¾ cup fresh or frozen cranberries (do not thaw)

⅓ cup dried cranberries

1 tablespoon unsalted butter

SERVES 8 TO 12

fine points

If you like your cornbread on the sweeter side, increase the honey to ⅓ cup.

A cast-iron skillet is my first choice here because it creates a rich golden-brown crust. If you don't have one, you can use a 9-inch glass pie dish. Preheat the dish at 400°F and bake the cornbread at the same temperature, about 20 minutes.

GLUTEN-FREE: Replace the spelt with 120 g brown rice flour for a more textured cornbread.

barley and wild rice dressing with fennel, apples, and marsala

BARLEY AND WILD RICE

3 cups low-sodium chicken or vegetable broth

3 cups water

1½ cups hulled (whole grain) barley, soaked overnight and drained

½ cup wild rice

2 sprigs thyme (optional)

VEGETABLES

1 cup chopped dried apples

½ cup golden raisins

½ cup Marsala wine

2 tablespoons extra-virgin olive oil

1 cup chopped yellow onion (1 small)

1 cup chopped celery (1 to 2 stalks)

2 cups fennel, cored, quartered lengthwise, and chopped into ½-inch pieces (about 1 large bulb), fronds chopped and reserved

2 cloves garlic, minced

2 tablespoons herbes de Provence (see page 249)

½ teaspoon fine sea salt

½ teaspoon freshly ground black pepper

½ cup chopped dried cranberries

2 tablespoons unsalted butter, cut into small pieces, or extra-virgin olive oil

½ cup coarsely chopped toasted walnuts

SERVES 8 TO 12

This mouthwatering side has become my go-to Thanksgiving dish. It makes a sizable amount that I believe will *never* be eaten, yet I have always been proven wrong. Responsible for the appeal of this dish is the marriage of earthy barley and chewy wild rice, infused with a medley of aromatics, fruit, vegetables, and toasted nuts. Most important to me: it comes together effortlessly.

Bring the broth and water to a boil in a large heavy saucepan. Add the barley. Decrease the heat to maintain a simmer, cover, and cook for 10 minutes. Stir in the wild rice and the thyme and return to a simmer. Cover and continue cooking until the barley is tender with a slight chewiness and the wild rice has split but retains some chew, 35 to 45 minutes more. Drain the grains and transfer them to a large bowl. Remove the thyme sprigs, if you can find them.

Once the barley has cooked for about 30 minutes, position a rack in the center of the oven and preheat to 325°F. Grease a 9 by 13-inch baking dish with olive oil or coat with cooking spray.

Add the apples and the raisins to a medium bowl and cover with the Marsala for 10 to 15 minutes, stirring once or twice in between. Drain, reserving the Marsala. Add the olive oil to a large skillet over medium heat and wait until it shimmers. Add the onion, celery, fennel, garlic, and 1 tablespoon of the herbes de Provence, salt, and pepper. Cook, stirring occasionally until the vegetables soften and the onion just starts to brown, about 5 minutes. Add the reserved Marsala and cook until it becomes syrupy, about 3 minutes, and take the pan off the heat.

Add the vegetables to the grains in the bowl together with the apple-raisin mixture and the cranberries. Sprinkle with the remaining 1 tablespoon herbes de Provence and stir to combine. Season with salt and pepper to taste. Transfer the mixture to the baking dish.

To finish, dot with the butter pieces (or drizzle with olive oil) and cover the pan tightly with aluminum foil. Bake until heated through, 25 to 30 minutes. Remove, sprinkle with the walnuts and the reserved fennel fronds, and serve.

fine points

During the holidays I resort to lazy grain-cooking methods—that's why both grains here cook in the same pot. Use the package time of your wild rice as a guide.

MAKE AHEAD The barley and wild rice mixture can be made up to 5 days ahead.

quinoa salad with roasted red beets, blood oranges, and pomegranate

This is the grain salad I serve during the holidays when I feel the need to please a crowd but have too much on my hands. It works for vegetarians and for guests who choose to go gluten-free—and it saves the cook because it can be made ahead.

Furthermore, the different shades of deep red, from beets, blood oranges, and pomegranate seeds, look stunning on any table. And the salad pairs beautifully with holiday classics, from turkey to ham and pork roast.

gluten-free

To prepare the beets, place a rack in the center of the oven and preheat to 425°F. Cut the greens off the beets (reserve for another use), leaving about 1 inch of stem. Rinse the beets and pat dry. Place the beets in an 8 by 8-inch baking dish, adding enough water to reach a depth of ¼ to ½ inch. Cover the pan tightly with aluminum foil and roast until the beets are tender (a knife should slide in easily), 45 to 60 minutes, depending on size. Remove from the oven and allow to cool. (If you're in a hurry, place the beets in a microwave-safe dish, add ¼ cup water, cover loosely, and microwave on high until they are tender, about 10 minutes, depending on size.)

Meanwhile, prepare the quinoa. Add the broth, water, quinoa, and salt to a large heavy saucepan and bring to a boil. Decrease the heat to maintain a simmer, cover, and cook until the liquid is absorbed, 15 to 20 minutes. Remove from the heat and set aside to steam, covered, for 5 minutes. Transfer the quinoa to a large serving bowl and spread to cool, about 20 minutes.

To make the salad, cut one orange in half crosswise. Peel 1½ oranges and cut the segments into ½-inch pieces; you will need a scant 1½ cups (reserve the rest for another use). Zest the remaining 1½ oranges until you have 1 tablespoon zest, then squeeze them until you have ¼ cup plus 2 tablespoons juice.

When the beets are cool enough to handle, peel and cut them into ½-inch wedges. Using a fork, stir the dates into the bowl with the quinoa, separating any chunks. Stir in the beets.

In a medium bowl, using a fork, combine the orange juice, zest, vinegar, salt, and pepper. Gradually beat in the olive oil in a thin stream until emulsified. Stir in the

BEETS AND QUINOA
3 medium red beets (about 1¼ pounds)

2 cups low-sodium vegetable broth

1½ cups water

2 cups quinoa, preferably red, well rinsed and drained, or 7 to 8 cups cooked

½ teaspoon fine sea salt

SALAD
3 blood oranges (can substitute regular oranges)

½ cup chopped pitted dates, preferably firm Deglet Noor

1 tablespoon sherry vinegar or freshly squeezed lemon juice

¾ teaspoon fine sea salt

½ teaspoon freshly ground black pepper

¼ cup extra-virgin olive oil

¼ cup plus 2 tablespoons finely chopped fresh flat-leaf parsley

⅔ cup pomegranate seeds (from 1 medium pomegranate)

¼ cup lightly toasted chopped pistachios for garnish

SERVES 8

continued >

¼ cup parsley. Pour the dressing over the salad and gently toss to combine. Season with salt and pepper to taste. Let sit at room temperature for 10 to 15 minutes to allow the flavors to meld.

Toss once more, then top with the oranges, sprinkle with the pomegranate seeds, pistachios, and the remaining 2 tablespoons parsley, and serve.

fine points

Deep red quinoa is worth seeking out here for its stunning hue, but more common white quinoa is a good stand-in.

For even more flair, serve the salad on a large platter of fresh spinach leaves. You will need about 4 ounces.

I just chop oranges into pieces without removing the pith and silky membranes between slices—I'm lazy, and I console myself with the fact that the pith contains valuable nutrients.

HOW TO SEED A POMEGRANATE There are many ways to seed a pomegranate. This one works well for me. First, be sure to wear an apron and have a medium bowl ready. Rinse the pomegranate and cut it lengthwise into quarters with a sharp serrated knife. Using both hands and working over the bowl, gently pull apart each piece to release all the seeds that are nestled between the skin "chambers." Remove any little skin pieces that might drop into the bowl.

MAKE AHEAD The quinoa can be prepared up to 5 days ahead. The beets can be roasted up to 2 days ahead. Chill separately, covered. The salad (except for the final topping of oranges, pomegranate seeds, pistachios, and parsley) can be prepared 4 hours ahead. Chill, covered. Bring to room temperature before serving and top with the remaining ingredients.

one good grain: saffron millet

I always get carried away in my passion for golden millet, a staple in Africa and India, and most underrated in the Western world. This mild quick-cooking grain is nourishing in a simple, blissful way. But toss in a few strands of majestic saffron and a good dab of butter, and you end up with a magnificent side dish to crown any meal.

To highlight the few good ingredients, I don't use any broth here, just plain water (see "One Pure Aroma," page 28). But I do ever so slightly toast the grains—it will make you reach for more. This is an inviting addition to fish or chicken breast. Try it someday also as a breakfast, in the Saffron Millet with Toasted Almonds and Cardamom (page 32). ⟣ gluten-free

....

Heat a heavy 2- or 3-quart saucepan over medium heat. Add the millet together with the saffron and cook, stirring often, until the millet crackles vividly, emits a toasty scent, and start to turn golden, 2 to 3 minutes. Watch closely so as to not burn the millet or the saffron.

Add the water (it will splatter!) and salt and bring to a boil. Decrease the heat to maintain a simmer, cover, and cook until the liquid is absorbed, 15 to 20 minutes. If the kernels have still a bit too much crunch to your liking, drizzle on a bit more water and continue cooking for a few minutes more.

Remove from the heat, cut up the butter into small chunks, distribute it across the top, and allow to sit, covered, for 5 minutes. Fluff with a fork and serve at once.

fine points

Saffron is expensive. So make this on occasion, for a special occasion. On regular weekdays, you can either omit the saffron—it will still be splendid—or add ½ teaspoon turmeric for a deep mustardy hue.

Black pepper could suffocate the delicate scent of saffron. Only white pepper with its winey scent will do here, just a few turns of it, and freshly ground.

1 cup millet

¼ to ½ teaspoon loosely packed saffron threads

1¾ cups water, plus a few tablespoons more as needed

½ teaspoon fine sea salt, or ¼ teaspoon if making this for breakfast

1 to 2 tablespoons unsalted butter

SERVES 4

soups and stews
for busy nights and slow weekends

just don't call it healthy

I always hesitate to bring up the topic of health and whole grains. It fills me with trepidation. After all, I have spent pretty much my whole adult life prodding friends, family, colleagues, and any unsuspecting stranger into trying whole grains for what they are: delicious. Yet so ingrained, pun unintended, is our perception of whole grains as healthy that it almost always dominates any conversation about my favorite food group.

Of course, much has changed since my first cookbook was published. Many of us now speak about whole or ancient grains with more nuance than just a few years ago. People across the country have started to appreciate their distinct textures and flavors, be it in the grains they explore for dinner or in the breads and baked goods they offer their families. Yet, health and healthy eating remains a mantra widely used to help us as a nation to improve our diet. This applies to whole grains but also to glorious green vegetables and fruits and many other good foods.

I am of a different mind here. I believe healthy eating comes naturally, by cooking often at home and by enjoying reasonable amounts of everything. For much of my life I have resisted labeling food as healthy. I felt that telling people, with a wagging finger that "you better eat well or else" is a dead-end street for something as sensual and satisfying as eating. Of course, I too want to live well and stay healthy. Who doesn't? But in my own life I find the only food I turn to, over and over again, is good home-cooked food, simple and well-prepared. I long for meals that are convincing by their very nature, with lots of different colors, textures, and flavors.

Needless to say, this is also how I get everyone who comes to my house to enjoy ancient grains. My personal rule has always been: don't talk about it, just serve it. And this, believe it or not, works with everyone, including children.

In this book, as in my first, children have tasted every single recipe and provided invaluable feedback. When parents say their kids don't eat healthy food, I say of course they do! Just serve them *good* food.

"Healthy" has become the one word I would like to ban in connection with eating altogether. More recently, fascinating research has emerged that shows that food labeled as healthy doesn't seem to nourish us adequately. *Eating Well* magazine summarized it in an eye-opening story by Rachael Moeller Gorman titled "The Whole-Grain, Reduced-Fat, Zero-Calorie, High-Fiber, Lightly Sweetened Truth about Food Labels." In it she describes several studies, one involving chocolate bars: One group received a piece of a "new health bar with high levels of protein, vitamins, and fiber, and no artificial sweeteners." The second group received a piece of a "very tasty and yummy bar with a chocolate raspberry core," and the third group received no bar. However, both the first and second group were given identical bars to eat. Guess what? The people who ate the "healthy" bar later reported being hungrier, not only than those who ate the "tasty" bar but than the people in the group who ate nothing.

Equally surprising, people who ate a slice of "healthy" bread ate more in a second experiment compared to those who ate a "tasty" bread (again, the slices of bread were identical). And a third study went even further and looked at a hormone that makes you feel hungry. The results were similar, again using identical milk shakes: it turned out that a shake advertised as "guilt-free" did not satisfy the people who drank it compared to the people who drank the "indulgent" milk shake. The indulgent group felt full and satiated, unlike the group that consumed the guilt-free milk shake.

Reading this article stopped me in my tracks. I felt vindicated—after disguising grains like millet and many whole grain flours for years inside tasty meals—always hoping to convince skeptics with the delicious food I was preparing rather than with a health claim.

I know, of course, I am truly very lucky. Having been raised in both Germany and Greece, many of the foods that we are touting as healthy today are part of the traditional diet. They were on our table simply as part of mouthwatering meals. This includes breakfast muesli and oatmeal in Germany, and rustic whole grain breads, often made with sourdough. And in Greece, we cherish grains such as bulgur and barley, and yogurt, legumes, and loads of wild greens. All these foods, it turns out, are also amazingly healthy, but no one ever had to tell me so.

It is in this spirit that I created the recipes in this book. In the soup chapter, for example, you can try a stunning Buckwheat and Beet Soup with Spicy Horseradish (page 141), an aromatic Chicken Stew with Honey-Balsamic Squash and Farro (page 154), or a flavorful Cumin-Scented Cauliflower Soup with Salmon (page 143). There are lots of vegetables, little fish or meat if any, and grains to provide you with long-lasting nourishment. What's not to love?

Yet we are just getting started. My hope is that one day, when I research a delicious grain like millet or a green vegetable such as watercress, a beautiful recipe will appear early on in the list of links—rather than a link to watercress as an "anticancer superfood" or any other "good for you" claim. Then, good eating will have won.

buckwheat and beet soup with spicy horseradish

This speedy and light yet nourishing soup is perfect in late summer or early autumn. It will feed you well without weighing you down. Beets lend a natural sweetness and opulent hue to the soup, transforming the earthy grains of buckwheat, making them look almost flamboyant. Please don't omit the topping: the thick Greek yogurt, spiked with horseradish, melds the flavors.

Because this soup is on the lighter side, I suggest you serve it with a few accompaniments: Smoked salmon is a classic flavor pairing; feta and olives work very well too. Also, add some rye crackers or whole grain toast, or, if you are so inclined, bake a quick loaf of good bread—we love it with the Irish Soda Bread with Amaranth, Cranberries, and Rosemary (page 68).

gluten-free

To make the soup, heat a large heavy saucepan over medium heat. Swirl in the oil and wait until it shimmers. Add the onion and ¼ teaspoon of the salt and cook, stirring occasionally, until the onion just starts to brown at the edges, about 5 minutes. Add the garlic, thyme, and savory and cook, stirring, until fragrant, about 1 minute. Watch closely so as not to burn the spices. Stir in the buckwheat and cook, stirring occasionally but watching closely, just until the grains take on some color, about 2 minutes. Add the broth (it will splatter!), the remaining ½ teaspoon salt, and the pepper and bring to a boil, scraping the bottom to release any toasted bits. Decrease the heat to maintain a simmer, cover, and cook until the buckwheat is tender, about 15 minutes.

Meanwhile, prepare the horseradish yogurt topping: Combine the yogurt, horseradish, salt, and pepper in a small bowl and beat until smooth, using a fork. Season with more salt and pepper to taste.

To finish, stir in the beets and 1 teaspoon of the honey and add about 1 cup water to reach the consistency you like. Remove the pot from the heat, cover, and allow to sit for 5 minutes for the vegetables to soften. Add the vinegar and taste for seasoning. Depending on the sweetness of your beets, you can add another teaspoon of honey and a bit more vinegar to balance it, perhaps a tad more salt and pepper. But don't fret over the seasoning too much, as the topping will bring the flavors together!

Ladle the soup into four bowls, garnish with a dollop of the yogurt topping, and serve at once.

SOUP

1 tablespoon extra-virgin olive oil

1½ cups chopped red onion (about 1 medium)

¾ teaspoon fine sea salt

2 teaspoons minced garlic (about 2 cloves)

¾ teaspoon dried thyme

¾ teaspoon dried savory, or ½ teaspoon more dried thyme

¾ cup raw buckwheat groats (not kasha)

4 cups low-sodium beef, chicken, or vegetable broth

¼ teaspoon freshly ground black pepper

2 cups raw shredded beets, preferably red (about 1 large or 2 small)

1 to 2 teaspoons honey

2 teaspoons sherry vinegar, or more as needed

HORSERADISH YOGURT

¾ cup whole milk or 2% Greek yogurt

3 tablespoons store-bought horseradish, with its liquid (or use fresh root; see sidebar)

¼ teaspoon fine sea salt

¼ teaspoon freshly ground black pepper

SERVES 4

continued >

fine points

Be sure to look for raw buckwheat groats with their clean grassy flavor for this soup, not toasted kasha.

Growing up in Germany, I learned to cherish the herb savory; if you love cooking soups, it is worth seeking out.

To save dishes, I shred small amounts of vegetables on the large holes of a box grater. Feel free to use a food processer, equipped with the shredding disc. And, of course, you can wear gloves when handling beets. I never bother, as I find that the crimson color washes off easily.

MAKE AHEAD The soup and topping can be prepared, separately, up to 2 days ahead. Chill, covered. Gently reheat over medium heat, stirring occasionally, adding a bit more broth or water to thin to your liking. The soup freezes well for up to 1 month.

FRESH HORSERADISH TOPPING

In Germany, a soup like this one would be served with a dollop of softly whipped cream, flavored with freshly grated horseradish. If you see the root in your market, try using it here. Peel a portion of the root and finely grate it. You will need 2 to 3 tablespoons for ¾ cup Greek yogurt, depending on your tolerance; add 1 to 1½ teaspoons apple cider vinegar and ¼ teaspoon salt and stir to combine. Make the topping at least half an hour ahead, as the enticing sharp heat of fresh horseradish needs time to infuse the yogurt.

The remaining root will last many weeks in the crisper drawer of your fridge. I wrap it in a paper towel and place it in an open plastic bag. This prevents the root from drying out while allowing air to circulate so it doesn't get moldy.

cumin-scented cauliflower soup with salmon

Millet is still a bird food to many people, and this soup showcases my favorite way of serving it: I hide it. My stealth-serving technique works well here, as the light golden grains blend in with the creamy-colored cauliflower, adding just the right amount of delicate texture. Naturally sweet salmon adds a gorgeous pink hue and brings the flavors together. And one day maybe millet can come out of the cupboard, undisguised. ✿ gluten-free

Heat a large Dutch oven or heavy saucepan over medium heat. Swirl in the oil and wait until it shimmers. Add the cumin seeds (they should sizzle!) and cook, stirring occasionally but watching closely (they can burn fast), until the seeds darken and become fragrant, 30 seconds to 1 minute. Add the onion, garlic, bay leaf, and ¼ teaspoon of the salt and cook, stirring frequently, until the onion just starts to brown at the edges, about 5 minutes.

Tip in the cauliflower, add the turmeric, and cook, stirring, until the florets are coated with color and the spice becomes fragrant, 1 to 2 minutes. Add the vermouth and cook until the liquid is almost evaporated, about 2 minutes. Add the broth, water, millet, preserved lemon, and ¼ teaspoon of the salt, and bring to a boil, scraping the bottom of the pot with a wooden spoon to loosen any browned bits. Decrease the heat to maintain a simmer, cover, and cook until the millet is tender, about 20 minutes.

When the millet is done, season the salmon pieces with the remaining ¼ teaspoon salt. Add the fish to the pot, stir gently, and return to a simmer. Cook, leaving the lid slightly askew, until the salmon is opaque throughout, about 3 minutes. Remove from the heat and add 1 tablespoon of the lemon juice. Season with salt and more lemon juice to taste. Serve right away in deep bowls, with lemon wedges on the side.

2 tablespoons extra-virgin olive oil

2 teaspoons whole cumin seeds

1½ cups chopped red onion (1 medium)

2 cloves garlic, minced

1 large bay leaf

¾ teaspoon fine sea salt

6 cups 1-inch cauliflower florets, (from about one 2-pound head)

¾ teaspoon turmeric

¼ cup dry vermouth (see page 248) or dry white wine

4 cups low-sodium vegetable broth

2 cups water

¼ cup millet

3 tablespoons finely chopped preserved lemon

12 ounces skinned salmon fillet, cut into 1-inch pieces

1 to 2 tablespoons lemon juice

1 lemon, cut into wedges, for serving

SERVES 6

fine points

Preserved lemons add complexity to this soup (see page 144, for sources see page 251).

MAKE AHEAD The soup, prior to adding the salmon, can be made up to 2 days ahead. Chill, covered. It will thicken. Just add a little more water or broth and reheat over medium to a gentle simmer before adding the salmon.

easy preserved lemons

2 medium or 3 small organic lemons (about 7 ounces total)

3 tablespoons (2 ounces) fine sea salt

About 1 cup water

MAKES ONE 1-PINT JAR; 12 TO 18 WEDGES

My mother uses lemons as a seasoning like other people use salt. She squeezes fresh lemon juice onto anything and everything, and in abundance. She might even squirt some onto chocolate pudding when no one is looking. Yet while I shake my head at her curious habit, I love the bright citrus almost as much and always have plenty on hand. And, inevitably at some point during winter, I will end up with too many fresh lemons in my crisper drawer. It is then that I make a large jar of preserved lemons.

Homemade preserved lemons have a superb clean taste, far superior to anything you find in a store. Their complex salty and tangy notes will almost jolt you out of your seat when you try them the first time—little do they resemble the acidic burst of fresh lemon juice. They are a staple of the Moroccan kitchen and can be used in countless recipes. Try, for example, the Minted Barley and Fennel Stew with Marinated Feta (page 149) or the Cumin-Scented Cauliflower Soup with Salmon (page 143). I also tuck them around chicken, together with potatoes and other vegetables I plan to roast. Or use the rind to add complexity to soups and salads. You can fill the cavity of a whole fish with them or top a fish fillet with a few tablespoons of chopped rind, olives, and parsley before roasting. Keep in mind, the wedges are salty—so give them a good rinse.

Some people don't like the soft mushy pulp of the preserved citrus. In my frugal kitchen I can't get myself to throw anything edible away, so I was relieved to come across a creative use in a restaurant a few years ago: coarsely chop up the pulp, drizzle with good-quality olive oil, and serve it on a small dipping plate, accompanied by warm pita or lavash bread. Divine!

This recipe, adapted from one in Germany's leading women's magazine *Brigitte*, is a cinch to make. All you need is a few minutes of prep, and then you have to wait for about 4 weeks. But your patience will be rewarded each time you walk by the jar of bright golden wedges on your kitchen counter.

This recipe makes a small sample if you are new to preserved lemons. Next time, double or quadruple the recipe as I do. After 4 weeks, transfer some wedges into small jars, top off with salty liquid, and share. They make a beautiful gift during the holiday season. gluten-free

Rinse the whole lemons well under hot running water and rub them dry. Cut each lemon into 6 wedges—first in half lengthwise, then each half into 3 pieces. At this point you can remove and discard the seeds (I have forgotten this more than once, and it was not a problem).

Add the lemon wedges to a medium bowl and toss with the salt. Pack them into a 1-pint jar, scraping in all the salt as well. Top off with water (I use filtered), leaving a bit of air space. Seal tightly and shake the jar to dissolve the salt. The lemons will start to float, which looks beautiful. Allow to sit at room temperature for 4 weeks. Occasionally shake the jar, a few times per week. The lemons will darken a bit as they mature.

fine points

Once you open the jar, store the preserved lemons in the refrigerator. They will last for up to 3 months. Make sure that they are always covered with liquid. Occasionally, your lemons can develop a white lacy substance. It is harmless; just rinse it off before using. For long-term storage in your pantry, be sure to follow proper canning instructions. Cathy Barrow's site is a great resource: www.mrswheelbarrow.com.

In any case, please keep your work surface, hands, jars, and spoons clean. While salt is a natural preservative, basic hygiene is always a good idea if you want your food to last.

freekeh soup with spicy harissa shrimp and dates

Toasting gives grains a brilliant boost. Yet for me, during the week, this is normally one step too many. Here is where freekeh comes in handy: this almost forest-green wheat adds a roasty aroma to your dinner without actually needing to toast it (more on freekeh, see page 9).

This nourishing grain and lentil soup is inspired by my travel to North Africa, where spicy hot chiles and sweet chewy dates are sometimes joined on a plate. My husband was a skeptic until he tried it—then I had to hide the dates.

gluten-free option

To make the soup, heat a large Dutch oven or heavy saucepan over medium heat. Swirl in the olive oil and wait until it shimmers. Add the onion, celery, bell pepper, garlic, sage, thyme, and ¼ teaspoon of the salt and cook, stirring occasionally, until the vegetables soften, about 5 minutes.

Stir in the broth, water, freekeh, and the remaining ¼ teaspoon salt and bring to a boil. Decrease the heat to maintain a simmer, cover, and cook until the freekeh is tender with a slight chewiness, 18 to 20 minutes. Stir in the lentils.

Meanwhile, prepare the shrimp: Place a rack about 4 inches from the broiler and heat on high for about 5 minutes. Grease a large rimmed baking sheet with olive oil or coat with cooking spray.

Combine 1 tablespoon harissa paste (more if you like it spicy), the olive oil, turmeric, Aleppo pepper, and salt in a small bowl. Place the shrimp in a medium bowl, gently rub in the harissa mixture, and allow to marinate for 10 to 15 minutes, or until the soup is almost done. Using paper towels, gently pat dry the shrimp and place on the baking sheet.

Broil until opaque throughout, 3 to 4 minutes, flipping them once in between with a metal spatula.

To finish, remove the soup from the heat and add the pepper and the lemon juice. Season with salt, pepper, and lemon juice to taste. Drizzle with a bit more olive oil and sprinkle with the ¼ cup parsley.

Divide between six wide shallow bowls and place 4 to 5 shrimp on top of each. Sprinkle each with ½ tablespoon of the dates, a bit of the remaining 2 tablespoons parsley, and serve at once, with lemon wedges on the side.

SOUP

2 tablespoons extra-virgin olive oil, plus more for drizzling

1½ cups chopped red onion (about 1 medium)

1½ cups chopped celery (½-inch pieces; about 3 stalks)

1½ cups chopped red bell pepper (½-inch chunks; about 1 bell pepper)

1 to 2 cloves garlic, peeled and slightly crushed

1 tablespoon minced fresh sage

2 teaspoons fresh thyme leaves

½ teaspoon fine sea salt

4 cups low-sodium vegetable broth

2 cups water, or cooking liquid from the lentils topped off with water

1 cup cracked freekeh

1½ cups cooked French lentils (see page 152), or 1 (15-ounce) can, rinsed and drained

SHRIMP

1 to 2 tablespoons harissa paste

1 tablespoon olive oil

½ teaspoon ground turmeric

½ teaspoon Aleppo pepper

¼ teaspoon fine sea salt

1 pound extra-large shrimp, shell-on (see page 248) or peeled and deveined

TO FINISH

¼ teaspoon freshly ground pepper

continued >

**2 tablespoons lemon juice,
or more as needed**

**¼ cup plus 2 tablespoons
coarsely chopped fresh flat-
leaf parsley**

**3 tablespoons finely chopped
firm dates, preferably Deglet
Noor**

**1 lemon, cut into 6 wedges,
for serving**

SERVES 6

fine points

You can cook the lentils while you prep your ingredients.

Harissa is a traditional Tunisian chile paste infused with spices such as garlic and coriander. Look for it in well-stocked supermarkets or Middle Eastern stores (see "Sources," page 251).

GLUTEN-FREE Millet, buckwheat, and quinoa can be substituted to make this gluten-free. If you like, toast them first (see page 17) in the empty saucepan. Immediately transfer to a medium bowl, and set aside until you're ready to cook the grains. These grains might be done a little faster than freekeh.

VEGETARIAN Drain a 14-ounce block of tofu (see page 118) and cut it into 12 triangles: first cut crosswise into 6 slices and then cut each slice in half into a triangle. Marinate like the shrimp and broil until puffed and nicely browned, about 10 minutes total, flipping once. Serve 2 triangles per person.

MAKE AHEAD The soup, prior to preparing the shrimp, can be made up to 2 days ahead. Allow to cool to room temperature; chill, covered. Add a little more water or broth to your liking and reheat over medium heat to a gentle simmer before fixing the shrimp.

minted barley and fennel stew with marinated feta

This homey winter meal is inspired by the simple bean stews of Greece. To stay with tradition, I've added barley, a grain served around the Mediterranean since antiquity, and lots of fresh fennel with its sweet licorice touch. This stew is easy and comes together in less than an hour. Thick and creamy, it is delicious even without the marinated feta. Serve with toasted pita wedges or crusty whole grain bread.

To prepare the barley, add the water, barley, bay leaf, and lemon zest to a small heavy saucepan and bring to a boil. Decrease the heat to maintain a simmer, cover, and cook until the barley is tender with a slight chew, 35 to 40 minutes. Remove the bay leaf and the zest and set aside, covered.

While the barley cooks, prepare the stew: Cut off the stems from the fennel, remove the fronds, and chop a few tablespoons for garnish (reserve the rest for another use). Cut the stems into ¼-inch-thick slices. Remove the tough outer leaves of the bulb and discard the fibrous core. Quarter and chop the bulb.

Heat a large Dutch oven or heavy saucepan over medium heat. Swirl in the olive oil and wait until it shimmers. Add the onion, celery, chopped fennel and stems, garlic, bay leaves, chile, and ¼ teaspoon of the salt. Cook, stirring occasionally, until the vegetables soften but don't brown, about 5 minutes. Add the ¼ cup mint and the oregano and cook, stirring, until the herbs become fragrant, about 30 seconds. Add the broth, wine, Parmesan, and preserved lemons, followed by the beans and the barley with any cooking liquid. Season with the remaining ¼ teaspoon salt and the pepper and bring to a boil. Reduce the heat to maintain a simmer, cover, and cook until the vegetables are tender and the flavors meld, 15 to 20 minutes.

Meanwhile, place the feta into a small bowl and sprinkle with the mint and the Aleppo pepper. Drizzle with the olive oil and set aside to marinate.

To finish, remove the rind, bay leaf, and chile. Thin with a bit more water or broth if you like. Stir in 1 tablespoon of the lemon juice. Season to taste with salt, pepper, and more lemon juice. Combine the chopped fennel fronds, the celery leaves, and the remaining 2 tablespoons mint in a bowl for garnish (use whatever you have, about ½ cup total). Ladle the stew into bowls. Garnish each serving with about 2 tablespoons of the marinated feta (or drizzle with a bit of olive oil if you don't use the feta) and some of the greens. Serve hot, passing more lemon juice around.

BARLEY

2 cups water

⅔ cup pearl barley, or 2½ cups cooked (see page 23)

½ bay leaf

1 (2-inch) strip lemon zest (optional)

STEW

1 large fennel bulb (scant 1 pound)

2 tablespoons extra-virgin olive oil

1½ cups chopped red onion (about 1 medium)

1½ cups chopped celery (about 3 stalks), plus a few tablespoons of chopped leaves, for garnish

2 cloves garlic, peeled and lightly crushed

2 small bay leaves

1 dried red chile pepper

½ teaspoon fine sea salt

¼ cup loosely packed torn fresh mint leaves, plus 2 tablespoons chopped for garnish

1 teaspoon dried crumbled oregano

2½ cups low-sodium vegetable or chicken broth

½ cup dry white wine or broth

1 (2-inch chunk) Parmesan rind (optional)

3 tablespoons finely chopped preserved lemons (see Fine Points)

1¾ cups cooked cannellini beans (see page 152), or 1 (15-ounce) can, rinsed and drained

continued >

minted barley and fennel stew
with marinated feta, continued

¼ teaspoon freshly ground
black pepper

1 to 2 tablespoons freshly
squeezed lemon juice, plus
more for serving

MARINATED FETA (OPTIONAL)

4 ounces feta, coarsely
crumbled

2 tablespoons chopped
fresh mint

½ teaspoon Aleppo pepper,
or ⅛ teaspoon dried red chile
flakes (optional)

2 tablespoons extra-virgin
olive oil

SERVES 4 TO 6

fine points

Pearl barley adds comforting starchiness; for more texture, use hulled (whole grain) barley soaked overnight and drained.

You can easily make your own preserved lemons (see page 144 or "Sources," page 251). Or follow my mom's lead and add a few thin lemon slices together with the broth for hints of bitterness from the pith and the peel and a mellowed tanginess from the flesh.

MAKE AHEAD You can make the stew completely ahead, up to 2 days; its aromas will deepen. Warm over medium heat, stirring occasionally and adding a bit more broth or water to thin as desired.

ONE VARIATION AND ONE SIMPLE MEAL FROM LEFTOVERS

Carrots are a nice replacement for the fennel. You will need about 4 medium, halved lengthwise if thick, and cut into ¼-inch slices (about 2½ cups). If you like, also add ½ bunch of chard, stems sliced ¼ inch thick and leaves chopped (about 2 cups). Add the stems together with the vegetables at the start, then stir in the leaves after the vegetable have simmered and allow them just to wilt, about 2 minutes. If you have carrot tops, chop up ¾ cup or so and add them in here as well.

If you have enough leftover soup (3 to 4 cups), add one 14-ounce can of diced tomatoes with their juices and perhaps a bit of water. Bring to a boil over medium heat, stirring occasionally, cover, and simmer for 10 minutes for the flavors to meld. Garnish with chopped parsley and drizzle with olive oil for a new effortless meal from leftovers.

how to cook your own "cans" of beans, chickpeas, and lentils

Everyone should have canned beans and lentils on hand for last-minute additions to meals. The legumes are delicious, nutritious, and feed you well. But over the years, I have found them so easy to make, flavorful, and with an appealing velvety texture, that I rarely resort to store-bought cans anymore. Instead, I cook a large amount ahead of time to always have a can-size stash of beans and chickpeas in the freezer. Plus, you can add flavorings and control how much salt you add (many cans contain a fair bit of sodium), and they are more economical as well.

Do this on a weekend; it's so easy that you will ask yourself why you haven't done this all your life.

You need 2-cup (475 ml) capacity glass or other freezer-safe containers. Microwave-safe containers allow you to thaw the legumes on the spot.

🍃 gluten-free

---

2 cups dried beans such as cannellini, black beans, or chickpeas, picked over, rinsed if you like (I never bother)

About 8 cups water

¾ teaspoon fine sea salt

½ yellow onion, peeled

2 cloves garlic, unpeeled (optional)

1 large bay leaf

1 dried red chile pepper (optional)

MAKES ABOUT 3 (14-OUNCE) CANS, EACH ABOUT 1¾ CUPS LEGUMES PLUS ¾ CUP COOKING LIQUID; PLUS A SCANT 1 CUP COOKING LIQUID AND A FEW SPOONS OF LEGUMES (EAT THEM!)

beans and chickpeas

The night before (or at least 6 hours ahead), add the beans or chickpeas together with the salt to a large heavy pot and add 6 cups of the water.

When you are ready to cook the legumes, or in the morning, add the remaining 2 cups water (or if you drain the water, add 6 to 7 cups water to cover by about 1½ inches and ½ teaspoon salt). Add the onion, garlic, bay leaf, and chile, cover, and bring to a boil over medium-high heat.

Uncover and boil for 5 minutes. Decrease the heat to maintain a simmer, cover, and cook until the beans are tender but not mushy, typically 50 to 60 minutes (fresh legumes from the last harvest can be ready in 35 minutes, older ones might take up to 80 minutes). Adjust salt at the end of cooking (or when you actually use the legumes in a dish).

Remove the onion (and eat it—it will be meltingly tender, sweet like jam), garlic, bay leaf, and chile. Remove the pot from the heat, uncover, and allow the legumes to cool in the cooking liquid, about 1 hour.

Once the legumes have cooled, add about 1¾ cups to each container and cover with about ¾ cup cooking liquid (or a bit less for smaller containers); leave a bit of room for the liquid to expand during freezing. Cover and chill for up to 5 days or freeze for up to 3 months. Defrost in the fridge overnight or in the microwave.

fine points

Adding salt during soaking softens the tough skins of legumes and results in creamier texture.

Draining the soaking liquid helps if beans give you lots of discomfort; it is not necessary.

Any extra cooking liquid can be used in soups. I often just drink it—it's flavorful and warming.

Unfortunately, most dried legumes still don't carry a harvest date. Look for them in bulk sections of health food stores with good turnaround.

You can now find fresh dried beans from the most recent harvest at some farmers' markets. Buy them if you see them!

lentils

For use in soups, I almost always buy green French lentils (*lentilles du Puy*) because they keep their shape better and stay toothsome compared to common brown lentils. Black lentils, also called beluga lentils, turn a beautiful shiny black when cooked—reminiscent of caviar, hence the name.

Add the water, lentils, shallot, bay leaf, and chile to a medium heavy saucepan and bring to a boil over medium-high heat. Decrease the heat to maintain a simmer, cover with the lid slightly ajar, and cook for 15 minutes.

Stir in the soy sauce and the salt and continue to simmer until the lentils are tender, 5 to 15 minutes more, depending on their freshness. Remove from the heat, remove the shallot, bay leaf, and chile, and stir in the pepper. Season with salt, soy sauce, and pepper to taste if you want to eat them right away (or adjust later). Drain, reserving the cooking liquid.

Once the lentils have cooled, add about 1¾ cups to each container and cover with about ¾ cup cooking liquid (or a bit less for smaller containers); leave a bit of room for the liquid to expand during freezing. Cover and chill for up to 5 days or freeze for up to 3 months. Defrost in the fridge overnight, or in the microwave.

3½ cups water

1 cup dried green French (Puy) lentils, brown lentils, or beluga lentils, picked over, rinsed if you like

1 small shallot, peeled

1 bay leaf

1 dried red chile (optional)

½ tablespoon low-sodium soy sauce, or more as needed

¼ teaspoon fine sea salt

¼ teaspoon freshly ground black pepper

MAKES ABOUT 2 (14-OUNCE) CANS, EACH ABOUT 1¾ CUPS LENTILS PLUS ¾ CUP COOKING LIQUID

chicken stew with honey-balsamic squash and farro

FARRO
2½ cups water

1 cup semipearled farro, or
3 cups cooked (see page 22)

Pinch of fine sea salt

STEW
3 skinless boneless chicken
breasts (also called halves), cut
in half crosswise for a total of
6 pieces (about 1½ pounds),
trimmed and patted dry

¾ teaspoon fine sea salt

½ teaspoon freshly ground
black pepper

2 tablespoons extra-virgin
olive oil, or more as needed

2 shallots, thinly sliced
(about ¾ cup)

1 to 2 cloves garlic, thinly sliced

5 cups cubed kabocha or
buttercup squash (¾- to 1-inch
cubes; from about 2¼ pounds)

½ cup dry white wine such
as Pinot Grigio

1 (28-ounce) can whole
tomatoes with their juices,
crushed

1 cup low-sodium chicken
broth

¼ cup white balsamic vinegar,
or more as needed

1 tablespoon honey, or more
as needed

¼ cup torn fresh basil leaves,
for garnish

SERVES 4 TO 6

As soon as bright orange–fleshed winter squash shows up in markets, my mom heads out to buy a heavy huge chunk and soon gets to work on a delectable stew. She never roasts the squash but just simmers it, together with onion and tomatoes, which highlights the delicate floral aroma of the winter vegetable. Her austere creation inspired this one-pot meal. And I kept making it again and again, even after the recipe was fully tested, because it comes together so easily and is all-around satisfying. My version is tangy with a hint of honey in the background to balance the gentle acidity of white balsamic vinegar. ⬤ gluten-free option

To prepare the farro, add the water, farro, and salt to a small heavy saucepan and bring to a boil. Decrease the heat to maintain a simmer, cover, and cook until the farro is tender with a slight chewiness, 20 to 25 minutes. Drain, return to the saucepan, cover, and set aside.

While the farro cooks, heat a large Dutch oven or heavy saucepan over medium-high heat. Season the chicken pieces with ¼ teaspoon of the salt and ¼ teaspoon of the pepper. Swirl 1 tablespoon of the olive oil into the pan and wait until it shimmers. Add 3 or 4 chicken pieces, with their round fleshy sides down and without touching, and cook them, undisturbed, until nicely golden brown on 1 side, 4 to 5 minutes. Lower the heat to medium if they darken too fast. Using a heatproof spatula, transfer the chicken to a large plate. Add the remaining 1 tablespoon of olive oil and repeat with any remaining chicken.

Add a bit more oil if the pan has become dry and continue over medium heat. Add the shallots, garlic, and ¼ teaspoon of the salt and cook until the shallots start to brown at the edges, stirring all the while with a wooden spoon, 1 to 2 minutes. Add the squash and cook, stirring, until the pieces are shiny and coated with oil, about 1 minute.

Add the wine (it will sizzle!) and cook until the liquid becomes syrupy and is almost evaporated, 2 to 4 minutes. Add the tomatoes, broth, vinegar, and the chicken with any juices. Season with the remaining ¼ teaspoon salt and ¼ teaspoon pepper and bring to a boil, scraping the bottom to release any browned bits. Decrease the heat to maintain a gentle simmer, cover, and cook for 15 minutes. Add the farro, return to a simmer, cover, and cook until the squash is tender and the chicken is cooked through, 7 to 12 minutes more.

To finish, stir in the honey and remove the pan from the heat. Season with salt and pepper to taste, adding perhaps a bit more honey or vinegar to balance flavors. I enjoy this stew with a nice tang and just a hint of sweetness from the honey. Serve, garnishing each portion with a few torn basil leaves.

fine points

This makes a comforting, nourishing stew for cold winter nights—for a lighter, thinner version, use 2 cups cooked farro.

I always brown tender chicken breast on one side only, which keeps the meat juicy while still providing enough browning for flavor.

You can use regular balsamic or sherry vinegar for the milder white balsamic vinegar, but you might need a bit more honey to balance.

GLUTEN-FREE Use 2 to 3 cups cooked wild rice, brown or black rice, or quinoa or only 1 to 2 cups cooked millet, as it tends to thicken liquids considerably (for cooking instructions, see page 22).

MAKE AHEAD The stew can be made up to 2 days ahead. Gently reheat over medium, stirring occasionally and adding a bit more broth or water as needed. The stew freezes well for up to 1 month.

spicy beef chili with amaranth and lime

STEW

1½ tablespoons extra-virgin olive oil, plus more as needed

½ pound lean ground beef, preferably grass-fed

½ teaspoon fine sea salt

¼ teaspoon freshly ground black pepper

1½ cups chopped yellow onion (about 1 medium)

2 cloves garlic, minced

½ serrano chile, minced, ribs and seeds removed for less heat (optional)

1½ teaspoons ground chili powder

1¼ teaspoons crushed dried oregano

1 teaspoon ground cumin

2 tablespoons tomato paste

2½ cups low-sodium beef or chicken broth

½ cup amaranth grains

1¾ cups cooked cannellini beans (see page 152), or 1 (15-ounce) can, rinsed and drained

1 (14.5-ounce) can whole tomatoes, crushed, with juices

TO FINISH

½ teaspoon granulated sugar

1 tablespoon low-sodium soy sauce, plus more as needed

1 tablespoon freshly squeezed lime juice, plus more as needed and for serving

¼ cup chopped fresh cilantro

SERVES 4 TO 6

One frigid night when the temperatures in Boston hit almost 0°F, this bone-warming aromatic stew bubbled away on my stove, introducing surprise dinner guests to amaranth. The gluten-free grain has an infamous sticky quality, gooey to some. But here its character shines, thickening the liquid and creating a satisfying stew, perfect for the depth of winter.

Don't let the long ingredient list deter you. This is a straightforward one-pot meal. As in most of my recipes, meat plays a second fiddle here to vegetables, grains, and beans. Serve with a dollop of sour cream or Greek yogurt and whole grain bread. I like to pair it with the Irish Soda Bread with Amaranth, Cranberries, and Rosemary (page 68). Or try it with the Olive Oil Biscuits with Cracked Pepper and Honey Glaze (page 66). ⌁ gluten-free

To make the stew, heat a large Dutch oven or heavy saucepan over medium-high heat. Swirl in the oil and wait until it shimmers. Add the beef and season it with ¼ teaspoon of the salt and the pepper. Cook, stirring occasionally and breaking up any large clumps, until the meat is nicely browned and no traces of pink remain, about 5 minutes. Remove the meat with a slotted spoon or spatula to a plate.

Reduce the heat to medium and add a bit more olive oil if the pan has become dry. Stir in the onion, garlic, chile, and the remaining ¼ teaspoon salt. Cook, stirring frequently and scraping the bottom with a wooden spoon, until the onion softens and starts to brown at the edges, about 5 minutes. If the pan blackens at the bottom, stir in 1 to 2 tablespoons water and scrape up the browned bits. Stir in the chili powder, oregano, and cumin and cook, stirring continuously, until the spices are fragrant, about 30 seconds. Watch so as not to burn the spices. Add the tomato paste and cook, stirring, until it darkens, about 30 seconds.

Add the broth (it might splatter!) and the amaranth and bring to a boil, scraping the bottom of the pot to release any browned bits. Cover, reduce the heat to maintain a simmer, and cook for 15 minutes.

Return the meat with any juices to the pot. Add the beans and tomatoes and return to a simmer. Cover and cook until the stew thickens, 25 to 30 minutes. Be sure to vigorously stir a few times, especially toward the end, as amaranth has a tendency to stick to the bottom.

To finish, remove the pan from the heat and stir in the sugar, soy sauce, and lime juice. Season to taste with a bit more lime juice and soy sauce (it can be salty!). Only then adjust for salt and pepper. Sprinkle with cilantro and serve in deep bowls, passing more lime juice at the table.

fine points

I prefer ground beef, 85% lean, for its richer flavor, but 91% lean works well.

MAKE AHEAD The stew can be made 1 day ahead, and like all stews, it tastes better when reheated. Leftovers freeze well for up to 1 month.

flemish beef stew with caramelized onions and rye

RYE

1½ cups water

¾ cup whole rye berries, soaked overnight and drained, or 2 cups cooked (see page 23)

1 bay leaf

1 dried red chile pepper (optional)

STEW

1¼ pounds beef stew meat such as chuck, trimmed of fat and cut into 1-inch cubes

½ teaspoon fine sea salt

½ teaspoon freshly ground black pepper

2 tablespoons extra-virgin olive oil, or more as needed

1½ pounds red onions, cut in half lengthwise and thinly sliced crosswise (about 6 cups)

1 tablespoon turbinado sugar or packed brown sugar

2 tablespoons white or regular whole wheat flour or all-purpose flour

2 (12-ounce) bottles oatmeal stout or other dark beer (about 3 cups)

1½ cups low-sodium beef broth, or a bit more if needed

2 tablespoons balsamic vinegar

4 sprigs fresh thyme

4 sprigs fresh flat-leaf parsley

2 bay leaves

SERVES 4

You will absolutely want to make this slow-cooking stew ahead. I admit I have never managed to do so because the scent emanating from the oven is impossible to resist, so we always end up eating it the same day. But if you can restrain yourself, it will be so much better.

My recipe is adapted from a Flemish carbonnade by the wonderful Anne Willan, internationally renowned cooking teacher and cookbook author. I added whole rye berries, as their slight natural tang is a beautiful match with the stew's deep aroma of dark beer and caramelized red onions, which melt into the rich concentrated broth. Triticale, spelt, and soft wheat berries are fine replacements. Serve with a crusty baguette or thick slices of sourdough bread, onto which you dab some good butter. Nothing else.

To prepare the rye, add the water, rye berries, bay leaf, and chile to a small heavy saucepan and bring to a boil. Decrease the heat to maintain a simmer, cover, and cook until the kernels are tender with a slight chew, 50 to 60 minutes. Take off the heat, remove the bay leaf and chile, cover, and set aside. There might be a bit of liquid left.

While the rye cooks, prepare the stew: Pat the beef dry with paper towels and season with ¼ teaspoon of the salt and ¼ teaspoon of the pepper. Heat a large Dutch oven or heavy saucepan over medium-high heat. Swirl in 1½ tablespoons of the olive oil and wait until it shimmers. Working in 2 or 3 batches, cook the meat until browned on all sides, turning it with tongs and adding the remaining ½ tablespoon oil if the pan goes dry, about 5 minutes per batch. Using a slotted spoon or spatula, transfer the beef to a plate and set aside.

Decrease the heat to medium, add a bit more oil if needed, and stir in the onions and the remaining ¼ teaspoon salt and ¼ teaspoon pepper. Cook, uncovered, stirring frequently and scraping the bottom to release any browned bits, until the onions become very soft, about 15 minutes. Decrease the heat to medium-low after about 5 minutes to brown the onions more slowly.

Meanwhile, position a rack in the center of the oven and preheat to 325°F.

Return to medium heat, stir in the sugar, and cook until the onions smell sweet and are caramelized, about 3 minutes. Sprinkle with the flour, stir, and cook until it emits a toasty scent, about 1 minute. Add the beer, broth, the beef with its juices, balsamic vinegar, thyme, parsley, and the bay leaves. Increase the heat to medium-high, scraping the bottom of the pot, and bring just to a boil.

Cover and transfer the saucepan to the oven and cook for 1½ hours. Stir in the rye berries with any remaining cooking liquid. There should be plenty of liquid to cover the meat, otherwise add ½ to 1 cup more broth or water and continue cooking until the beef is fork-tender, about ½ hour more, or a bit longer.

To finish, discard the bay leaves and the herb twigs if you can find them (otherwise don't worry). Now take a moment to inhale the aromas of the concentrated dark liquid. To my mind the plentiful broth is so amazing at this point I pretty much leave it alone. But, by all means, season with more salt and pepper to taste. Serve and swoon, or allow to cool and chill.

fine points

If you cook the rye berries as soon as you start prepping ingredients, you can practically walk away when the stew goes into the oven.

Leaner top round roast is a good choice if you wish to lighten this up.

MAKE AHEAD The whole stew can be made up to 2 days ahead. Allow to cool to room temperature; chill, covered. Gently reheat over medium heat, stirring occasionally. The stew also freezes well for up to 1 month.

pasta
from ancient grains to modern heirlooms

one serious passion for pasta

Allow me to sing the praises of pasta, ancient and new. To my mind, there are few things more speedy and satisfying than a bowl of pasta on a busy weeknight. Home-cooked pasta is nourishing soul food, first-class. Its beauty lies in its simplicity. Even if your cupboards are bare, you can create an alluring meal in minutes.

The most remarkable pasta dishes are often austere creations. They provide a bridge to the roots of our table, connecting us to people the world over who created memorable meals out of scarcity. In Germany we call this *Arme Leute Küche*; the Italians refer to it as *cucina povera*. Think risotto with just Parmesan and a dab of butter, a panzanella using day-old bread, onions, and garlic, or—in Germany—a soup of beans or lentils with a slice of good whole-grain bread. To me, these meals always stand out—they are honest and simple, easy and comforting. This is how I like to eat.

These creations have timeless appeal, with a long, fascinating history. The oldest pasta dates back about four thousand years. And, unlike what you might think, it was *not* made from hard durum wheat like today's classic strands, but from gluten-free millet. Furthermore, these ancient noodles were found *not* in Italy, but excavated in China in 2005. Since then I have been equally mystified *and* impressed by how the yard-long strands held up, given that millet has no gluten. And held up they did, thousands of years. I have more recently learned from Rachel Laudan's fascinating book *Cuisine and Empire* how this miracle was performed. The dough, she writes, was poured through a sieve into boiling water to set the mixture. This, of course, reminds me of a classic German noodle dish, spaetzle, which too is pressed into a pot of simmering water, either through a spaetzle press or, for lack of one, a simple colander.

With this chapter I invite you to explore the exhilarating textures and aromas of whole and ancient grain pasta, this traditional and often meatless meal. Many cultures treasure pasta from ancient grains. My random list includes dark buckwheat soba from Japan, Germany's *Dinkelnudeln* made from spelt, Italy's traditional buckwheat pizzoccheri and trendy farro pasta. Today, you find myriads of high-quality 100% whole grain pasta creations on store shelves, offering slowly digested nutrient-rich complex carbohydrates. Little do these resemble the harsh cardboard strands of the 1970s and 1980s. The fast-growing choices include lots of gluten-free pasta options, made from quinoa to brown rice.

Naturally, in choosing pasta, I look to Italy first. Italian companies with their centuries-old understanding of the craft make, without a doubt, some of the best pasta all around. If you want to go all the way, look for slow, low-temperature drying pasta, extruded through bronze dyes, which leave a rough surface on the pasta, allowing sauces to cling better to the strands.

But there is more: if you are passionate about supporting local grains and farmers, there are fascinating new players on the block. Community Grains, based in Oakland, California, offers exquisite pasta from freshly milled grain, grown locally in the state. Their whole wheat pasta is in a class of its own, beautifully textured and deeply wheaty in a pleasing way. Or check out Baia Pasta, also Oakland-based, which uses organic American-grown flour for their whole spelt, Kamut, and whole durum wheat pasta (see "Sources," page 251).

Pasta is well suited to our busy lives and can be part of a balanced diet. My recipes are normally not cheese-laden creations but rather nourishing and satisfying meals with loads of fresh vegetables woven in. The vegetables are not an afterthought but an integral part of the meal to round out the flavors—this is how I *love* my pasta, no fuss, simple, and delicious. And I make sure to pair these unique new pasta flavors with ingredients that highlight their character and heighten their appeal.

I hope some creations will surprise you, for example, a pasta with parsnips that has become a favorite (see page 174). I'm also thrilled about a citrusy honeyed pesto (see page 168), and my new tomato sauce, mellowed with sweet shallots and infused with saffron (see page 172).

I didn't change the character of classic *cacio e pepe*, which is a minimalist's indulgence, as the name suggests, of cheese and pepper. But I pair mine with traditional farro pasta, which, in my mind, makes for a more appealing composition (see page 173). Last but not least, I bring you my mac and cheese, tested during icy winter nights in Boston—with two surprise ingredients: meltingly tender sweet leeks replace some of the carbohydrates, and Greek yogurt makes for a lighter take on this all-time favorite (see page 177).

All of the meals in this chapter are an invitation to a modern and moderate indulgence, for all of the days when your soul longs to spool strands around a fork and a spoon. My own passion was probably instilled by my Greek mom, who doesn't let a week go by without making a quick pasta dinner. To this day, she laments the fact that she never asked my late *yiayia*, her mother and my grandma, for her recipe for *koulakia*. Hers were sizable pasta pockets, ravioli-style, filled with fresh cheese and dripping with melted butter. Alas my *yiayia* took the recipe with her, to please only the angels now.

fusilli with tahini yogurt sauce and nigella seeds

Thick Greek yogurt and whole grain pasta are a perfect match in my food heaven—the creamy yogurt enveloping the pasta in an appealing and comforting blanket, thus lightening its rustic look and feel. This pasta with earthy tahini (sesame butter) and a sprinkling of deeply aromatic nigella seeds is my husband's favorite and has been on our table for years. Its sauce is spicy, with a good amount of raw garlic (use less only if you must!). And it thrives next to grilled steak, burgers, and lamb chops but is just as good with chicken; or serve it on its own, next to a peppery arugula salad. *gluten-free option*

Bring a large pot of water to a rolling boil. Add salt as you see fit and then the pasta, stirring a few times. Return to a boil with the lid on; uncover and cook at a gentle boil until the pasta is al dente, according to the package directions.

While the water is coming to a boil, add the sesame, cumin, and nigella seeds to a medium skillet over medium heat. Toast, stirring frequently, until the seeds turn fragrant and the sesame becomes golden, 3 to 5 minutes. Immediately scrape the seeds onto a plate.

Cut half of the chile into fine rings and set aside. Add the remaining chile and the garlic to the bowl of a food processor, fitted with the metal blade. Process until minced, scraping down the sides as needed. Add the yogurt and sour cream and blend until creamy. Add the tahini, lemon juice, and salt and process until smooth. Season with salt to taste.

While the pasta is cooking, transfer the sauce to a 12-inch skillet. Gently heat over medium-low, stirring occasionally, until warmed through, about 5 minutes (do not bring to a boil, as the yogurt will curdle).

To finish, dip a heatproof measuring cup into the pasta pot to reserve ¾ cup cooking liquid. Drain the pasta and add it to the skillet with the sauce. Add about half of the reserved liquid. Toss vigorously to combine for 1 to 2 minutes, adding a bit more cooking liquid as needed, until you have a creamy sauce. Sprinkle with the seed mixture, the chile rings, and the parsley. Serve at once.

fine points

If you don't like the sharpness of fresh red chile, omit it and sprinkle the pasta at the end with a bit of mild Aleppo pepper (see "Sources," page 251) or sweet paprika.

MAKE AHEAD The yogurt tahini sauce can be prepared 1 day ahead; chill, covered.

Fine sea salt

12 ounces whole grain fusilli, rotelle, or other pasta shells (gluten-free if desired)

2 tablespoons sesame seeds

1 teaspoon whole cumin seeds

1 teaspoon nigella seeds (optional; see page 248)

1 or 2 fresh hot red chiles, depending on your preference, seeds and veins removed for less heat

4 cloves garlic, peeled

1 cup plain whole milk or 2% Greek yogurt (do not use nonfat)

1 cup low-fat sour cream

¼ cup plus 2 tablespoons tahini

¼ cup freshly squeezed lemon juice (1 to 2 lemons)

½ teaspoon fine sea salt

¼ cup chopped fresh flat-leaf parsley, for garnish

SERVES 4 AS A MAIN, OR 6 AS A SIDE

simple summer farfalle with roasted golden peppers

ROASTED PEPPERS

3 yellow or a mixture of red, yellow, and green bell peppers, cut in half lengthwise, cored, and seeded (about 1¼ pounds)

1 or 2 cloves garlic, thinly sliced

3 tablespoons extra-virgin olive oil

1 tablespoon balsamic vinegar

½ teaspoon fine sea salt

¼ teaspoon freshly ground black pepper

¼ teaspoon dried red chile flakes (optional)

½ cup lightly packed coarsely chopped fresh flat-leaf parsley

PASTA

Fine sea salt

12 ounces whole spelt or whole wheat farfalle, penne, or other short-cut pasta (gluten-free if desired)

2 ounces (about 1 cup) finely grated Grana Padano cheese or Parmesan, plus more for serving

SERVES 4 TO 6

This is one of those elementary creations only a bare fridge can inspire. On a hot day in late summer, after I had neglected grocery shopping for too long, the one thing left in the fridge at dinnertime were some bell peppers I had stuck under the broiler the day before because I didn't want them to spoil. I guess this is dinner, I mumbled to myself, not sure what to do. A little while later we were gobbling up this homey pasta meal. It was the perfect ending to the day, with the charred sweetness of the marinated peppers enveloping and elevating the nutty pasta. When I later posted a picture on Facebook, I was surprised by how many people commented or requested a recipe for this simple summer meal. So I wrote it down.

If you make the peppers ahead, dinner is ready in minutes. Leftovers are great for lunch the next day. Pack them together with a slice of feta as we do in Greece. Or, if you are at home, panfry some pasta and place a poached egg on top. ⟫ gluten-free option

To prepare the roasted peppers, place a rack 4 inches away from the heat and preheat the broiler on high for about 5 minutes. Place the bell pepper halves, cut side down, in the bottom of a large broiler pan or on a large rimmed baking sheet.

Broil until nicely charred and blistered, 12 to 15 minutes, rotating the pan once for even heat. Using tongs, transfer the peppers to a wooden cutting board, piling them on top of each other. When cool enough to handle, after 5 to 7 minutes, scrape or peel off the skin with your hands or a paring knife (a bit of skin or charred flecks may remain). Do not rinse the peppers, as they will lose their sweet aroma. Cut each half into 4 to 5 strips of a scant 1 inch, and each strip into 1-inch pieces.

Place the peppers and the garlic in a medium bowl. Drizzle with the olive oil and vinegar. Sprinkle with the salt, pepper, and chile flakes, and toss to combine. Allow to sit at room temperature for 15 minutes for the flavors to come together (or cover and chill if making ahead).

Meanwhile, bring a large pot of water to a rolling boil. Add salt as you see fit and then the pasta, stirring a few times. Return to a boil with the lid on; uncover and cook at a gentle boil until the pasta is al dente, according to the package directions.

To finish, dip a heatproof measuring cup into the pasta pot to remove ½ cup of cooking liquid. Drain the pasta and transfer it to a large serving bowl. Add the peppers and the parsley together with a scant ¼ cup of the reserved cooking liquid. Toss to combine, adding perhaps a tad more cooking liquid to loosen. Sprinkle with half of the cheese. Serve at once, passing the remaining cheese or more around.

fine points

This is most amazing when bell peppers are sweetest, in season—of course!

VARIATION Add ¼ cup pitted kalamata or other good-quality black or mixed olives.

MAKE AHEAD The roasted bell peppers can be prepared up to 3 days ahead. Sweet pepper juices will accumulate in your container—don't toss them out. Instead, add a drizzle of olive oil and sop up with some baguette. The whole mixture, with the garlic and seasonings, can be made 1 day ahead. Chill, covered; remove it from the fridge when you start boiling the pasta water.

COOKING PASTA IN LESS WATER WORKS VERY WELL INDEED

All my adult life I have often cooked pasta, against tradition, in so little water any proud Italian would cringe. But in the exhausted rush to dinner after long workdays, I frankly couldn't care less. I was hungry. And to my mind, my pasta turned out just fine, thank you very much. Or course, I never would have publicly confessed this habit; after all, Italians swear by cooking pasta in huge vats of boiling water, with enough salt to resemble the salinity of the Mediterranean.

Notice my surprise when the eminent food scientist Harold McGee wrote in the New York Times a few years ago about cooking pasta in minimal water. It not only worked for him. It also gave him a surprising "dividend," thick starchy cooking liquid. Restaurants get this supreme liquid by not changing the water in their pasta cooker so it goes from "clear to cloudy to muddy" over the course of an evening. Chefs prize it, writes McGee—because it binds the ingredients together, acting like a flavorful thickener. The only downside: You have to stir a bit more often. Of course, I knew that already from my own secret habit. McGee goes further, calling the aromatic full-bodied water "good enough to sip." This is especially true when you cook pasta from enticing ancient wheat varieties such as farro, einkorn, or Kamut!

According to McGee, this method works particularly well with short shapes. For long strands and ribbons, he recommends a quick wetting with cold water before you add them to the boiling water and then more frequent stirring at the start for a minute or so. In my day-to-day home cooking, I often use only about 6 cups of water for 12 ounces pasta because it is fast and easy. And now I don't have to hide it anymore. Oh, I love the science of food.

whole wheat spaghetti with orange walnut pesto

PASTA

Fine sea salt

12 ounces whole wheat spaghetti (gluten-free if desired)

1 tablespoon extra-virgin olive oil

3 cups chopped green onions, white and dark green parts (about 12)

½ teaspoon fine sea salt

½ teaspoon freshly ground black pepper

3 ounces (about 1½ cups) finely grated Parmesan, for serving

ORANGE WALNUT PESTO

2 cups (2 ounces) lightly packed basil leaves, rinsed and patted dry

½ cup (2 ounces) coarsely chopped toasted walnuts

3 tablespoons extra-virgin olive oil

2 tablespoons honey

1 tablespoon finely grated orange zest (from 1 orange, preferably organic)

1 teaspoon lemon juice, or more as needed

¼ teaspoon fine sea salt

SERVES 4

Some recipes are created in a moment of stove top bliss. Others take huge detours—this is one of them. An idea I considered ingenious evaporated in trial after trial. But suddenly it hit me: could this perhaps become a pesto? I'm happy to report this creation is as simple as it is divine. The orange-scented pesto with the lightly toasted walnuts is a magnificent match with nutty whole grain pasta. Its gentle kiss of honey paired with a cloudlike heaping of Parmesan brings you savory, salty, and delicately sweet in one bite. What's not to love?

This unusual pesto has many uses. I have set it out as a spread with bread and a cheese plate with aged Gouda, a sharp Cheddar, a blue cheese, or a mild Gorgonzola Dolce. We spoon it into a simple red lentil stew and use it as a garnish on roasted squash soup. It gives a nice boost stirred into plain brown rice or dolloped on sautéed zucchini. I can't get enough of it.

gluten-free option

Bring a large pot of water to a rolling boil. Add salt as you see fit, then the pasta, stirring a few times. Return to a boil with the lid on, uncover, and cook at a gentle boil until the pasta is 1 minute short of al dente, according to the package directions.

While the water is coming to a boil, prepare the pesto: Place the basil in the bowl of a food processor, fitted with a metal blade, and sprinkle the walnuts across. Pulse until the mixture is coarsely ground, about fifteen 1-second pulses. Drizzle the olive oil and honey across. Sprinkle with the orange zest, lemon juice, and salt and process briefly until you have a chunky paste, about 3 seconds. Feel free to whirl it a bit longer for a smoother, more homogenous pesto. Season with a bit more lemon juice and salt to taste. You will need ⅓ cup for the pasta.

When you add the pasta to the water, heat a 12-inch skillet over medium heat. Swirl in the olive oil and wait until it shimmers. Add the green onions and salt and decrease the heat to medium-low. Cook, stirring occasionally, until softened but not browned, 5 to 7 minutes. Stir in the pepper. Set aside if your pasta is not ready.

To finish, dip a heatproof measuring cup into the pasta pot to reserve ¾ cup cooking liquid. Drain the pasta. Add about ½ of the cooking liquid to the skillet with the green onions and bring to a simmer. Stir in the pesto, add the pasta, and decrease the heat to medium-low. Toss vigorously for 1 to 2 minutes, adding a bit more cooking liquid as needed, until you have a creamy sauce. Serve at once, grinding more black pepper on top and passing generous amounts of grated cheese around the table. The emphasis is on the word *generous*. Trust me on that.

fine points

For a pesto spread, use 3 (instead of 2) tablespoons of honey, or more to taste.

VARIATION Tangerine zest makes for a nice change.

MAKE AHEAD This recipe makes ¾ cup of pesto, enough for 2 meals. The pesto can be made ahead. Transfer to a ½-pint jar or other lidded container, cover with a thin layer of olive oil, and wipe the rim with a clean dish cloth, dipped in hot water; it will keep, chilled, for up to 7 days. Or freeze the pesto for up to 3 months.

kamut spaghetti with saffron-infused tomato sauce

Fine sea salt

12 ounces Kamut or other whole grain spaghetti (gluten-free if desired)

3 cups saffron-infused tomato sauce (½ recipe; page 172)

2 tablespoons unsalted butter

8 ounces (about 1 cup) whole milk ricotta cheese, preferably fresh (optional)

Freshly ground white pepper (see Fine Points, page 135), for serving

Finely grated Parmesan cheese, for serving

SERVES 4

By transforming classic pasta sauce with saffron, I have been secretly plotting to give you a reason to make this peasant meal into a feast—and to try any of the new ancient wheat pasta varieties that have been showing up on store shelves. Be it farro (emmer), Kamut, or einkorn, they all share an enticing light wheatiness that will make you long for more (see "Sources," page 251). *Buon appetito!* ⚭ gluten-free option

Bring a large saucepan of water to a rolling boil. Add salt as you see fit and then the pasta, stirring a few times. Return to a boil with the lid on; uncover and cook at a gentle boil until the pasta is al dente, according to the package directions.

Meanwhile, add the tomato sauce to a small saucepan and gently reheat over medium heat, stirring a few times. Season with salt to taste.

To finish, dip a heatproof measuring cup into the pasta water to remove ½ cup cooking liquid. Drain the pasta and return it to the pot or to a large serving bowl. Add the tomato sauce and the butter. Toss well, adding cooking liquid by the tablespoon (depending on the thickness of your sauce) until the pasta strands are well coated.

Immediately divide the pasta between four shallow plates. Spoon on some ricotta and serve at once, passing the pepper mill and the Parmesan around.

fine points

I love this plain and simple just as much as with chunks of fresh ricotta on top. Try it both ways.

saffron-infused tomato sauce with vermouth

3 tablespoons extra-virgin olive oil

6 shallots, thinly sliced crosswise (about 2 cups)

3 cloves garlic, peeled and lightly crushed

2 bay leaves

½ teaspoon loosely packed saffron threads

¼ teaspoon fine sea salt

Scant ½ cup dry vermouth (see page 248)

2 (28-ounce) cans whole peeled tomatoes with their juices, crushed

1 to 2 teaspoons sugar

MAKES ABOUT 6 CUPS; ENOUGH FOR 2 DINNERS FOR 4

fine points

Because this sauce uses so few ingredients, quality matters; get the best you can afford.

I used the famed and pricey San Marzano tomatoes, but good-quality canned organic tomatoes are fine.

No saffron? No problem—the sauce will still be worth your time.

Black pepper will mask the fine scent. If you must, use a bit of freshly ground white pepper.

MAKE AHEAD Cool the sauce to room temperature and chill, covered, for up to 5 days. Reheat over medium heat, adding water as needed. It freezes well for 3 months.

Created entirely by accident, this tomato sauce is an intoxicating blend of elusive flavors. I had bought too many sweet shallots, so I threw them in a pot. On the counter I found a tiny container of saffron from a different recipe—so I tossed some in as well. And then I opened a fresh bottle of vermouth, with its faint botanical scent, and in went a good glug. A little while later I almost danced on the counter as these aromas mingled and emerged from my pot.

This simple sauce takes a little time, mostly unsupervised, and is best made ahead, which allows the flavors to intensify. It is lovely after 20 minutes of cooking, but a slow simmer of 40 to 45 minutes is better. And if at any moment you wonder why on earth you are bothering to make homemade tomato sauce in the first place, just take a whiff as the sauce slowly simmers away and the sweet herbal scent wafts through the house—that's why. This makes enough sauce to use in two meals, the Kamut Spaghetti with Saffron-Infused Tomato Sauce (page 171) and the Baked Feta Fingers in Saffron Quinoa with Tomatoes (page 82). ⁓⁓ gluten-free option

Heat a large Dutch oven or heavy saucepan over medium heat. Swirl in the olive oil and wait until it shimmers. Add the shallots, garlic, bay leaves, saffron, and salt and cook, stirring often, until the shallots soften and turn golden, about 5 minutes. Watch closely and err on the side of stirring more rather than less because you don't want any browning or bitterness from burning the shallots, garlic, or saffron. Everything should stay golden, which means it will be sweet.

Add the vermouth and cook, stirring once or twice, until it becomes syrupy and is almost evaporated, 1 to 2 minutes. Add the tomatoes with their juices and 1 teaspoon of the sugar and bring to a boil over medium-high heat, stirring a few times. Decrease the heat to maintain a steady simmer, cover with the lid askew about 1 inch, and cook for 20 minutes.

Uncover, stir through, and continue cooking at a steady simmer, stirring once or twice, until nicely thickened, about 20 minutes more. Remove the bay leaves and fish out the garlic if you like (I always eat the sweetened cloves on the spot, sharing with no one). Season with the remaining 1 teaspoon of sugar if needed and perhaps a bit of salt (canned tomatoes are often salted, so you might not need much, if any). Be sure to inhale the subtle flavors—before you serve it.

farro pasta cacio e pepe

I turn to this recipe when I'm famished on a busy weeknight and don't know what to cook. It exudes its magic with minimal ingredients and labor. Traditional farro (emmer) or einkorn pasta (see "Sources," page 251) is a natural match, unpolished in the best of ways. But any good-quality whole grain pasta makes this a treat.

Serve this homey pasta with a simple dark leaf salad or my superfast broiled asparagus (page 107). If you have no greens with it, I'm afraid you have to make much more pasta—here's talking from experience. ⟫ gluten-free option

Fine sea salt

12 ounces farro, einkorn, or other whole grain spaghetti (gluten-free if desired)

1 tablespoon extra-virgin olive oil

2 teaspoons very coarsely ground or crushed black pepper (see Fine Points), plus more for serving

1 tablespoon unsalted butter or olive oil

3 ounces (about 1½ cups) freshly and finely grated Pecorino, plus more for serving

SERVES 4

Bring a large pot of water to a rolling boil. Add salt as you see fit and then the pasta, stirring a few times. Return to a boil with the lid on; uncover and cook at a gentle boil until the pasta is about 1 minute shy of al dente, according to the package directions.

A few minutes before your pasta is ready, heat the olive oil in a 12-inch skillet (I always use cast iron) over medium heat until it shimmers. Add the pepper and cook, stirring, until fragrant, about 60 seconds. Take off the heat and set aside.

To finish, dip a heatproof measuring cup into the pasta pot to reserve 1 scant cup cooking liquid. Drain the pasta. Return the skillet to the heat over medium-low to low. Add about ½ of the reserved cooking liquid, the butter, and the pasta and about two-thirds of the cheese and toss vigorously, using tongs. Gradually add the remaining cheese and a bit more pasta water by the tablespoon until a creamy sauce clings to the pasta, about 2 minutes. Divide between plates, warmed if you like, and serve at once, grinding on more pepper and passing more cheese at the table.

fine points

If possible, use Italian Pecorino Romano, made with 100% sheep's milk. Less harsh than domestic, it enhances the farro pasta with a savory sweet nuttiness.

I keep it simple during the week. Feel free to swap grated Parmesan for half of the cheese for a more complex aroma.

My new pepper mill delivers perfect coarse pepper for this dish. I have previously tried crushing whole peppercorns with a cast-iron skillet and with a mortar and pestle, but neither are easy or work very well. My best solution is a clean coffee mill: add the 2 teaspoons peppercorns, briefly pulse the button (don't hold it down), and immediately let go. After five or six times, you will have great coarse pepper for this dish, the lazy way.

spelt spaghetti with lemony parsnips and olives

Fine sea salt

8 ounces whole wheat
or other whole grain spaghetti
(gluten-free if desired)

3 small parsnips (about
12 ounces)

1 lemon, preferably organic

1 tablespoon extra-virgin
olive oil

1 tablespoon anchovy oil,
from the jar or can, or olive oil

2 large shallots, thinly sliced
crosswise (about 1 cup)

¼ teaspoon fine sea salt

2 teaspoons chopped oil-
packed anchovies (about 3)

½ cup mixed good-quality
olives, pitted (about 20)

2 teaspoons minced fresh
thyme, or ¾ teaspoon dried

¼ teaspoon freshly ground
black pepper

⅔ cup dry white wine such as
Pinot Grigio or vegetable broth

1 ounce (about ½ cup)
finely grated Parmesan,
plus more for serving

3 tablespoons chopped fresh
flat-leaf parsley, for garnish

SERVES 4

This unusual pairing of ingredients was born in the blizzard of 2013. We were stranded in California for days on end while the East Coast and my hometown of Boston were snowed in. When we finally made it home, I found nothing in the fridge but a few parsnip roots, lemons, and olives that I had covered with olive oil before our departure to preserve them. After the steaming pasta dish was heaped onto our plates, all conversation stopped—this is when I knew I was onto something . . .

If roasting is your first choice for coaxing flavor out of earthy parsnips, I invite you to try them crisp-sautéed. They will fill your fork with fragrant hints of pear and apple. Don't be surprised by the small amount of pasta—this is an unintended low-carb meal from a high-carb fan. Any leftover pasta is delicious fried in a little olive oil until nicely browned and topped with an egg, sunny-side up, or with a slice of grilled salmon. ⁓ gluten-free option

Bring a large pot of water to a rolling boil. Add salt as you see fit, then the pasta, stirring a few times. Return to a boil with the lid on, uncover, and cook at a gentle boil until the pasta is 1 minute short of al dente, according to the package directions.

Scrub the parsnips well under cold running water and trim on both ends. Cut each root in half lengthwise, then cut the thick top half again lengthwise to get equal-size pieces. Add the parsnips to the feed tube of a food processor fitted with the shredding blade. Process until shredded and use 3½ cups. Finely grate the zest of the lemon until you have 1½ teaspoons, then squeeze the lemon. Set the zest and the juice aside.

While the pasta is cooking, heat both oils in a 12-inch skillet over medium heat until shimmering. Add the shallots and salt and cook, stirring frequently, until the shallots just start to caramelize, 2 to 3 minutes. Move the shallots to the sides and add the anchovies to the center of the skillet. Cook, pressing on the fillets with a wooden spoon and stirring, until they disintegrate, about 30 seconds.

Add the parsnips, olives, thyme, and pepper and cook, stirring, for 1 minute. Add the wine (it will sizzle!), cover, and decrease the temperature to maintain a lively simmer. Cook until the parsnips are tender, retaining just a slight crunch, and the wine has almost evaporated, about 5 minutes. Stir in the lemon zest and 1½ tablespoons lemon juice. Remove from the heat and season to taste with salt, pepper, and a bit more lemon juice if you like. Cover and set aside if the pasta is not ready.

continued >

To finish, dip a heatproof measuring cup into the pasta pot to reserve ¾ cup cooking liquid and drain the pasta. Return the skillet to medium-low heat. Add half of the cooking liquid to the parsnip mixture, sprinkle with the Parmesan, and add the pasta. Toss to combine for about 1 minute, adding a tad more cooking liquid to loosen the pasta if needed. Garnish with the parsley and serve right away, grinding on more black pepper and passing the Parmesan around.

fine points

Anchovies add deep umami flavor without tasting fishy—so please don't omit them.

No need to remove the core of parsnips because the vegetable is shredded (of course, you may, if you wish).

VEGETARIAN Add 1 tablespoon low-sodium soy sauce (instead of the anchovies) to the pan and allow the liquid to cook off, 30 seconds.

my mac and cheese with greek yogurt and leeks

Introducing a new mac and cheese—with natural creaminess from Greek yogurt, less cheese than many recipes, and a surprise ingredient: naturally sweet leeks, infused and softened in a brief simmer with white wine, orange, and thyme, thus highlighting one of my favorite winter vegetables and lightening this comfort dish at the same time.

My cheese mix is comprised of mild Gouda, with Parmesan tossed in for umami, and chunks of fresh mozzarella for creaminess. For a more pronounced aroma, use aged Cheddar instead of the Gouda. Pasta shells are my first choice here because their exposed edges crisp up beautifully on top, and they turn into succulent bonbons in the creamy sauce. gluten-free option

Place a rack in the center of the oven and preheat to 400°F. Lightly oil a broiler-safe 9 by 13 by 2-inch porcelain or ceramic casserole dish (do not use glass, as it can shatter under the broiler).

To prepare the pasta, bring a large heavy pot of water to a rolling boil. Add salt as you see fit, then the pasta, stirring a few times. Return to a boil with the lid on, uncover, and cook at a gentle boil, until the pasta is 2 minutes shy of al dente, according to the package directions. Dip in a heatproof measuring cup and remove 1 cup cooking liquid, then drain the pasta and transfer it to a large bowl. If using cooked leftover pasta (you will need about 6 cups), loosen it with your hands.

Meanwhile, add the leeks, wine, thyme, zest, sage, and ¼ teaspoon of the salt to a large skillet and bring to a boil. Decrease the heat to maintain a simmer, cover, and cook until the leeks are soft, 5 to 7 minutes. Remove the thyme, zest, and sage and season with ¼ teaspoon of the pepper. Drain (I always drink the aromatic cooking liquid!) and set aside.

Add the half-and-half to the now empty pasta saucepan and bring to a simmer over medium heat. Toss the Gouda with the flour and whisk into the sauce until melted. Add half of the Parmesan and continue whisking vigorously until the mixture returns to a simmer. Keep whisking until all of the cheese is melted and the sauce is creamy and smooth, about 1 minute. Whisk in the nutmeg, the remaining ¼ teaspoon salt, and ¼ teaspoon pepper.

Stir a scant ½ cup of the reserved cooking liquid into the bowl with the pasta, followed by the leeks and the yogurt. Stir in the sauce as well, adding a few more tablespoons of cooking liquid to loosen if needed—you want the mixture to be

Fine sea salt

8 ounces whole grain pasta shells (chicciole) or penne (gluten-free if desired)

2 leeks, well rinsed, cut in half lengthwise, then crosswise into ¾-inch slices (about 4 cups)

½ cup dry white wine or vegetable broth

2 or 3 sprigs fresh thyme, or 1 teaspoon dried

1 (2-inch) piece of orange zest, white pith removed (optional)

2 fresh sage leaves, or ¼ teaspoon dried (optional)

½ teaspoon fine sea salt

½ teaspoon freshly ground black pepper

2 cups half-and-half or whole milk

5 ounces (about 2 cups) coarsely grated Gouda

2 tablespoons white or regular whole wheat flour (use gluten-free if desired)

4 ounces (about 2 cups) finely grated Parmesan

1 teaspoon freshly ground nutmeg

1 cup whole milk or 2% Greek yogurt

5 ounces (about 1 cup) fresh mozzarella, torn into ½-inch chunks (optional)

¼ cup whole wheat panko bread crumbs

1½ teaspoons fresh thyme leaves

SERVES 4 TO 6 AS A MAIN, OR 8 AS A SIDE

continued >

slightly soupy. Transfer to the prepared pan. Sprinkle with the mozzarella and the remaining Parmesan.

Bake until the mac and cheese is heated through and bubbles gently, 15 to 20 minutes. Remove the pan and turn on the broiler with a rack 4 inches below the heat. Combine the bread crumbs and the thyme in a small bowl. Sprinkle the mixture evenly across the top and place under the broiler. Cook, watching closely, just until the crumbs start to brown, 1 to 2 minutes. Allow to sit for a few minutes before serving.

fine points

Cook the pasta while you prep your ingredients to speed up dinner.

Whole milk (instead of half-and-half) works but will not be as richly rewarding—I'd rather eat a little less.

I have provided weight measures for the cheese for the best outcome, as different grating methods can lead to fairly sizable differences. You can use the shredding disc in your food processor to grate the Gouda and half of the Parmesan. For sprinkling on top, I prefer a fine grind for better distribution.

MAKE AHEAD The pasta and leeks can be made up to 2 days ahead. Chill, covered, in separate containers. Reserve the pasta liquid separately, or use water. You can make the whole dish ahead and transfer to the pan, but don't sprinkle with cheeses. Chill, covered. Remove from the fridge while preheating the oven. Add the mozzarella and continue from there.

simply mains
for busy nights and slow weekends

more than one good wheat

Have you ever seen a reddish round spelt berry? A slender bronze-colored Kamut kernel? A birch-colored einkorn, the smallest of wheats and one of the oldest? No, never even heard of Kamut or einkorn? You are not alone. And I can't blame you. Because these grains are part of a group of ancient types of wheat that have largely disappeared from our plates. And, in fact, almost vanished from the face of the earth.

To me, these ancient wheats are a delicacy. I have long been smitten by their subtle, splendid flavors and sublime textures. Compared to chewy modern wheat, these kernels from the days of yore are in a class of their own: they look different, they taste different, and they offer a new culinary revelation in each meal. I find them mesmerizing all around.

Yet, they are also part of the large wheat family. And wheat has become a cause of concern for many. Since the early 1960s, increasing numbers of people have been diagnosed with the autoimmune disorder celiac disease. In addition, there are countless people who suffer from gluten intolerance or wheat allergies. These sensitivities too seem to have risen starkly during the same time frame, according to Peter Green, a gastroenterologist at Columbia University. It thus comes as no surprise that many people—already struggling with a multitude of diet, weight, and health concerns—have stopped eating any products with gluten-containing wheat—from bread to pasta, cookies, and cake.

Throughout the history of modern humans, locally grown grains—from wheat and barley, to corn and rice—have played a significant role in traditional diets. And from what we can extrapolate today, the gluten-containing grains—wheat, barley, and rye—seem to have been tolerated "with relative ease," as the journalist Todd Oppenheimer put it so well in his article "Our Daily Bread."

So what has happened? Why is gluten suddenly making us sick? And is all gluten the same? Or, for that matter, are all wheats the same? The science on this topic is fast evolving, and as I'm writing this, researchers around the globe are working feverishly to understand the reasons for the explosion of gluten-related health issues. One thing is certain: celiac disease and gluten sensitivities have increased globally. More important, it has risen in parallel to a change in the way we grow and process wheat.

In the early 1960s, a new type of wheat was introduced that benefited from heavy application of fertilizers. Since then, high-yield wheat varieties have spread around the globe. These uniform modern wheats have been dwarfed to be easy to harvest. And their protein structure (aka gluten structure) has been altered so they can be used in huge dough mixers in industrial settings—to create the fluffy processed breads we often crave.

Heirloom and ancient wheat varieties have since largely fallen by the wayside because they are more labor-intensive to grow and harder to harvest and hull (removing the outer, inedible husk). These include the smallest ancient wheat, einkorn, and also emmer (better known as farro), Kamut, and spelt. These ancient wheats derive from grasses and haven't changed much through history. They are much taller than modern wheat and have a significantly larger root system, which enables them to take in more nutrients from the soil. This explains why ancient wheats are higher in protein and also in vitamins, minerals, and antioxidants, yet also have less gluten.

More important, they might be easier to digest for people who experience gluten sensitivities such as discomfort or mild digestive issues. Peter Green of Columbia suggests there is good evidence that ancient grains "didn't have anything like the toxicity that current wheat does." Stay tuned, as the research is quickly evolving. Of course, if you have serious health concerns or allergies, consult with your doctor. And if you've been diagnosed with celiac disease, please do not try any of the wheat varieties I rave about. Nor should you eat barley or rye, two other grains with gluten. But you will still be able to enjoy most of my recipes, as I have provided countless alternatives, keeping the needs of gluten-free readers in mind.

Needless to say, I'm thrilled that many of these older wheat varieties are experiencing a comeback, spurred on by farmers, chefs, and homemakers alike. Just like me, they are intrigued by their enthralling textures and alluring flavors as much as by their health benefits. There is more to look forward to. The ways we are growing, processing, and baking wheat into bread are also changing. Thanks to artisan bakers across the country, grains are again freshly grown and locally milled into good flour, containing all their natural parts (see "The Revival of Heirloom Wheat and Grains," page 15).

Traditional slow fermentation and baking techniques are also being revived and reinvented. Chad Robertson of Tartine Bakery fame is at the forefront of this revolution. Working with naturally fermented sourdough, he and others achieve lighter textures even in 100% whole grain breads. And sourdough might even offer hope to gluten-affected guts. According to one peer-reviewed study, in thoroughly fermented wheat bread the amount of gluten fell from roughly 75,000 parts per million to 12, a level that is considered gluten-free.

In this spirit, I invite you to explore as many different types of ancient wheat as you can (see "Ancient Grains A to Z," page 8). I hope they all find their way back to our tables, to satisfy our cravings for good bread, cakes, pancakes, and pasta. In this chapter, be sure to try my favorite einkorn recipe, which is also a most simple creation, Just Tomatoes and Farro Piccolo (page 207). Or cook the Roasted Eggplant Fan with Tomatoes, Spelt, and Mozzarella (page 202). Other recipes using these ancient wheats are used throughout the book, in salads and sides (chapter 3) and also in baked goods, for example, the Farro Scones with Almonds, Apples, and Thyme (page 57).

Each time I spill some of these original kernels onto my kitchen counter, I take a close look and marvel at their shapes, their cinnamon and milk-coffee hues. I remember how far back they have nourished us. I ponder their significance in the diet of our ancestors, as they provided sustenance through harsh winters when fresh food was hard to come by. And I think of the many farmers who are working hard to return these ancient wheats to our tables today. It is then that I stop in my tracks and pause. And I look forward to dinner.

new england cider mussels with fresh cranberries and bulgur

This speedy dinner is my love song to New England, my adopted home. It combines two types of cranberries with fresh mussels, local hard cider, and my favorite quick-cooking grain, bulgur. It makes for a dazzling visual feast—with the spectacular red berries appearing between the dark glistening mussels and, again, in the grain.

Adding fresh cranberries to mussels was inspired by my friend JJ Gonson, a Boston-area caterer and the most dedicated locavore I know. She once mentioned that she uses local cranberries during the winter months as a replacement for lemons. Suddenly, I saw fresh cranberries anew and they became a serious cooking ingredient rather than an obligatory part of my Thanksgiving repertoire. Soon enough, I found myself tossing a handful into a pot of mussels. For someone not raised in the Northeast, where mussels and cranberries are celebrated, combining them was a revelation—it has become one of our favorite last-minute meals. ⟫⟫ gluten-free option

To prepare the bulgur, add the water to a small heavy saucepan and bring to a boil. Stir in the bulgur, dried cranberries, olive oil, and salt and return to a boil. Decrease the heat to maintain a simmer, cover, and cook until the water is absorbed, 11 to 15 minutes. Remove from the heat, cover, and set aside to steam for 5 minutes. Taste and adjust for salt (keep in mind that the juices of mussels can be salty).

Meanwhile, heat a large Dutch oven or heavy saucepan over medium heat. Swirl in 2 tablespoons of the oil and wait until it shimmers. Add the shallots, celery, and salt. Cook, stirring frequently, until the shallots start to brown at the edges, 2 to 3 minutes. Increase the heat to medium-high. Add the chile and stir for 15 seconds or so to unleash its flavorful heat (but don't burn the spice!). Add the cider, mussels, and fresh cranberries and bring to a boil. Cover and cook until the mussels open, 4 to 8 minutes, shaking the pan a few times in between.

To finish, remove the pan from the heat and discard any unopened mussels. Grind a good dose of pepper on top, garnish with the celery leaves, and drizzle with the remaining 1 tablespoon olive oil.

Divide the bulgur between shallow rimmed bowls and top with some of the mussels and their juices. Serve at once, passing the lemon wedges around for a bit more tang.

BULGUR

1¾ cups water

1 cup medium-coarse bulgur (use quinoa for gluten-free)

⅓ cup dried cranberries

1 tablespoon extra-virgin olive oil

½ teaspoon fine sea salt

MUSSELS

3 tablespoons extra-virgin olive oil

⅓ cup thinly sliced shallots, cut crosswise (about 1 large)

½ cup chopped celery (1 to 2 stalks), plus ¼ cup chopped leaves, for garnish

¼ teaspoon fine sea salt

¼ teaspoon dried chile flakes (optional)

1 cup good-quality hard cider

2 pounds mussels, cleaned (see sidebar, page 81)

¾ cup fresh or frozen cranberries (do not thaw)

Freshly ground black pepper

1 lemon, cut into 6 wedges, for serving

SERVES 4 AS A STARTER, OR 2 AS A MAIN

fine points

To speed up dinner, clean the mussels while you simmer the bulgur.

Smaller, wild-caught, and very fresh mussels cook faster, 2 to 3 minutes.

roasted portobello mushrooms with hazelnut buckwheat stuffing

4 large portobello mushrooms with 5-inch-diameter caps, wiped clean (about 1 pound)

3 tablespoons extra-virgin olive oil

¾ cup kasha (whole toasted buckwheat, not raw groats)

⅓ cup, heaped, coarsely chopped hazelnuts

2 cloves garlic, pressed or minced

1 tablespoon fresh thyme leaves, or 1 teaspoon dried, plus 4 small twigs for garnish

½ teaspoon Aleppo pepper, or ¼ teaspoon dried chile flakes (optional)

¼ teaspoon fine sea salt

1 ounce (about ½ cup) finely grated Parmesan

TO FINISH
4 thin slices (about 2 ounces) prosciutto

Balsamic vinegar, for drizzling

Freshly ground black pepper

SERVES 4 AS A LIGHT MEAL

fine points

Large portobello mushrooms are key here so you have enough room for the filling.

VEGETARIAN Omit the prosciutto and double the amount of Parmesan.

During the week, I often step into my kitchen after an exhausting day at the computer, hungry and impatient all at once. This mouthwatering dinner is the result of one such night. The stuffing of earthy kasha and aromatic hazelnuts crisps up beautifully under the broiler and is the perfect foil for meaty portobello mushrooms. Plus, it has deep richness from the combination of mushrooms, Parmesan, and prosciutto. All told, it has enough star power even when surprise dinner guests show up at the door. ➽ gluten-free

Place a rack about 6 inches away from the heat and preheat the broiler on high for about 5 minutes. Grease a large rimmed baking sheet with olive oil or cooking spray. Remove the stems of the mushrooms, slicing close to the base (reserve for another use such as in a broth or vegetable stir-fry). Rub the mushrooms, inside and out, with 2 tablespoons of the olive oil. Season generously with salt and pepper.

Place the mushrooms, gill side up, on the baking sheet and broil for 5 minutes (7 minutes for thick mushrooms).

Meanwhile, add the kasha, hazelnuts, garlic, thyme, Aleppo pepper, and salt to a medium bowl. Drizzle with the remaining 1 tablespoon olive oil and stir with a fork to combine well. Season the stuffing with salt to taste.

Remove the baking sheet with the mushrooms and carefully heap about ¼ cup of the buckwheat filling into the center of each mushroom. Spread the filling with the back of a spoon, gently pressing it down. Sprinkle the Parmesan across the top.

Rotate the baking sheet and return it to the oven. Continue broiling until the mushrooms are tender and the cheese becomes crisp and starts to brown, 3 to 5 minutes more, watching closely so as not to burn the Parmesan (this can happen within 30 seconds—I've been there!).

To finish, remove the baking sheet. Loosely fold a slice of prosciutto and immediately place it into the center of a stuffed mushroom so the residual heat can soften it. Repeat with the remaining prosciutto. Garnish each mushroom with a twig of thyme, drizzle with balsamic vinegar, and grind a bit of black pepper on top. Serve right away.

spicy honey and habanero shrimp with cherry couscous

This is the dinner I make on a Friday night when I want the week to end on a sparkling note without all of the trouble. It brings you a fast, succulent meal with loads of flavor—a nice kick of heat from habanero chile, a kiss of honey in pan-seared shrimp, all served over lemony couscous with bits of mild goat cheese melting in. Sauté some fresh chard or spinach in a little olive oil, as a simple side dish, and you will be *fine dining* at home. Vegetarians can replace the shrimp with cooked chickpeas and heap on the goat cheese.

gluten-free option

To make the couscous, add the broth, the 2 teaspoons olive oil, and the 2 teaspoons honey to a heavy 2-quart saucepan over medium-high heat and bring to a boil. Remove from the heat, stir in the couscous, cherries, and ½ teaspoon of the salt. Cover and let sit until the liquid is absorbed, about 10 minutes.

Meanwhile, finely grate the lemon until you have 1 teaspoon zest. Squeeze the lemon and set aside the juice. Season the shrimp with the remaining ½ teaspoon salt and the chile flakes.

Turn on the exhaust fan. Heat the 1 tablespoon olive oil in a 12-inch skillet over high heat until it shimmers. Add the shrimp in one layer and cook, undisturbed, until they turn golden, about 2 minutes. Flip them with tongs or a metal spatula, stir in the habanero, and cook until the shrimp are just opaque, about 1 minute more. Decrease the heat to medium and carefully (!) add the wine. Cook until only a thin layer of liquid remains, about 2 minutes. Move the shrimp to the sides, reduce the heat to medium-low, and stir or whisk the butter pieces into the center, one at a time, until smooth. Stir in the 1 tablespoon honey. Remove the pan from the heat and discard the habanero.

To finish, stir the lemon zest and 1 tablespoon of the lemon juice into the couscous. Season with salt to taste. Fluff with two forks and transfer to a large serving platter. Top with the shrimp and drizzle on the pan sauce. Sprinkle with the goat cheese and garnish with the pine nuts and basil. Serve at once, passing lemon juice around.

COUSCOUS AND SHRIMP

1¼ cups low-sodium vegetable broth

1 tablespoon plus 2 teaspoons extra-virgin olive oil

1 tablespoon plus 2 teaspoons honey

1 cup whole wheat couscous

⅓ cup tart dried cherries

1 teaspoon fine sea salt

1 lemon

12 ounces extra-jumbo shell-on shrimp (see page 248) deveined and patted dry

¼ to ½ teaspoon dried red chile flakes

1 small fresh habanero chile, seeds removed and thinly sliced crosswise into rings (optional; wear gloves)

½ cup dry white wine

2 tablespoons chilled unsalted butter, cut into 3 pieces

TO FINISH

½ cup (2 ounces) mild crumbled goat cheese

2 to 3 tablespoons lightly toasted pine nuts

3 tablespoons torn fresh basil leaves

SERVES 4

fine points

GLUTEN-FREE Cook 1 cup quinoa instead of couscous (see page 22).

bulgur with chard and saffron-infused yogurt

Scant ¼ teaspoon loosely packed saffron threads

1 tablespoon hot water

1 bunch chard, preferably Swiss rainbow

1 tablespoon extra-virgin olive oil

¾ cup chopped green onions, white and dark green parts (about 3)

½ teaspoon fine sea salt

1 cup medium-coarse bulgur (use quinoa for gluten-free)

1¾ cups low-sodium vegetable or chicken broth

¼ teaspoon freshly ground black pepper

2 cloves garlic, peeled and pressed

½ teaspoon Aleppo pepper, or ⅛ teaspoon dried red chile flakes, or more as needed (optional)

1 cup whole milk yogurt or low-fat yogurt

¼ cup toasted sliced almonds

SERVES 4

fine points

For best flavor, make the saffron yogurt ahead, a few hours or up to 1 day.

VARIATION Young tender kale can be substituted for the chard.

When I entertain, I always want to get away with a stunning yet stupendously easy main course. This is one of them. If you've tried bulgur only in tabbouleh, this one-pot meal is just as enjoyable. Pouring the deep orange saffron-infused yogurt on top of the bulgur, flecked with colorful rainbow chard, always makes me pause in my tracks. Don't hesitate to use freshly pressed garlic—any harshness is mellowed by the yogurt, bringing all the flavors together.

This is a versatile dish. Enjoy it as a terrific light vegetarian meal or serve it next to roast chicken, grilled lamb chops, salmon, or trout. It also makes a lovely side for a potluck or picnic (keep the yogurt and almonds separate until ready to serve). And it doubles beautifully. 〰 gluten-free option

Add the saffron to a small bowl and cover with the hot water. Set aside for about 15 minutes.

Meanwhile, trim the chard stems and chop them into ¼-inch pieces; roll the leaves into a tight bundle and cut into ½-inch ribbons; if the leaves are large, cut the ribbons crosswise a few times as well.

Heat a large heavy saucepan over medium heat. Swirl in the oil and wait until it's shimmering. Add the green onions, the chard stems, and ¼ teaspoon of the salt and cook, stirring frequently, until the onions wilt and the stems soften, about 2 minutes. Stir in the bulgur until all grains are coated, and cook, stirring often and watching closely until the grains smell toasty and the bottom of the pot turns dry, 2 to 3 minutes. Add the broth (it will splatter!), the remaining ¼ teaspoon salt, and the black pepper and bring to a boil. Reduce the heat to maintain a simmer, cover, and cook until the water is absorbed and the bulgur is tender with a bit of a chew, 10 to 12 minutes. Stir in the chard leaves and remove the pot from the heat. Set aside for 3 to 5 minutes for the leaves to wilt.

Stir in the garlic and Aleppo pepper. Season to taste with Aleppo pepper, salt, and pepper.

To finish, add the yogurt to a small bowl. Stir the saffron-infused water into the yogurt and beat well to create a smooth, golden cream. When ready to serve, spoon the bulgur mixture onto a large rimmed serving plate and pour the saffron yogurt on top. Sprinkle with the almonds and serve at once.

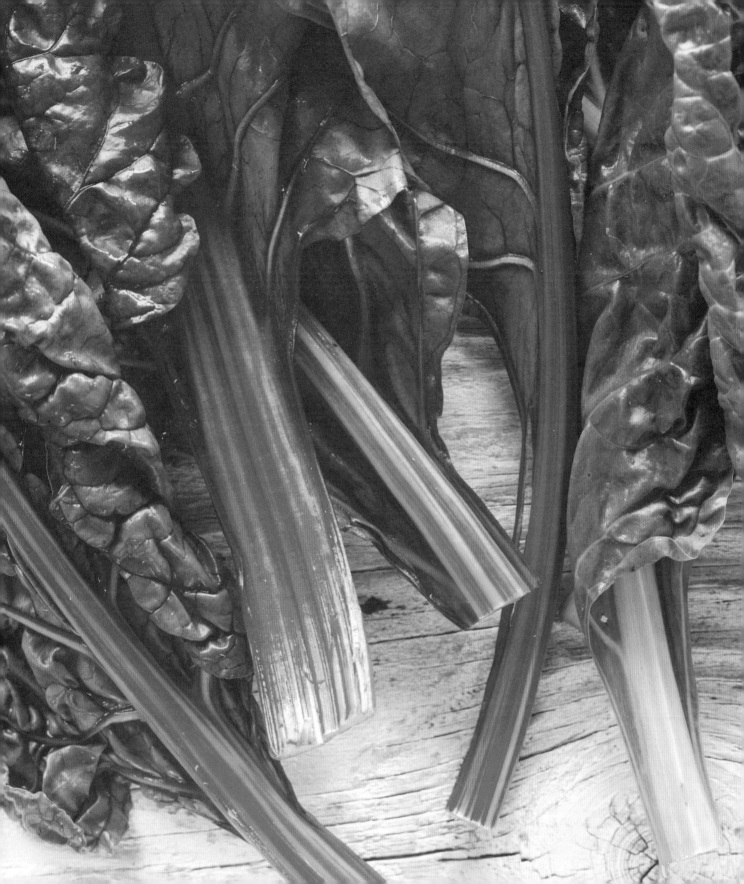

prosciutto-wrapped roasted bass with teff polenta

TEFF POLENTA

1½ cups low-sodium chicken or vegetable broth

1½ cups water, a bit more if needed

1 cup teff grains

BASS

4 small striped bass fillets, about 1½ inches thick, preferably skin-on (about 1¼ pounds total)

2 teaspoons extra-virgin olive oil

2 teaspoons Dijon mustard

½ teaspoon freshly ground black pepper

¼ teaspoon dried red chile flakes (optional)

5 teaspoons fresh thyme leaves

4 or 8 slices prosciutto (2 to 4 ounces)

1 to 2 tablespoons unsalted butter

1 tablespoon low-sodium soy sauce, or more as needed

Fine sea salt

SERVES 4

It is my secret dream to turn the minuscule nutty-sweet seeds of teff into the next hip grain on our tables. For me, this creation was a turning point. It is as easy as it is refined. While the teff simmers, you broil the fish, and soon you will marvel at the feast on your plate: a sizzling fork-tender fillet, enveloped in crisp umami-rich prosciutto—gorgeously nestled on a bed of soft coffee-colored teff.

I've become a huge fan of bluefish—its gorgeous dark meat is superb with the grain. I like to pair this entrée with My Go-To Greens (page 96), but any simple sautéed spinach or chard that you perk up with a good drizzle of red wine or sherry vinegar will work. ⁕ gluten-free

To make the teff polenta, add the broth, water, and teff to a large heavy saucepan and bring to a boil. Decrease the heat to maintain a simmer, cover, and cook for 10 minutes. Stir well with a wooden spoon, breaking up any lumps and scraping the bottom and sides of the pan to loosen any stuck grains. Cover and simmer until the teff has the creamy consistency of polenta, 8 to 10 minutes more, stirring vigorously once or twice. The grains have a tendency to stick to the bottom—that's normal. If your pan bottom runs dry, just add a few tablespoons of water.

Meanwhile, prepare the bass. Place the fillets on a large cutting board, check for bones, and remove any with tweezers. Add the olive oil, mustard, ¼ teaspoon of the pepper, and chile flakes to a small bowl and beat with a fork until emulsified. Stir in 4 teaspoons of the thyme. Gently rub the mixture all over the fillets and set aside.

Generously brush a 12-inch cast-iron skillet or a large rimmed baking sheet with olive oil (don't be stingy here—this will make your fish packages sizzle!). Place an oven rack about 6 inches from the heat and set the skillet on it while you preheat the broiler on high for 5 minutes.

Once the broiler is preheated, wrap one slice of prosciutto lengthwise around each fillet (two for a more luxurious "fish in a blanket"). Wearing thick oven mitts, carefully remove the skillet. Using a spatula, place the fillets into the hot skillet (it will sizzle!).

Broil until the prosciutto starts to crisp at the edges and a paring knife, inserted into the thickest part of a fillet for 3 seconds, is warm when held against your lip, about 8 minutes, depending on the thickness.

To finish, carefully remove the hot skillet from the oven. Stir the butter, soy sauce, and the remaining ¼ teaspoon pepper into the teff. Naturally, 2 tablespoons butter taste better than 1. Season with a bit more soy sauce or salt and pepper to taste. Spoon some teff onto each plate and, using a spatula, place a fish fillet on top. Garnish each serving with a sprinkle of the remaining 1 teaspoon thyme. Serve at once.

fine points

Mackerel is a good replacement, as are cod and haddock. Of course, salmon works as well.

I really enjoy crisp fish skin, so I leave it on, but do as you like.

greek-inspired fresh artichokes with barley and tomatoes

If you are comfortable cleaning artichokes, this one-pot meal comes together with ease. If you are not, try it once and you might want to clean artichokes every day (see sidebar, page 186). I like this dish best in spring when fresh heavy globe artichokes show up in stores. But if you need to make it in the dead of winter, I see nothing wrong with using frozen or canned artichokes until then.

I have paired the artichokes with chewy whole grain barley because this ancient grain has been traditionally used around the Mediterranean since antiquity. Make this ahead to impress guests for dinner—this allows the flavors to deepen as well. Or make it on a Sunday to enjoy later in the week. My husband and I often have it as a light meal one day and use leftovers as a side next to grilled chicken or steak. One is as good as the other.

🍃 gluten-free option

To prepare the barley, bring the water, barley, bay leaf, and salt to a boil in a small heavy saucepan. Decrease the heat to maintain a simmer, cover, and cook until the grain is tender but still slightly chewy, 50 to 60 minutes. If you have time, remove from the heat and let sit, covered, for 5 to 10 minutes. Drain, if needed.

Meanwhile, to make the stew, heat a large Dutch oven or heavy saucepan over medium heat. Swirl in 2 tablespoons of the olive oil and wait until it shimmers. Add the onion, garlic, bay leaves, chile, and salt and cook, stirring occasionally, until the onions soften but do not brown, 3 to 5 minutes. Add the soy sauce and cook, stirring, until it evaporates, about 30 seconds. Add the wine and cook, uncovered, until the liquid is syrupy and almost evaporated, about 5 minutes. Add the broth. Nestle the artichokes into the liquid, cut side down, and return to a boil. Decrease the heat to maintain a simmer, cover, and cook until the stems and the hearts of the artichokes are soft when pierced with a paring knife, 12 to 15 minutes.

Using tongs, remove the artichoke pieces to a plate, holding them at their firmer centers (you don't want the stem to break!). Stir the barley and the tomatoes with their juices into the pot. Stir in the pepper and return the artichokes to the pot, nestling them in as you see fit. Add a little more broth or water if needed for a slightly soupy consistency.

Return to a simmer, cover, and cook for at least 5 and up to 15 minutes more for the flavors to meld. Remove the bay leaves and the chile if you like. Drizzle with the

continued >

BARLEY
1¾ cup water

½ cup hulled whole grain barley, soaked overnight and drained, or 1½ to 2 cups cooked (see page 23)

½ bay leaf

Pinch of fine sea salt

ARTICHOKES
3 tablespoons extra-virgin olive oil

2 cups chopped yellow onion (about 2 small)

2 cloves garlic, peeled and slightly crushed

2 bay leaves

1 whole dried chile

¼ teaspoon fine sea salt

2 tablespoons low-sodium soy sauce

½ cup dry white wine

1½ cups low-sodium vegetable or chicken broth, or more as needed

3 globe artichokes, cleaned and quartered

1 (14-ounce) can whole tomatoes, crushed, with juices

¼ teaspoon freshly ground black pepper

1 tablespoon freshly squeezed lemon juice, or more as needed

1 cup (4 ounces) coarsely crumbled Greek feta, preferably sheep's milk

¼ cup chopped fresh flat-leaf parsley

SERVES 4 AS A LIGHT MAIN, OR 6 AS A SIDE

fine points

Globe artichokes are my first choice because they have soft, large tender hearts, but other types of artichokes can be used.

I add the tomatoes later on, as their acidity can slow down cooking.

GLUTEN-FREE Black quinoa looks spectacular. I enjoy the crunch it adds to this soupy dish, but any quinoa works. Millet and brown rice are fine replacements; so is chewy sorghum. You will need 1½ to 2 cups cooked grain.

MAKE AHEAD The whole meal, up to the finishing step, can be made ahead. Gently rewarm over medium heat until it simmers, adding a bit more water if needed, then finish as indicated.

VARIATIONS Pearl barley, soft wheat berries, or farro are delicious as well.

You can use one 12-ounce package frozen quartered artichokes, or about 1½ cans or jars (12 to 14 ounces each) artichoke hearts, in water or in a simple marinade. Add only about 1 cup of broth together with the artichokes, omit the simmering step, stir in the grains and tomatoes, and continue as described, simmering for 10 minutes, adding more broth as needed.

lemon juice. Season to taste with a bit more lemon juice, salt, and pepper (keeping in mind that feta can be salty).

To finish, remove the pot from the heat, sprinkle with the feta, and cover for 2 minutes to allow the cheese to soften. Sprinkle with the parsley. Spoon into shallow rimmed plates, drizzling with the remaining 1 tablespoon olive oil and grinding some black pepper on top.

HOW TO CLEAN ARTICHOKES

I admit coming late to cooking fresh artichokes at home. Not because I didn't like them but because of what I perceived was a hassle cleaning them. Marinated or frozen artichokes were good enough until—well, until I did it once! It tasted so good that I asked myself, what took you so long? Of course, it takes a bit of time so try this for the first time on a weekend. Once you figure out which tools in your kitchen are best for the job, you will find it much less tedious. You might actually enjoy the cleaning as a little ritual given the pleasures that await.

Use a sharp serrated knife and cut about one-third off the top of each globe artichoke. Tear off the outer leaves until you reach a bright, fresh-looking layer. Trim the stem at the bottom. Use a paring knife or a vegetable peeler to remove first the tough outer layer of the stem, then the hard leaf stubs all around the base (a bit tedious but worth it). Last but not least, cut each artichoke in half with the serrated knife and remove the choke, the fuzzy inner core and small spiky leaves, using a spoon, a melon baller, or a grapefruit spoon. I found a little pointed cheese knife in a drawer, which works beautifully. Try what works best for you. Cut each cleaned half again into quarters. I streamline the task by doing each step for all artichokes at the same time instead of preparing one artichoke after the other. But that's up to you.

Many recipes call for adding the cut artichokes to a bowl of acidulated water (adding the juice of 1 lemon to a large bowl of cold water) until you cook them to prevent browning. I find this step unnecessary in a meal where the grains and the tomato sauce cover the vegetables anyway.

roasted one-pan chicken with leeks and barley

This is a scrumptious one-skillet meal, easy to put together yet with enough panache to make dinner guests happy too. Tender leeks first roast in the aromatic juices of your chicken. While the chicken rests, you add some barley and allow the sweet leeks with their burnished edges to melt into the chewy grains. There are a few simple steps, but I have streamlined them for you to make it easy. ⁓ gluten-free option

To prepare the citrus rub, finely grate the zest of the lemon and the orange. Reserve the orange for another use. Cut the lemon in half crosswise, and cut one half into 2 pieces (reserve the other half for another use); set aside. Add both types of zest, the fennel, thyme, pepper, and salt to a small bowl and combine well with a fork.

To prepare the chicken, pat it dry and trim any excess fat. Spread some citrus rub all over the skin and sprinkle inside the cavity. Using your fingers, gently loosen the skin from the breast meat and both thighs to create pockets so you can spread some of the citrus rub there as well. Place the 2 lemon pieces and the garlic inside the cavity and close it with kitchen twine. Place the chicken on a plate in the fridge without touching anything. Chill, uncovered, for at least 4 hours and up to 24 hours.

About 2½ hours before you want to eat, remove the chicken from the fridge and allow it to come to room temperature. After half an hour, place a rack in the center of the oven and preheat to 475°F. Brush a 12-inch cast-iron skillet (or a similar-size roasting pan) with oil.

Once the oven is preheated, add the leeks to a large bowl. Sprinkle with the fennel seeds, ¼ teaspoon of the salt, and the pepper. Drizzle with 2 tablespoons of the olive oil and toss with your hands until the vegetables are well coated. Spread the leeks across the bottom of the skillet. Rub the remaining 1 to 2 tablespoons olive oil across the skin of the chicken, and sprinkle with the remaining ¼ teaspoon salt. Place the chicken, breast side up, on top of the leeks in the center of the skillet. Tie the legs together and tuck the wing tips under the body. If you have a meat thermometer with an attached rope, insert it now into the thickest part of the thigh.

Roast the chicken for 25 minutes. Reduce the oven temperature to 400°F and continue roasting until the thermometer registers 165°F, 35 to 40 minutes more, depending on size.

While the chicken is roasting, cook the barley: Add the water, barley, zest, and bay leaf to a 2-quart heavy saucepan and bring to a boil. Decrease the heat to maintain

CITRUS AND FENNEL SALT RUB

1 lemon

1 orange

1 teaspoon dried fennel seeds

1 teaspoon dried thyme

¼ teaspoon freshly ground black pepper

2 teaspoons fine sea salt

CHICKEN AND LEEKS

1 (4- to 4½-pound) chicken, preferably organic

1 to 2 cloves garlic, peeled

7 cups leeks, white and light green parts, cut crosswise into ¾-inch slices (3 to 4 stalks; see page 248)

1½ teaspoons whole fennel seeds

½ teaspoon fine sea salt

¼ teaspoon freshly ground black pepper

3 to 4 tablespoons extra-virgin olive oil

BARLEY

3 cups water

1 cup pearl barley, or about 3½ cups cooked (see page 23)

1 (3-inch) strip lemon zest (optional)

1 bay leaf (optional)

TO FINISH

1 teaspoon dried thyme

¼ to ½ cup dry white wine, or chicken broth

SERVES 4

continued >

a simmer, cover, and cook until the grains are tender with a bit of a chew, 30 to
40 minutes. Remove the zest and the bay leaf. Drain and set aside.

Wearing thick oven mitts, carefully remove the skillet from the oven and transfer
the chicken to a large cutting board, loosely tent with aluminum foil, and allow to
rest for at least 15 minutes; your meat will be so much juicier.

While the chicken rests, add the cooked grains to the leeks in the skillet and
sprinkle with the thyme. Pour in the wine—just enough to nicely moisten the grains
and vegetables—and stir well to combine. Return the pan to the oven for about
10 minutes, until the grains are heated through, then turn off the oven and keep the
door ajar until ready to serve.

To finish, carve the chicken. Remove the leek and barley mixture from the oven, stir
through once, and season to taste with salt and pepper. Serve each portion of leeks
and barley with a piece of the chicken.

fine points

I am a huge fan of flavoring roasted chicken with a salt rub at least 4 hours and up
to 24 hours ahead—it makes for superbly crisp skin and aromatic meat. If you don't
have the time to make the rub, pat the chicken dry, remove excess fat, and leave it to
sit in the fridge, uncovered and without touching anything, for 1 day—this helps dry
out the skin for more crispness. The next day, after you rub the chicken with oil,
sprinkle with 1½ teaspoons salt (instead of ¼ teaspoon) and with ¼ teaspoon pepper.
Continue as described.

GLUTEN-FREE Chewy sorghum is a beautiful replacement for the barley here (see
page 23).

VARIATION Feel free to use hulled (whole grain) barley or spelt or whole wheat
berries, soaked overnight, and cooked for 50 to 60 minutes.

mediterranean meat loaf with fresh herbs and tangy tomato glaze

BULGUR

½ cup medium-coarse bulgur

1 cup hot water

MEAT LOAF

1 pound ground beef, 85% to 90% lean, preferably grass-fed

1 large egg

½ cup grated yellow onion (about 1 small)

2 tablespoons tomato paste

2 cloves garlic, minced

1 cup loosely packed chopped flat-leaf parsley, plus a few whole leaves for garnish

2 tablespoons finely chopped fresh mint, or 1½ teaspoons dried mint

1 tablespoon finely chopped fresh oregano, or 1 teaspoon dried

1 tablespoon fresh thyme leaves, or 1 teaspoon dried

¾ teaspoon fine sea salt

½ teaspoon Aleppo pepper, or ⅛ teaspoon dried chile flakes

¼ teaspoon freshly ground black pepper

GLAZE, AND TO FINISH

1 (28-ounce) can diced tomatoes, with their juices

1½ tablespoons extra-virgin olive oil

2 tablespoons turbinado sugar

2 tablespoons cider vinegar

2 tablespoons tomato paste

½ to 1 teaspoon Sriracha sauce (optional)

Tender, moist, and profusely aromatic with fresh and dried herbs—this is the meat loaf you would be served if you visit my mom in Greece. Needless to say, this is the meat loaf I crave. I have made just a few tweaks to my mother's creation. I added bulgur, traditionally done to stretch your meat—today it allows me to buy fine grass-fed beef, which adds its own deep flavor. In this country, I've been introduced to the concept of a glazed meat loaf. So I added my own tangy one with just a touch of sweetness. My mom's best secret: she shapes the loaves ahead of time to allow the aromas to permeate the meat, and working ahead makes life easier too.

In the winter months, I pair this with sautéed leeks. In the summer, I slice fresh cucumbers into a simple salad with olives, feta, and a bright lemony olive oil dressing. 🌾 gluten-free option

At least 2 hours ahead: Place the bulgur in a small bowl and cover with the hot water. Let sit at room temperature until much of the water is absorbed and the kernels are tender with a bit of chew, 20 to 30 minutes. Grease a 9 by 13 by 2-inch ceramic or glass baking pan with olive oil or cooking spray. Place a rack in the center of the oven and preheat to 350°F.

Drain the bulgur in a fine-mesh sieve, pressing the grains with the back of a spoon to squeeze out as much water as you can. Add the bulgur and all of the meat loaf ingredients to a large bowl and combine well but gently—I start with a fork (it helps with the herbs!) before I switch to my hands so I can feel the mixture holding together. Divide in half and form into two evenly shaped elongated loaves, about 5½ inches long and 3½ inches wide. Place them, without touching, crosswise, into the pan. If you have time, cover with plastic wrap and chill.

To prepare the glaze: Drain the canned tomatoes (about 2½ cups), reserving the liquid (about 1¼ cups). If you don't have fresh tomatoes for garnish, put a few tablespoons of the diced tomatoes aside. Add the liquid to a small saucepan. Stir in the olive oil, sugar, vinegar, and tomato paste and bring to a boil over medium-high heat, stirring occasionally to dissolve the sugar. Decrease the heat to maintain a simmer and cook, uncovered, to thicken slightly, about 5 minutes. Stir in the Sriracha.

Spoon the diced tomatoes around the meat. Remove 2 tablespoons of the glaze to a small bowl and brush the loaves with it (discard any leftovers). Place 1 or 2 fresh tomato slices on top of each loaf (or the reserved diced tomatoes) and garnish with a few leaves of parsley.

Bake until the loaves are nicely browned and a thermometer inserted into the center reaches 160°F, 60 to 70 minutes. Remove and allow to sit for 5 minutes.

To finish, briefly reheat the remaining glaze over medium heat, stirring a few times. Slice the loaves with a large sharp knife. Serve the slices with a few tablespoons of tomatoes and a bit of glaze spooned on top.

fine points

If you have good-quality crumbled oregano and dried mint, preferably spearmint (see page 247), don't hesitate to use it here.

To save time, soak the bulgur while you prep your ingredients. And mince the onion, garlic, parsley, and fresh herbs in a mini food processor if you like.

GLUTEN-FREE You can use 1½ cups cooked millet instead of the bulgur (see page 22).

MAKE AHEAD You can shape the loaves a few hours and up to 1 day ahead. Remove from the fridge when you preheat the oven. The glaze can be made 1 day ahead as well. Chill, covered. Stir well before removing the 2 tablespoons for glazing the loaves.

A few slices fresh tomatoes, for garnish (optional)

MAKES 2 SMALL MEAT LOAVES, TO SERVE 8

oven-roasted chicken with minted summer squash and bulgur

8 chicken drumsticks and thighs (4 each), skin-on and bone-in (about 2 pounds)

¾ teaspoon fine sea salt

½ teaspoon freshly ground black pepper

2 tablespoons extra-virgin olive oil, or more as needed

3 cups chopped green onions, light and dark green parts (about 12)

3 cloves garlic, peeled and lightly crushed

4 cups (about 1¼ pound) yellow squash or zucchini, cut into 1-inch cubes

½ cup lightly packed and torn fresh mint leaves, plus 2 tablespoons finely chopped, for garnish

½ cup dry white wine

3 cups (about 1¼ pounds) coarsely chopped ripe tomatoes, measured with their juices, or 1 (14-ounce) can whole peeled tomatoes, crushed, with juices

1 cup medium-coarse bulgur

About 1 cup low-sodium chicken broth if using fresh tomatoes, or about 1½ cups if using canned tomatoes

1 to 2 tablespoons freshly squeezed lemon juice

1 lemon, cut into wedges, for serving

SERVES 6

I come to recipes one of two ways. I either mull over an idea for days, weeks, even months until inspiration strikes, often in the middle of the night. The second is the confluence of too few or too many ingredients in my kitchen. This recipe is the result of a late summer visit to the farmers' market that yielded an abundance of produce. All of it went into this meal for out-of-town guests. There was not a forkful left.

While this recipe takes a little time, it is a straightforward preparation. On a warm summer evening, serve it with a bit of minted whole milk yogurt drizzled on top. gluten-free option

---

Place a rack in the center of the oven and preheat to 350°F. Grease a 9 by 13 by 2-inch glass baking pan with olive oil or cooking spray.

Gently pat dry the chicken pieces and season with ½ teaspoon of the salt and ¼ teaspoon of the pepper. Heat a large Dutch oven or other heavy saucepan over medium-high heat. Swirl in 1½ tablespoons of the olive oil and wait until a wisp of smoke appears. Add half of the chicken pieces, skin side down and without touching, and cook them until they are nicely browned, turning them once with tongs—about 10 minutes total. Transfer the chicken to a clean plate. Add a bit more oil if your pan has become dry and repeat with the remaining chicken.

Reduce the heat to medium and add the green onions, garlic, and the remaining ¼ teaspoon salt. Cook, stirring and scraping the bottom, until the green onions wilt, 1 to 2 minutes—you don't want them to darken, as they become bitter. Stir in the squash and ¼ cup of the mint. Cook, stirring only every 2 minutes or so, to allow the squash to turn golden, 4 to 6 minutes.

Add the wine, scrape the bottom again, and cook at a lively simmer, uncovered, until the liquid is evaporated and the squash has softened, about 5 minutes. Take the saucepan off the heat. Gently stir in the tomatoes, bulgur, and the remaining ¼ cup mint. Slowly add the broth—the mixture should be similar to a thick soup. But don't fret over it, as bulgur is quite forgiving. Season with the remaining ¼ teaspoon pepper and to taste with salt.

Tip the bulgur and vegetables into the baking pan. Gently nestle in the chicken pieces, skin side up, and drizzle with any of its juices.

Roast until a meat thermometer, inserted into the center of a thigh (and not touching the bone), reaches 165°F, or until the juices run clear when you cut into one piece with a knife, 20 to 25 minutes. Any liquid in the pan will be gone by then or absorbed during resting.

Remove the pan and allow to sit for 5 minutes. Drizzle with the lemon juice and garnish with the 2 tablespoons mint. Serve warm, passing the lemon wedges around.

fine points

I love the acidity yellow tomatoes add to this meal, but you might enjoy it more with sweet red summer tomatoes.

Buying 4 chicken legs and cutting them into drumsticks and thighs is the most economical. Some chickens release a lot of fat, which you can drain after browning the chicken. You just need about 1 tablespoon in the pan.

GLUTEN-FREE 1 cup raw quinoa or ¾ cup raw millet is a great replacement for the bulgur.

roasted eggplant fan with tomatoes, spelt, and mozzarella

SPELT

1¾ cups water

1 cup whole grain spelt berries, soaked overnight and drained, or about 3 cups cooked (see page 23)

EGGPLANT

2 globe eggplants (2 to 2½ pounds total)

2 teaspoons fine sea salt

2 tablespoons extra-virgin olive oil, plus 2 teaspoons, for drizzling

3 cups (½ recipe) Saffron-Infused Tomato Sauce with Vermouth (page 172) or store-bought plain or basil tomato sauce (one 25-ounce jar)

½ cup loosely packed torn fresh basil leaves

8 to 12 ounces fresh mozzarella, cut into ¼-inch-thick slices

SERVES 4 TO 6

The first time I saw an eggplant, cut into thin slices and fanned out like a hand of cards, I was smitten. This image in a German magazine stayed with me for years. And while it seemed perfectly natural to cut the plump summer fruit (yes, eggplants are a fruit, botanically speaking) into slices to fan out, I had never thought about it—nor could I forget about it.

This makes a stunning presentation to impress dinner guests, but it is just as lovely on a weekend in summer. Needless to say, it tastes best with homemade sauce and when eggplants are in season. I like it as a side with grilled meat, or serve it on its own if you are vegetarian. Any grain berries from the wheat family are splendid here, from emmer (farro) to soft whole wheat and einkorn. ➳ gluten-free option

To prepare the spelt, add the water and spelt to a small heavy saucepan and bring to a boil. Decrease the heat to maintain a simmer, cover, and cook until the berries are tender with a slight chew, 45 to 55 minutes. Drain any remaining water, or just set aside to steam for 10 minutes or so—all of the water might be absorbed.

Meanwhile, prepare the eggplant: Cut each eggplant lengthwise into ½- to ¾-inch slices, about 6 each, without cutting through the stem. You want to be able to open the eggplant like a fan. Carefully lift the slices and spread the salt between them, about 1 teaspoon per eggplant. Place a large colander in the sink and set the eggplants inside, on top of each other. Put a small plate on top, to fit inside the colander, and weigh it down with a large can. Allow to drain for about 25 minutes.

Meanwhile, place a rack in the center of the oven and preheat to 450°F. Grease a large rimmed baking sheet and a 9 by 13-inch casserole pan with olive oil or cooking spray.

Carefully rinse and pat the eggplants dry, again taking care not to wreck the fan. (If you are not salt-sensitive, just thoroughly (!) wipe off the salt with paper towels). Brush the slices of each eggplant with about 1 tablespoon olive oil. Place next to each other on the baking sheet. Gently push down the eggplants to spread each to about 6½ inches wide.

Roast for 35 to 40 minutes, carefully turning each fan—using a large spatula and holding them at the stem with oven mitts—once halfway, until the eggplants have collapsed and the flesh is soft and browned in places. Remove from the oven and decrease the temperature to 400°F.

While the eggplants cool a bit, add the tomato sauce to a large bowl and stir in the cooked spelt and ¼ cup of the basil leaves. Add about ¼ cup water to loosen the sauce, if needed. Spread the mixture into the prepared pan. Drizzle the 2 teaspoons olive oil across the sauce. Using a spatula, carefully transfer the eggplants and place them next to each other on top of the mixture, with the fan opening in opposite directions (it helps to have the pans close!). Gently lift the eggplant slices and slide 1 to 2 mozzarella slices, depending on your preference, in between.

Bake until the sauce is bubbly and the mozzarella is melted, 15 to 20 minutes. If you like (and if your pan is broiler-safe—not with glass!), place the pan under the broiler (no need to preheat) to brown the cheese, watching closely, 1 to 3 minutes. Allow to sit for a few minutes, then garnish with the remaining ¼ cup basil leaves.

To finish, using a sharp knife, cut off the stem of the eggplant to separate the slices. Using a spatula, place about 2 cheese-filled slices per person on a plate. Spoon some of the tomato spelt berries on the side and serve.

fine points

Salting or not salting eggplants? I'm a fierce proponent of salting because it alters the texture of the fruit to make the flesh more supple and mouthwatering.

VARIATION For a change, use 1¼ cups (about 5 ounces) crumbled feta instead of the mozzarella.

GLUTEN-FREE Use about 3 cups cooked quinoa or 2½ cups cooked millet (see page 22).

MAKE AHEAD The eggplant can be roasted 1 day ahead. Allow to cool and chill, covered. The whole dish, up to the baking step, can be made 1 day ahead; chill, covered. Remove from the fridge when you preheat the oven and bake.

vegetarian wild rice paella with sweet potatoes, tart cherries, and gorgonzola

WILD RICE

2 cups low-sodium vegetable broth

2 cups water

1½ cups wild rice

1 dried red chile pepper (optional)

PAELLA

2 tablespoons extra-virgin olive oil

1½ cups chopped red onion, ¼-inch dice (about 1 medium)

½ teaspoon fine sea salt

1½ cups sliced carrots (¼-inch pieces, from about 3 medium carrots)

2 cups cubed sweet potato (½-inch pieces, from about ½ large sweet potato)

1 cup chopped red or yellow bell pepper (½-inch pieces, from about ½ bell pepper)

1 tablespoon minced garlic (about 3 cloves)

1 tablespoon smoked paprika (sweet pimentón) or sweet paprika

½ teaspoon loosely packed saffron threads

2 tablespoons tomato paste

½ cup Madeira, preferably medium dry, or sherry

¾ cup tart dried cherries

1 (14.5-ounce) can fire-roasted diced tomatoes

¾ cup coarsely crumbled Gorgonzola

½ cup loosely packed chopped fresh flat-leaf parsley

SERVES 4 AS A LIGHT MAIN, 8 AS A SIDE

If you are looking for eye candy on a festive table, this one-skillet dinner is for you. I use the term *paella* for this vegetable-rich wild rice dish loosely, because I borrow some of its classic flavors such as pimentón and saffron and it is a similarly stunning presentation. It's a nourishing vegetarian meal as is. But it also pairs beautifully with turkey and chicken during the holidays, and it is a knockout—tested and tried courtesy of our generous neighbors—next to grilled rib eye. gluten-free

To parboil the wild rice, add the broth, water, wild rice, and chile pepper to a large heavy saucepan and bring to a boil. Decrease the heat to maintain a simmer, cover, and cook for 30 minutes (or two-thirds of the recommended cooking time on your package). Drain, reserving the cooking liquid in a large measuring cup and topping with water to reach 2½ cups if needed. Remove the chile.

Meanwhile, make the paella: Heat the olive oil in a 12-inch skillet over medium heat until it shimmers. Add the onion and ¼ teaspoon of the salt and cook, stirring occasionally, until the onion caramelizes at the edges, 5 to 7 minutes. Add the carrots, sweet potato, bell pepper, and garlic and cook, stirring frequently, until the vegetables start to soften, about 5 minutes. Sprinkle the pimentón and the saffron across, then stir in the tomato paste. Cook, stirring, until aromatic and the tomato paste turns dark, about 1 minute. Add the Madeira (it will sizzle!) and cook until it turns syrupy and is almost absorbed, 1 to 2 minutes.

Add the wild rice, its reserved liquid, and the remaining ¼ teaspoon salt and bring to a boil. Decrease the heat to maintain a brisk simmer and cook, with the lid ajar about 1 inch, for 15 minutes, gently stirring once. Stir in the cherries and the tomatoes with their liquid. Return to a brisk simmer and continue cooking, leaving the lid ajar, until the vegetables are tender and the wild rice is cooked but retains some chew, 15 to 20 minutes more, adding ½ cup or a bit more water as needed—the final dish should retain a little juiciness. Season with salt to taste.

To finish, turn off the heat, sprinkle the dish with the Gorgonzola, and cover for 2 minutes to get it to melt a bit. Sprinkle with the parsley and serve.

fine points

Parboil the wild rice while you prep the ingredients to get a head start.

one good grain: just tomatoes and farro piccolo

Help out a passionate chef by giving her some local grains and get a mouth-watering recipe idea in return—this is the story of this side dish. Divine in its simplicity, it is a mesmerizing introduction to farro piccolo, ancient einkorn wheat (see page 13). Its small plump grains add just the right subtle bite to the saucy-sweet tomatoes.

Locavore chef and caterer JJ Gonson was preparing an event dinner and couldn't find grains. I handed her all of my remaining supplies from the lovely farmers at Four Star Farms in Massachusetts. Later JJ told me that she simply added the soft wheat to a crockpot together with tomatoes, cooked them for 4 hours, and left it at that. The austerity of her recipe intrigued me. But since not everyone has a crockpot, I came up with the overnight soak in the fridge, which works like a charm. ⟶ gluten-free option

1 large (28-ounce) can good-quality whole peeled tomatoes, with juices, crushed

1 cup farro piccolo (einkorn)

1 dried red chile pepper (optional)

2 tablespoons unsalted butter or extra-virgin olive oil

Fine sea salt or low-sodium soy sauce

Freshly ground black pepper

SERVES 4 TO 6

step one
At least 8 hours and up to 24 hours ahead: Add the tomatoes, farro piccolo, and chile to a heavy 4-quart saucepan. Swirl out the tomato can with ¾ cup water and add that as well. Cover, and chill.

step two
When you are ready to cook the grain, bring everything to a boil over medium-high heat, stirring once or twice so the grains don't get stuck to the bottom of the pot. Reduce the heat to maintain a simmer, cover, and cook until the einkorn is tender with a slight chew, 15 to 20 minutes for lighter-colored types, and up to 40 minutes for other varieties. Depending on the amount of liquid left, uncover and cook for a few minutes more, until slightly thickened. Remove the dried chile. Stir in the butter, season with salt or soy sauce, and serve with a nice dose of black pepper.

fine points
For an exquisite meaty variation, cook 2 ounces chopped pancetta over medium to medium-low heat until browned and crisp, 5 to 7 minutes. Stir the fat into the grains (instead of the butter) and top with the crisped bits.

GLUTEN-FREE AND VARIATIONS Other ancient wheats such as spelt and Kamut can be used but will need 65 to 75 minutes cooking time, as does gluten-free sorghum.

VEGETARIAN Add 1¾ cups or one 15-ounce can cooked chickpeas (see page 152) or top it with Greek yogurt, crumbled ricotta salata, or feta.

simple and sweet
desserts for every day and for the holidays

glorious dried fruit

If you think I have a store-worthy display of ancient grains in my kitchen, I invite you to take a look at my pantry. There you will find not only grains but also a veritable lineup of jars filled with dried fruit. The content of the jars is always changing, but I typically have an ample collection to show off. Soft caramel brown figs from Turkey or Greece and denser dark Mission figs from California, huge intensely sweet Medjool dates and their cousin, the firm, slim, less sugary Deglet Noor. There are always golden and dark raisins, often luscious jumbo or giant raisins, chewy dehydrated apple rings, shriveled aromatic prunes, and two types of dried apricots, intensely sweet ones from Turkey and tangy Blenheim from California. Never amiss—I live in New England—a jar of ruby-red cranberries plus, a more recent addition, their acidic kin, supremely sour barberries from Iran. Furthermore, I rely on a constant supply of exquisite candied oranges, citron, and lemon rinds for winter baking and summer desserts.

My dried fruit pantry has always been central to my cooking and baking and at the heart of my ancient grains kitchen. I consider it a candy store of yore, full of concentrated nuggets of summer. The dehydrated fruit can take an everyday meal from pedestrian to royal in a cinch. I use them in warm oatmeal, in leafy greens and grain salads, and in countless meat and even fish dishes. They transform my breakfast, lunch, and dinner with their riveting textures and intense nuanced aromas.

Yet, I have often wondered if anyone shares my devotion. Thus one day, on a whim, I put a question to my Facebook friends, many in the food community, to find out which dried fruits were in their pantry at the moment. Within a day the thread grew a mile long with over 100 passionate responses. I learned two things from it: the pantries of food pros are filled with dried fruit during the holidays, similar to mine, but in many home kitchens they seem generally less appreciated—yielding perhaps just a cardboard box of Sun-Maid raisins or a forgotten pack of dates or dried-out figs.

The venerable food writer Russ Parsons put it to the point: pastry chefs he spoke with told him that putting dried fruit on the restaurant menu was a "sure kiss of death." But if they were simply part of a dessert or cake without being advertised, no one would complain. Another colleague confirmed this dire observation, all of which inspired this essay.

In that moment it became clear to me that dried fruit has a serious image problem. Perhaps not unlike the status of whole grains just a few years ago: in the good-for-you-but-taste-like-hell-drawer. That's why they end up in the last corner of the cupboard. Where we stack food we don't know what to do with. Or food we feel bad tossing out because we *should* eat it.

Which leads straight to the question, why is there such disdain for dried fruit? Throughout history, and across cultures, the concentrated sweetness of these morsels was revered, not least because sugar was hard to come by. Until the nineteenth century sugar was a luxury item, kept under lock and key. As a result, farmers and homemakers preserved summer's bounty by drying any extra fruit they had to sweeten long winters without fresh produce. No wonder raisins, dried apricots, figs, or dates were once treasured as exquisite and intricate parts of special meals.

They were used not only in familiar holiday treats but also for celebration. Persian jeweled rice, studded with raisins, dried apricots, and barberries, is one famous example. The festive Indian biryani and countless rice pilafs in Turkey, Greece, and the Eastern Mediterranean likely derived from this glorious dish.

Prunes, figs, apricots, and dates have been added to chicken, lamb, or pork for centuries in cuisines as diverse as French, Middle Eastern, and Chinese. Not to forget fish: North Africans, for example, stuff their bellies with raisin-laced couscous. I was surprised by this unusual combination until I tried it—needless to say, it is divine.

This appreciation extended to the United States. According to Russ Parsons, until the 1870s, for example, almost all raisins were considered exotic ingredients, reserved for special occasions. In 1960 Napa's prunes were more valuable than the valley's grapes.

Unlike sugar, with its in-your-face cloying sweetness, dried fruits have nuanced complexity. Their sweetness is often subtle, even in the background in their natural state. They force you to pause, to notice their character.

But as cheap sugar replaced some of the more traditional sweeteners such as honey or molasses in desserts and baked goods, good-quality dried fruit seems to have disappeared from store shelves as well. Supermarkets sometimes offer sugar-coated flavorless morsels not worth your attention. Or they bring you strange presoftened prunes and apricots, geared to the healthy-minded. No wonder dried fruit has an image problem. This disregard—I would like to call it disrespect—extends to candied fruits, another exquisite traditional food preservation. I will never forget the first time I picked up a package of candied cherries, eye-popping disco green and red, during the holidays years ago. I almost started to cry. How am I supposed to bake with these artificial sugary bits? At this moment, I understood the countless jokes about doorstop fruitcakes I had heard before.

I have to thank my Greek mom, who inspired a deep appreciation of these frugal treats. She selects her dried fruits with the same care she exercises for fresh fruits, vegetables, bread, and cheese. They are an integral ingredient in her cooking, and their quality matters—just like any other food she selects for preparation.

In my own ancient grains kitchen, dried fruits play a starring role. Grain dishes get an instant facelift with a handful of colorful dried fruits tossed in—they play off other flavors, add satisfying chew, and bring just enough sweetness to give earthy grains a kick. And if you plump or stew dried fruits in a bit of alcohol, their aroma amplifies and transforms everyday sweets. In this spirit, I have developed the Just Fruit Holiday Cake (page 240). Barely sweetened, with just a little whole wheat flour to hold it together, it has no resemblance to the sugar-laden concoctions you might have had. Instead, I hope, it will change your mind about this festive treat.

Last but not least, dried fruits make the most amazing portable snacks. On plane and car rides or if you love to hike, nothing is as convenient and nourishing as a small bag of dried fruit and nuts—chewy and satisfying, with just the right sweetness. Or grab a handful of walnuts and a fat Medjool date to nourish your brain during a long workday or to tide yourself over until dinner.

Most important, go hunting for best-quality dried fruits just as you would for good cheese and wine. Do some tasting and some more tasting to discover their nuances, and use them in your cooking and baking all day long.

light lemon custard with blackberries and pomegranate molasses

3 or 4 lemons, preferably organic

3 tablespoons unsalted butter, softened

½ cup plus 1 tablespoon superfine sugar

3 large eggs, whites and yolks separated, at room temperature

½ cup whole milk

1 tablespoon limoncello

3 tablespoons (20 g) whole grain spelt flour, white whole wheat flour, or Kamut flour

Pinch of fine sea salt

About 1½ cups fresh or frozen blackberries (no need to thaw)

1½ tablespoons pomegranate molasses (see page 249)

About 3 tablespoons crème fraîche, for garnish

Confectioners' sugar, for sprinkling

SERVES 6

This bright tangy citrus dessert is a standby in my house. I have made variations of it for years—this new twist yields an astonishing transformation. Adding just a few blackberries and a drizzle of pomegranate molasses into the ramekins not only is visually striking but also adds complexity. Delicate spelt flour intensifies the aromas. To me, these little creamy custard cakes are the perfect ending to a main course of seafood, but they can be dessert any day.

Please don't expect me to use a water bath here. Just giving the ramekins a little rest with a cracked-open oven door after baking preserves the beauty of this homey dessert in an old-fashioned way. Plus, it's much less work.

Place a rack one level below (!) the center of the oven and preheat to 350°F. Butter six 6-ounce ramekins and place them in the fridge. Finely grate the lemons until you have 4 teaspoons zest, then squeeze the fruit to get ½ cup of juice.

In a large bowl and using a hand mixer at medium speed, beat the butter until smooth, about 30 seconds. Gradually add the ½ cup sugar and beat until light and fluffy, 1 to 2 minutes. Beat in 1 egg yolk at a time, blending well with each addition and scraping the sides of the bowl with a spatula as needed. Decrease the speed to low and beat in the lemon juice and the zest. The mixture might look curdly. Blend in the milk and the liqueur, then lightly sprinkle the spelt flour across and beat until just incorporated.

Add the egg whites and the salt to a medium bowl. Switch to the whisk attachment and whip the whites at medium-low speed until foamy, about 1 minute. Increase the speed to medium-high and slowly drizzle in the 1 tablespoon sugar and continue beating until soft glossy peaks form, about 1 minute more. Whisk one-third of the whites into the batter to lighten, then switch to a spatula and gently but thoroughly fold in the remaining whites in two more additions until no streaks remain.

Place the ramekins on a rimmed baking sheet for easier handling. Place 6 blackberries (about ¼ cup) into the bottom of each ramekin and drizzle ¾ teaspoon pomegranate molasses across each. Divide the batter among the ramekins, using a scant 1 cup, filling them almost to the rim.

Bake until the custard cakes turn light golden brown and a cake tester or toothpick inserted into the center comes out dry or with faint streaks, about 25 minutes. Turn off the oven and open the door a crack. (If needed, slide a wooden spoon in sidewise to prop it open 1 or 2 inches.) Leave the ramekins in the oven for 10 more minutes. Remove and, using tongs, transfer the ramekins to a cooling rack until warm, about 20 minutes.

To finish, top each ramekin with a dollop of crème fraîche and dust with confectioners' sugar.

fine points

You can make your own superfine sugar in a food processor, fitted with a metal blade. Add 1 cup granulated sugar and process until very fine, about 3 minutes; this will yield more than you will need for this recipe.

Separate the egg yolks and egg whites right after you remove them from the fridge—it's easier.

MAKE AHEAD Custard cakes can be baked up to 1 day ahead. Let cool to room temperature, about 1 hour, cover loosely with plastic wrap, and chill; serve chilled or at room temperature. Alternately, if you prefer your dessert warm from the oven, you can prepare the batter and fill the ramekins up to 3 hours ahead. Cover with plastic wrap and chill. Bake straight from the fridge; custards will rise a little less.

almond polenta tart with sherried plum compote

Somehow this dessert hugs my German-Greek heart, with its warm Mediterranean feel and its touch of northern European cool. It is a pleasing ending to summer meal—the warm, lightly sweetened honeyed polenta with a crisp layer of buttery almonds, accompanied by chilled sherried plums.

Adapted from a recipe in the German magazine *Schöner Essen*, it introduced me to polenta as a dessert when I started out in my own kitchen. I've since made it countless times without ever tiring of it. It is best during plum season, throughout summer into the cool of early fall, and even better with aromatic farmers' market fruit. Don't forget to dollop it with a little softly whipped cream or vanilla ice cream. ⬥ gluten-free

....

To make the polenta, add the water, milk, honey, and salt to a large heavy saucepan and bring to a bare simmer over medium-high heat, stirring occasionally. Using a large whisk, slowly add the polenta in a thin stream and continue whisking for 1 minute more, decreasing the heat if the mixture bubbles up. Decrease the heat further to maintain a gentle bubble, cover, and cook for 10 minutes, stirring vigorously with a wooden spoon every few minutes to keep the polenta from sticking to the bottom. Remove the saucepan from the heat and let sit, covered, for 10 minutes, stirring well once or twice.

Meanwhile, butter a 10-inch ceramic tart pan and place it on a wire rack. Have a tall glass of cold water ready. Transfer the polenta to the pan, spreading it evenly across the bottom with the back of a wooden spoon, dipping the spoon into the water as needed to help distribute the mixture. Set aside at room temperature to cool and firm up, 45 minutes to 1 hour. Using the round end of the spoon, poke about a dozen holes into the polenta—hold the spoon at a 45-degree angle and insert it while turning to keep the polenta from sticking to the spoon. This prevents the polenta from heaving in the oven later.

About 1 hour before you want to serve the dessert, position a rack in the center of the oven and preheat to 400°F.

Meanwhile, prepare the compote: Add the plums to a large bowl and sprinkle with the cinnamon. Add 2 tablespoons of the honey, the sherry, brandy, and the 1 tablespoon thyme leaves. Gently toss to combine; taste and add a bit more honey if you like. Cover the bowl and chill to macerate, stirring once or twice.

Add the butter and the remaining 2 tablespoons honey to a medium skillet. Heat over medium heat, stirring occasionally with a wooden spoon, until well blended.

POLENTA
2 cups water

1½ cups whole or low-fat milk

¼ cup honey

½ teaspoon fine sea salt

1 cup (150 g) polenta, preferably medium grind

COMPOTE, AND TO FINISH
2 pounds fresh plums, pits removed, and cut into ½- to ¾-inch pieces (if the plums are small, cut into 8 wedges)

½ teaspoon ground cinnamon

4 tablespoons honey, or more as needed

¼ cup dry sherry or apple juice

1 tablespoon brandy (optional)

1 tablespoon plus 1 teaspoon fresh thyme leaves

4 tablespoons (¼ cup) unsalted butter, preferably European-style

1 cup sliced almonds

Softly whipped heavy cream, for serving

SERVES 8

continued >

Add the almonds and stir until they are warmed through and the mixture becomes foamy, 1 to 2 minutes. Immediately spread the almond mixture over the polenta, using the back of the spoon.

Bake until small bubbles appear around the edges and the almond topping turns a glistening golden brown, about 20 minutes. Transfer the pan to a wire rack and allow to set before cutting, at least 20 minutes.

To finish, cut the tart into 8 wedges, using a sharp knife. Place each wedge on a dessert plate and spoon some of the chilled compote with a bit of its juices on top. Garnish each serving with a few leaves of the 1 teaspoon thyme and a dollop of cream.

fine points

For types of polenta, see page 8. Stone-ground medium cornmeal can be used but will take 50 minutes to set before cutting, and will be creamier, not toothsome like polenta; be sure to use weight measures for best results.

VARIATIONS This is just as delicious with a compote of fresh or (thawed) frozen peaches.

MAKE AHEAD For best results, prepare the polenta and spread it in the tart pan at least a few hours or up to 1 day ahead—this allows the cornmeal to firm up. Cool to room temperature, chill uncovered for a couple of hours, then cover loosely with plastic wrap.

Leftover polenta wedges reheat well in the microwave—yes, I sometimes have one for breakfast.

simple maple pudding with farro piccolo

Farro piccolo, a superb supple and starchy ancient wheat, seems destined for pudding. Ever since I tasted it for the first time, I have been mesmerized by this smallest of the ancient wheats. The roundish grains plump up beautifully yet retain a delicate toothsomeness, which makes them uniquely suited for this simple dessert.

To prepare the farro piccolo, add the water, farro piccolo, and cinnamon stick to a medium heavy saucepan and bring to a boil. Decrease the heat to maintain a simmer, cover, and cook until the kernels are tender with a slight chewiness, 25 to 35 minutes, depending on the type. A fair bit of the kernels should burst and show their starchy centers, and there will be water left (do not drain).

To make the pudding, add the half-and-half, 2 tablespoons of the maple syrup, the lemon zest, vanilla, and salt to the farro. Return to a boil over medium-high heat, stirring a few times and pressing on the lemon strips to release their etheric oil. Decrease the heat to maintain a gentle bubble and cook, uncovered and stirring occasionally, until the pudding thickens to a creamy consistency and the grains swell, about 20 minutes more. It should still be a bit soupy.

To finish, take the saucepan off the heat and remove the cinnamon stick and the zest. Stir in the remaining 1 tablespoon maple syrup, or more to taste. Spoon into individual dessert bowls or cups and serve warm. Or, spoon the pudding into a medium bowl and press a piece of parchment paper or plastic wrap right on top to avoid skin formation. Cool to room temperature and chill for about 2 hours. The pudding will continue to thicken—you may need to add a bit of half-and-half before serving to loosen it. Spoon into individual bowls.

Garnish each bowl with a dollop of whipped cream and sprinkle with cinnamon.

fine points

For types of einkorn (farro piccolo), see page 13. For Sources, see page 251. Semipearled farro (emmer) can be used, using the shorter cooking time.

I use Grade B maple syrup in all of my cooking and baking. It is worth seeking out for its dark amber hue and deeper aroma.

The pudding can be made up to 1 day ahead; chill as instructed.

FARRO PICCOLO

1¼ cups water

½ cup farro piccolo (einkorn)

1 (2-inch) cinnamon stick

PUDDING

1¼ cups half-and-half, plus more as needed

3 tablespoons maple syrup, preferably the darker Grade B, or more as needed

2 (3-inch) strips of lemon zest

1 teaspoon vanilla extract

¼ teaspoon fine sea salt

Softly whipped cream, for serving

Ground cinnamon, for sprinkling

SERVES 4

rum raisin ice cream with kamut berries

½ cup dark raisins

3 tablespoons rum, preferably white

2¼ cups whole milk Greek yogurt

¾ cup heavy whipping cream

¼ cup plus 2 tablespoons maple syrup, preferably Grade B

1 teaspoon vanilla extract

1 teaspoon ground cinnamon

½ cup cooked Kamut berries (see page 23)

MAKES ABOUT 2 PINTS

fine points

Remove from the freezer about 20 minutes before serving.

I chose the grain Kamut because I happen to adore the bronze-colored ancient wheat, but cooked whole grain spelt, farro, or soft wheat berries are fine replacements.

Using chilled ingredients speeds up freezing. Adding a bit of alcohol to ice cream lowers its freezing point, resulting in a smoother texture. Use apple juice if making this for children.

Ice cream will last for about 1 week.

The first time I stirred a handful of ancient wheat berries into an early version of this ice cream, I remember mumbling to myself, "What on earth—this is dessert, not breakfast!" Yet I continued, inspired by a recent trip to the corner convenience store. There I had seen many tubs of ice cream with chewy cookies, which made me wonder, wouldn't chewy grains be just as divine? Frankly, even I wasn't convinced. Yet the leftover grains went into the creamy mixture anyway—and a few hours later everyone around the dinner table that night fell silent, spooning in and trying to identify the secret ingredient. Here is the fine-tuned treat. I hope you try it for yourself, but be sure not to reveal the hidden grain.

This ice cream is lovely on its own, but if you feel up to it, it pairs nicely with the Walnut Spelt Biscotti (page 223).

Add the raisins to a small bowl, drizzle with 2 tablespoons of the rum, cover, and chill until ready to use.

Add the Greek yogurt, whipping cream, maple syrup, vanilla, and cinnamon to a medium bowl and whisk together well. Whisk in the remaining 1 tablespoon rum. Cover with a lid or with plastic wrap and refrigerate until well chilled, at least 2 hours.

Transfer the yogurt mixture to an ice cream maker and churn until almost frozen, about 15 minutes. Stir in the plumped rum raisins with any liquid and the Kamut berries and continue until frozen, about 3 minutes more.

If you don't have an ice cream maker, cover and place the bowl in the freezer for about 1½ hours. Beat until smooth with a handheld mixer, scraping down the sides of the bowl with a spatula. This prevents the formation of ice crystals. Return to the freezer and repeat every 1½ hours or so until the mixture is almost frozen and has thickened enough so you can lift it with the beaters. Stir in the plumped raisins with any liquid and the grains and continue freezing until frozen, 1 to 2 hours more (for a total of about 6 hours, depending on your freezer).

greek yogurt chocolate mousse

This luscious dessert is for the days when dinner guests are almost at your doorstep and you need an after-dinner bite *now*. Prepared in minutes, it can hold its own next to the sophisticated French dessert. Intensely rich, with a dense chocolate mouthfeel, it has an appealing slight tanginess from the Greek yogurt. My recipe was inspired by one in the Greek magazine *Glykes Istories (Sweet Stories)*. I added a glug of Grand Marnier, which rounds out the flavors, and I used chocolate with 70 percent cocoa, as I'm partial to its bitter notes. Dark or bittersweet chocolate with 50 to 60 percent cocoa makes for a more mellow spoonful, especially if you make this for children. ◀ gluten-free

Put the chocolate into a medium bowl. In a small heavy saucepan bring the milk just to a simmer over medium heat. Pour the hot milk over the chocolate and allow to sit for 1 to 2 minutes. Stir with a wooden spoon until you have a smooth liquid, then add 1 tablespoon of the Grand Marnier. If you like a boozy dessert, add the second tablespoon.

Put the Greek yogurt in a small bowl and beat with a fork until smooth. Add the yogurt to the chocolate mixture, folding in, using a spatula, until thoroughly combined.

Spoon the mousse into four small cups or bowls and chill until firm, at least 1 hour. Garnish each serving with about 1 teaspoon of jam.

About 1¼ cups (6 ounces) finely chopped good-quality dark chocolate (I use a sharp serrated knife; you can use the food processor)

½ cup whole milk

1 or 2 tablespoons Grand Marnier or other good-quality orange liqueur (optional)

1 cup whole milk Greek yogurt

1 to 2 tablespoons kumquat jam or orange marmalade

SERVES 4

fine points

This recipe can easily be doubled, quadrupled, and more for a crowd.

Whole milk Greek yogurt is my first choice here. Since there is no cream in this treat, no eggs, and no added sugar, it needs a little richness to taste like, well, dessert. Don't use nonfat yogurt, but 2% Greek yogurt is fine.

MAKE AHEAD You can prepare the dessert (without the topping) 1 day ahead. Cover the bowls with plastic wrap; garnish when ready to serve.

lemony millet pudding with caramelized grapes

MILLET

1 cup water

½ cup millet

⅔ cup whole or low-fat milk

½ teaspoon vanilla extract

Pinch of fine sea salt

PUDDING

¾ cup dry white wine such as Pinot Grigio, or apple juice

¼ cup honey

2 tablespoons turbinado sugar

2 cups halved seedless grapes, preferably red or purple (about 10 ounces), plus about ¼ cup (2 ounces) for garnish

3 whole cloves or a pinch of ground cloves

1 (4 by ½-inch) strip lemon zest, white pith removed

1½ cups whole milk Greek yogurt

2 tablespoons limoncello or apple juice, or more as needed

1½ teaspoons finely grated lemon zest, plus a little more for garnish

SERVES 6

fine points

To stand out in the creamy mixture, dark red or black grapes are my first choice here.

MAKE AHEAD This dessert can be made up to 4 hours ahead. It tastes best on the day it is made, as millet tends to harden. However, gently warming leftovers—on the stove top over low heat, or at 50 percent power in the microwave—makes a deliriously good breakfast.

Creamy desserts are a perfect foil to showcase millet—they provide enough cover to hide the small grain from plain view yet plenty of appeal to highlight its delicate, toothsome texture. This nimble lemon-infused dessert, similar to rice pudding, is a case in point. Aromatic white wine syrup caramelizes the grapes and ties the ingredients together, showing off this comforting ancient grain. ⟫ gluten-free

To prepare the millet, add the water and the millet to a small heavy saucepan and bring to a boil. Decrease the heat to maintain a simmer, cover, and cook until the water is absorbed, 18 to 20 minutes. Stir in the milk, vanilla, and salt. Return to a simmer, cover, and cook until the liquid is absorbed, about 10 minutes more. Remove from the heat and let sit, covered, for 5 minutes. Uncover and allow to cool for about 25 minutes.

While the millet is cooling, make the pudding. Add the wine, honey, sugar, grapes, cloves, and the zest strip to a heavy medium saucepan. Bring to a boil over medium-high heat, stirring gently a few times for the sugars to dissolve, then cook at a lively simmer for about 2 minutes to just soften the grapes.

Gently tip the grapes into a sieve, placed over a medium bowl to retain the liquid. Return the liquid, including the cloves and the zest, to the pot and bring to a boil. Cook at a vigorous simmer, adjusting the heat as needed, until the syrup starts to caramelize and turns a deep amber color, 7 to 9 minutes. Remove the pan from the heat and set aside to cool for about 15 minutes.

To finish the pudding, be sure that both the millet and the syrup are not more than slightly warm to the touch. Remove the zest strip and the cloves from the syrup (you will have about ½ cup); set aside 2 tablespoons of the syrup for garnish. Add the remaining syrup, the yogurt, limoncello, and grated zest to a medium bowl and beat with a wooden spoon until smooth. Fluff the millet with a fork and stir it into the yogurt mixture. Gently stir in the grapes as well. Divide the dessert between six bowls and chill, covered with plastic wrap, for 2 hours to allow the flavors to mingle.

When ready to serve, garnish each bowl with a few grape halves. Spoon a bit of the reserved syrup on top (stir in a teaspoon of boiling water to loosen it if needed) and garnish with a bit of lemon zest.

cardamom-scented barley cake with grapes and rose petals

¾ cup plus 1 tablespoon (90 g) whole grain spelt flour

¾ cup plus 1 tablespoon (90 g) whole grain barley flour

1¼ teaspoons baking powder

1 teaspoon cardamom, preferably freshly ground

⅛ teaspoon fine sea salt

2 large eggs, at room temperature

¾ cup chilled heavy whipping cream, plus a few tablespoons more as needed

½ cup plus 2 tablespoons (125 g) turbinado sugar

1 teaspoon finely grated orange zest, preferable organic

¼ teaspoon vanilla extract

About 1½ cups (250 g) seedless red or other dark grapes, preferably small

¼ cup (30 g) coarsely chopped toasted hazelnuts

1½ teaspoons dried edible rose petals, for sprinkling (optional; see "Sources," page 251)

Confectioners' sugar, for dusting

MAKES 1 ROUND 9-INCH CAKE, TO SERVE 8

fine points

MAKE AHEAD The cake can be baked 1 day ahead. Store under a cake dome or turned-over bowl at cool room temperature.

Witness a miraculous transformation of ingredients in this easy German-inspired cake. There is not a drop of butter or oil—instead, after a mighty good beating of eggs and heavy cream, a striking creation will emerge from your oven, light yet moist with a fine crumb. And I'm now convinced that crunchy hazelnuts were destined to be combined with cardamom and sweet-malty barley flour. A dollop of unsweetened softly whipped cream or a bit of vanilla ice cream is highly recommended.

Position a rack in the center of the oven and preheat to 350°F. Butter and flour a 9½-inch metal tart pan with removable bottom, shaking out excess. Set the pan on a large rimless baking sheet for easier handling.

Whisk together both flours, the baking powder, cardamom, and salt in a medium bowl.

Add the eggs, cream, and ½ cup (100 g) of the sugar to a medium bowl with tall sides. Beat the ingredients, using an electric hand mixer on high, 3 to 4 minutes, scraping the sides once—the mixture should about double in volume, turn lighter in color, and thicken slightly, and the sugar should be completely dissolved. Beat in the zest and the vanilla. Reduce speed to low and gradually beat in the flour mixture in four additions until just combined. The batter should be creamy, and you should be able to spoon and spread it. If not, blend in a little more cream by the tablespoon. Using a spatula, stir through, scraping the bottom of the bowl to make sure all ingredients are blended. Scrape the batter into the tart form and gently spread it across, evening the top.

Carefully place the baking sheet with the tart pan in the oven (it can slide!) and bake for 7 minutes.

Remove the pan and distribute the grapes evenly across the surface. Sprinkle with the hazelnuts, the 2 tablespoons (25 g) sugar, and the rose petals.

Return to the oven and bake until the cake turns lightly golden around the edges, firms up when gently pressed, and a cake tester or toothpick inserted into the center comes out clean, 20 to 25 minutes more.

Carefully slide the tart pan onto a wire rack. Cover with a clean dishcloth to help retain moisture and allow to cool completely, about 2 hours. When ready to serve, unmold, lightly dust with confectioners' sugar, and cut into 8 pieces.

walnut spelt biscotti with olive oil

The beauty of biscotti is that they last—this to me means a lot, as not a day goes by that I won't long for a sweet treat with my cup of coffee. Sipping coffee by itself is boring, and a whole slice of cake on a regular Monday too much. But a biscotti? Never! So when my magnificent colleague, cookbook author and blogger Domenica Marchetti, asked whether I would create a spelt biscotti for a book she was working on, I said, "Yes, of course!"

These olive oil biscotti, chock-full of walnuts and scented with lemon, are firmly rooted in the Mediterranean. Enjoy them with your morning or afternoon cuppa or dunk one into a glass of sweet wine for dessert. They are also a terrific match with the Rum Raisin Ice Cream with Kamut Berries (page 218).

Whisk together the flour, sugar, baking powder, and salt in a large bowl. Make a well in the center. In a medium bowl, lightly beat the eggs with a fork. Gradually stir in the olive oil until well blended, followed by the limoncello, vanilla, and zest. Pour the olive oil mixture into the center of the flour mixture. Using a dough whisk (see page 21) or a wooden spoon, and stirring from the center, gradually combine the ingredients until a soft dough just comes together.

Add the nuts to the bowl. Using your hands, gently incorporate them into the dough—there are lots of them!—while forming a ball. If the mixture becomes sticky, moisten your hands with water. Cover the bowl with a plate and set aside for 25 to 30 minutes. This allows the bran to soften for a more appealing texture.

Meanwhile, place a rack in the center of the oven and preheat to 350°F. Line a large rimless baking sheet with parchment paper. Lightly grease your work surface with olive oil.

Cut the dough inside the bowl into 4 equal pieces. Lightly knead each piece and gently roll into a log, about 9 inches long, pressing in any protruding nuts and moistening your hands with water if needed. Place the logs crosswise on the baking sheet, leaving at least 2 inches in between. Gently pat down the top of each log until it is about 1¾ inches wide. Sprinkle each log with a scant teaspoon sugar.

Bake until the logs firm up, small cracks appear on top, and their edges turn golden brown, about 25 minutes. Remove the baking sheet from the oven and carefully slide the parchment paper with the logs onto a wire rack. Allow to cool for 25 to 30 minutes.

Leave the oven on and reduce the temperature to 300°F. Place a fresh sheet of parchment on the baking sheet for easier cleanup. Transfer the logs to a cutting

2 cups plus 2 tablespoons (240 g) whole grain spelt flour

1 cup (200 g) turbinado sugar, plus more for sprinkling

1 teaspoon baking powder

¼ teaspoon fine sea salt

2 large eggs, at room temperature

½ cup extra-virgin olive oil

1 tablespoon limoncello or brandy

1 teaspoon vanilla extract

4 teaspoons finely grated lemon zest (from about 2 lemons, preferably organic)

1¾ cups (200 g) coarsely chopped toasted walnuts

MAKES ABOUT 62 SMALL BISCOTTI

continued >

board (loosen them with a metal spatula if needed). Using a large serrated knife, cut each log diagonally into ½-inch-thick slices. Place the slices, cut side down, onto the baking sheet without touching.

Bake until the biscotti feel dry to the touch, emit a lovely toasty scent, and start to brown around the edges, 30 to 35 minutes. Carefully slide the parchment paper with the biscotti to a wire rack to cool completely before storing.

fine points

These biscotti taste best after 1 day when their flavors have time to meld. Store in an airtight container for up to 2 weeks.

kamut shortbread with hazelnuts

This is a divine melt-in-your-mouth treat, tender and crisp at the same time, with a seductive nuttiness. Yet it is as easy as can be. My shortbread is inspired by a recipe from Faith Durand, executive editor of The Kitchn and author of the mouthwatering dessert cookbook *Bakeless Sweets.*

    I swapped the all-purpose flour for whole grain flour—both spelt and Kamut are enticing—and used less processed turbinado sugar. Instead of the sweet lemon glaze, I opted for a sprinkling of toasted nuts and a bit of flaked sea salt. The result is as versatile as it is addictive: it's a treat with your breakfast or afternoon coffee but just as terrific with a cheese plate after dinner.

Cut and place a piece of parchment paper into the bottom of an 8 by 8-inch square baking pan. (No need to grease the paper, but you can smear a bit of oil into the corners of the pan to help the paper adhere.)

Combine the olive oil and the vanilla in a small bowl. Set aside.

Add the nuts to the bowl of a food processor, fitted with a steel blade. Process until the mixture looks like coarse sand, with many pieces the size of steel-cut oats, 15 to 20 seconds. You will have 1⅓ cups ground nuts. Remove 1 tablespoon of the nuts and set aside.

If continuing by food processor, add the flour, both sugars, salt, and the lemon zest to the bowl with the nuts. Process until combined, about 10 seconds. Drizzle the olive oil mixture across the top and pulse just until a soft dough forms, about five 1-second pulses. Cover with a plate and allow to sit for 15 to 20 minutes while you preheat the oven.

If continuing by hand, transfer the ground nuts to a medium bowl. Add the flour, both sugars, salt, and the lemon zest and whisk until well combined. Be sure to dissolve any clumps of confectioners' sugar with your fingers. Make a well in the center and pour the olive oil mixture into it. Stir, using a dough whisk (see page 21) or a spatula, until no dry streaks remain; the dough will be soft. Cover with a plate and allow to sit for 15 to 20 minutes while you preheat the oven.

Meanwhile, position a rack in the center of the oven and preheat to 375°F.

Transfer and press the dough firmly into the baking pan, evening out the top. I like to first spread it across with the bottom of a measuring cup and finish with my fingers. Sprinkle with the remaining 1 tablespoon ground hazelnuts.

½ cup extra-virgin olive oil

¾ teaspoon vanilla extract

1 cup (130 g) slightly heaped whole toasted hazelnuts

⅔ cup (85 g) whole grain Kamut or spelt flour

¼ cup (50 g) turbinado sugar

¼ cup (30 g) confectioners' sugar, unsifted

¼ teaspoon (30 g) fine sea salt

2 teaspoons finely grated lemon zest (from 1 lemon, preferably organic)

2 small pinches flaked sea salt, for sprinkling

MAKES 16 SQUARES

continued >

Bake until the top firms up when gently pressed and the shortbread is golden brown across with darker edges, 25 to 30 minutes. Watch closely, as these can darken fast. Transfer the pan to a wire rack. While still warm, cut into 16 squares and sprinkle with the salt flakes, crushing larger ones between your fingers. Allow to cool completely in the pan, about 1 hour. Use a slim spatula or a thin-bladed knife to gently slide under each piece, lifting it out of the pan.

fine points

If using a glass pan, reduce the oven temperature to 350°F.

MAKE AHEAD Shortbread can be made 1 day ahead. It will retain its aroma and crispness when stored in an airtight container or metal cookie tin for at least 5 days.

greek sesame tahini cake with spelt

If tahini, the intensely nutty sesame butter, is not yet in your pantry, try this cake and get ready to stock up. The cake comes together in a flash, powered just by your hands and two bowls—yet the outcome is superb: aromatic and dense yet with a delicate crumb. My recipe is adapted from a creation by Greek superstar pastry chef Stelios Parliaros, whose work I adore. To serve, keep it simple with a dollop of unsweetened softly whipped cream.

Position a rack in the center of the oven and preheat to 350°F. Lightly butter a 9-inch round metal baking pan. Line the bottom with parchment paper and lightly butter the paper as well. Dust the pan with flour, tapping out excess.

Combine the dried fruit and the liqueur in a small bowl and set aside to plump a bit while you prep the ingredients, stirring once or twice.

Whisk together the flour, baking powder, and salt in a medium bowl. In a large bowl, whisk the sugar, tahini, and water to combine—it will look broken initially—then whisk vigorously for 1 to 2 minutes until amalgamated and glistening.

Gradually and slowly add the flour mixture, gently whisking until just combined. Do not overmix. Fold the dried fruit, including any liquid, into the batter. The batter should be creamy with a thick pourable consistency. Gently stir in 1 or 2 tablespoons more flour if it is too liquidy. Scrape the batter into the pan and even out the top, gently spreading into the corners. Sprinkle with the sesame seeds.

Bake for 20 minutes. Reduce the oven temperature to 325°F and continue baking until the cake barely starts to brown at the edges and a toothpick inserted into the center comes out clean, about 15 minutes more.

Transfer the pan to a wire rack to cool for 10 minutes. Loosen the cake around the edges with a paring knife. Invert the cake onto a plate, remove the parchment paper and carefully return the cake right side up to the rack to cool completely. When ready to serve, sprinkle lightly with confectioners' sugar. Cut with a long sharp knife, dipped into hot water and wiped clean between each cut, into 8 to 12 wedges.

1 cup (130 g) finely chopped dried fruits

1 tablespoon limoncello or brandy

1¾ cups (200 g) whole grain spelt flour

1¼ teaspoons baking powder

¼ teaspoon fine sea salt

1¾ cups (200 g) confectioners' sugar, unsifted, plus more for dusting

½ cup plus 2 tablespoons (150 g) tahini, preferably organic

¾ cup water, at room temperature

1 tablespoon sesame seeds, for sprinkling (optional)

MAKES 1 ROUND 9-INCH CAKE, TO SERVE 8 TO 12

fine points

A combination of candied lemon peel with currants adds beautiful complexity to this cake but only if you can get something other than supermarket-brand peel, which is often one-dimensional and cloyingly sweet (see "Sources," page 251). Other good combinations are tangy Blenheim apricots with currants or dried figs, or prunes and dried figs.

MAKE AHEAD This cake can be baked 1 day ahead—its flavor will only intensify. Store in an airtight container or under a cake dome at room temperature.

dark chocolate cherry cake with marsala cream

My favorite chocolate cakes are pitch-dark and more bitter than sweet in the best of ways. Morsels of tart cherries take this one up a notch, and buttery whole grain Kamut flour in the background only intensifies its dark richness. This is a grown-up cake that, to everyone's surprise, the children of all of my friends devoured. *Always* make the Marsala Cream (page 230) for grown-ups—just do it.

Position a rack in the center of the oven and preheat to 350°F. Add the cherries and wine to a small bowl while you prep your ingredients, leaving to macerate for about 15 minutes, stirring once. Lightly butter a 9 by 5-inch loaf pan. Line the bottom of the pan with parchment paper and lightly butter the paper as well. Dust the pan with cocoa, tapping out excess.

Drain and gently pat dry the cherries and toss with 1 tablespoon of the flour. In a medium bowl, thoroughly whisk together the remaining flour, the cocoa, baking powder, baking soda, and salt. Be sure to loosen any lumps of cocoa with your dry fingers.

In a large bowl, beat the butter with an electric mixer at medium speed until smooth, about 30 seconds. Gradually add the sugar and continue beating until lighter in color and fluffy, about 3 minutes, scraping the sides with a silicone spatula a few times as needed. Beat in the honey. Add one egg at a time, beating until well incorporated, 30 seconds per egg, and scraping the sides each time. Beat in the vanilla. Reduce the speed to low and gradually add one-third of the flour mixture (a ½-cup measuring cup helps!), followed by half of the buttermilk, repeating once, and ending with the remaining one-third of the flour mixture. Scrape down the sides, then beat at medium speed to blend, about 10 seconds.

Loosen the cherries with your fingers if they have clumped together. Using a spatula, gently fold them in with any flour, followed by the chocolate. Scrape the batter into the pan and smooth the top, gently spreading all the way to the edges.

Bake until the cake has risen, springs back when gently pressed, and a cake taster or toothpick comes out with just a few moist crumbs, 50 to 55 minutes. Transfer the pan to a wire rack to cool for about 10 minutes. Using a paring knife, loosen the cake around the edges and unmold. Peel off the parchment, turn it right side up, and return to the rack to cool completely before cutting, at least 2 hours.

½ cup (65 g) finely chopped dried tart cherries

2 tablespoons Marsala wine or apple juice

1 cup (130 g) whole grain Kamut flour

½ cup (40 g) unsweetened Dutch-process cocoa powder

¾ teaspoon baking powder

¼ teaspoon baking soda

¼ teaspoon fine sea salt

½ cup (8 tablespoons) unsalted butter, softened

1 cup (200 g) granulated sugar

1 tablespoon honey

4 large eggs, at room temperature

2 teaspoons vanilla extract

½ cup well-shaken low-fat buttermilk

½ cup (75 g) finely chopped dark chocolate (70 percent cocoa)

MAKES 1 LOAF, TO SERVE 12 TO 16

continued >

½ cup dried tart cherries

**¼ cup dry or medium-dry
Marsala wine**

1½ cups heavy whipping cream

2 tablespoons granulated sugar

marsala cream

For best outcome, soak the cherries in the morning, at least 6 hours ahead, or the day before.

Add the cherries and the Marsala to a small bowl and allow to macerate for at least 6 hours or overnight. (If you're in a rush, you can add them to a microwave-safe bowl and heat on high until hot, about 25 seconds. Allow to cool.) Drain, reserving the wine.

Add the cream and the sugar and 1 tablespoon of the soaking liquid to a medium bowl and whip, using an electric mixer at medium speed, until soft peaks form. Gently fold in the cherries with a spatula.

Serve each slice of the cake with a dollop of the cream.

fine points

Be sure to chop cherries and chocolate into ¼-inch pieces so they distribute better.

MAKE AHEAD The cake's flavor improves if made at least a few hours ahead or the day before. Store in an airtight container at room temperature or wrap in plastic wrap. It will be terrific for at least 3 days and freezes beautifully for 1 month. Thaw at room temperature and refresh in the microwave for 15 seconds or so per slice.

lemon-scented blondies with millet and white chocolate

Needless to say that serving a sweet treat is an effortless way of introducing family and friends to new grains. Tiny golden millet, often decried as bird food, shines beautifully in these mouthwatering fudgy and dense blondies. I use two types of the grain here: the flour with its interesting bittersweet edge and the whole seeds. Their slight crunch enhances the texture of these bites; the seeds on top make them pop. gluten-free

---

Position a rack in the center of the oven and preheat to 350°F. Lightly butter the bottom of an 8 by 8 by 2-inch square baking pan. Place a 13 by 13-inch piece of parchment paper in the pan, folding it into the corners with a bit of overhang all around.

In a medium bowl, whisk together the flour, 2 tablespoons of the millet seeds, baking powder, and salt. In a large bowl, using an electric mixer at medium speed, beat the almond butter and the butter until smooth, about 30 seconds. Add the brown sugar gradually and continue beating until creamy, about 1 minute, scraping the sides as needed. Beat in the eggs, one at a time, until well blended, followed by the limoncello, zest, and vanilla. Decrease the speed to low and gradually add the flour mixture until just blended. Fold in the chocolate with a spatula. Scrape the thick batter into the pan, evening out the top. Sprinkle with the remaining 1 tablespoon millet and the turbinado sugar.

Bake until the edges turn light golden brown and a cake tester or toothpick inserted into the center comes out just with a few moist crumbs, about 25 minutes.

Transfer the pan to a wire rack to cool completely, at least 1 hour before cutting. Grabbing the parchment, carefully lift the blondies out of the pan. Peel off the parchment paper and transfer to a wooden board. Cut with a long, sharp thin-bladed knife into 16 squares, or 24 smaller pieces if you prefer.

fine points

I learned, growing up in Germany and Greece, that a minuscule amount of alcohol, much of which will bake out, rounds out flavors in baked goods. Omit if you must.

¾ cup plus 1 tablespoon (100 g) whole-grain millet flour

3 tablespoons (35 g) uncooked millet seeds

1 teaspoon baking powder

¼ teaspoon fine sea salt

¾ cup (200 g) creamy almond butter, preferably toasted

¼ cup (4 tablespoons) unsalted butter, cut into 4 pieces, softened

¾ cup minus 2 tablespoons (125 g) packed light brown sugar

2 large eggs, at room temperature

1 tablespoon limoncello or brandy

2 teaspoons finely grated lemon zest (from about 1 lemon, preferably organic)

½ teaspoon vanilla extract

⅔ cup (100 g) coarsely chopped white chocolate (about ½-inch pieces)

About 1 tablespoon turbinado sugar, for sprinkling

MAKES 16 SQUARES, OR 24 SMALLER BITES

jugu cakes: east african–indian peanut biscotti

3 cups (375 g) whole roasted
unsalted peanuts

1 cup plus 2 tablespoons (225 g)
granulated sugar, plus 2 to
3 teaspoons for sprinkling

2 cups minus 2 tablespoons
(225 g) white whole wheat flour

1 teaspoon cardamom,
preferably freshly ground

1¼ teaspoons baking powder

¾ teaspoon baking soda

½ teaspoon fine sea salt

6 tablespoons (85 g) chilled
unsalted butter, cut into
½-inch pieces

½ cup whole or low-fat milk,
plus a few tablespoons more,
as needed

1 large egg, lightly beaten with
2 teaspoons water, for the egg
wash

**MAKES ABOUT 36 SIX-INCH
BISCOTTI**

This biscotti has traveled halfway around the world. It is called a jugu cake in my husband's family, and I have been enamored with it from my first bite—by its tender texture, but also by the combination of ingredients. And what a biscotti it is, with the roots of my husband's family baked right into it (see sidebar).

During a visit to Toronto, I asked my mother-in-law to help me with a whole grain version. Jugu cakes are typically baked only once, which creates an enchanting soft cookie with a more pronounced peanut flavor. As a result, I usually remove some of the cookies to a tight-fitting container to be eaten within 5 days or so. I then double-bake the rest to keep longer, like a traditional Italian biscotti (*biscotti* literally means "twice-baked").

Place parchment paper or a nonstick liner on a large rimless baking sheet. Add the peanuts and 6 tablespoons of the sugar to the bowl of a food processor, fitted with a steel blade. Process until the nuts are ground, not too fine, stopping once in between to stir with a spatula, 18 to 20 seconds total. The mixture should look like pinhead oatmeal.

Tip the nut-sugar mixture into a large bowl. Add the remaining ¾ cup sugar, the flour, cardamom, baking powder, baking soda, and salt and whisk well to combine. Distribute the butter across the surface and, using your fingers or a pastry blender, quickly rub the butter into the dry ingredients until it is well distributed and the mixture resembles coarse bread crumbs with a few pea-size pebbles. Drizzle the milk across, in two additions, and stir with a spatula until you have a lumpy dough. Very lightly oil your hands and gently knead to combine until you have a soft smooth dough, adding a bit more milk by the tablespoon if needed. The dough will be slightly sticky.

Divide the dough in half. Lightly grease your work surface with olive oil or cooking spray. Very lightly oil your hands as well and gently roll each piece into a log, about 15 inches long. (If your dough is a bit too sticky to handle, use lightly floured hands and a lightly floured surface instead.) Place the logs lengthwise next to each other onto the baking sheet, leaving at least 3 inches in between (logs will spread!) Gently pat them down to about 2 inches wide. Chill the baking sheet with the logs for 30 minutes.

Meanwhile, place a rack in the center of the oven and preheat to 350°F.

Once the logs are chilled, brush each with some of the egg wash and sprinkle with sugar.

Bake until the tops of the logs are golden brown with many cracks—they will still be soft when gently pressed, about 30 minutes. The logs will spread to about 5 inches wide and 17 inches long.

Remove and carefully slide the parchment paper with the logs to a wire rack to cool for 30 minutes. Meanwhile, line two baking sheets with parchment paper and place one rack in the top third of the oven and one in the bottom third. Decrease the oven temperature to 300°F.

Carefully loosen the logs from the parchment paper with a wide spatula or the flat side of a large knife, and transfer them to a large cutting board. Using a long serrated knife, cut each log on the diagonal into ¾-inch-thick slices. Handle gently, as the dough might still be a bit soft. Transfer the slices to the baking sheets cut side down.

Bake until the biscotti are firm to the touch and turn golden brown on top, 25 to 30 minutes more, rotating the baking sheets halfway, front to back and top to bottom, for even baking. Remove and carefully slide the parchment paper with the biscotti onto a cooling rack and allow to cool completely before storing.

fine points

These are delicious right away, but even better starting the next day as the flavors meld.

My mother-in-law uses raw skin-on peanuts, which add their own distinct, slightly bitter note. If you find some, you can use them instead of the roasted kind—no need to toast them ahead.

JUGU CAKES

My husband's roots span the globe like the jugu cake biscotti I learned to love in his family. His entrepreneurial grandfather traveled to East Africa from a small village in India as a young man looking for work. Soon he labored on a plantation in Zanzibar, eventually buying a clove farm with a business partner. (For reasons that will be forever mysterious to me, one of the few places around the world I always wanted to visit was Zanzibar, well before I ever met my husband.) He also ran a bicycle rental, started with a loan from a wealthy man people called the King of Kigoma. Later he built a general store in Tabora, the town where my husband was born.

Political turmoil in neighboring Uganda forced many Indians to flee East Africa in 1972, including my in-laws, who ended up in Toronto to start a challenging new life. The biscotti recipe traveled with them, a family favorite that is always baked in abundance when we visit.

My mother-in-law remembers first having jugu cakes, also called peanut or karanga ja biscuits, growing up in Dar es Salaam in Tanzania. On holidays, her family would flock to a popular bakery to pick up sweets, including these soft biscotti-style treats with the flavors of India and Africa baked right into them.

When she taught me her recipe, I posted a picture of her retro forest-green kitchen scale on Instagram. People loved it, I told her later on the phone, after we had returned home to the Boston area. There was a pause. Visibly moved, she said quietly no one ever had asked for her jugu cake recipe.

nantucket cranberry cake with currants and grand marnier

½ cup (65 g) dried currants

3 tablespoons (30 g) finely chopped candied orange

2 tablespoons Grand Marnier or brandy or freshly squeezed orange juice

2 cups (200 g) fresh or frozen cranberries (do not thaw if using frozen)

½ cup plus 2 tablespoons (125 g) granulated sugar, plus 2 teaspoons for sprinkling

2 teaspoons finely grated orange zest

1 cup (110 g) whole wheat pastry flour

¼ teaspoon fine sea salt

2 tablespoons honey

½ teaspoon vanilla extract

6 tablespoons (85 g) unsalted butter, preferably higher-fat Irish butter or Plugrá, melted and cooled

2 large eggs, at room temperature, lightly beaten

1 to 3 tablespoons heavy cream, as needed

MAKES ONE 8-INCH CAKE, TO SERVE 8

fine points

If you can't get good-quality candied orange (see "Sources," page 251), increase the amount of orange zest to 1 tablespoon and use ¼ cup (50 g) sugar (instead of 2 tablespoons) for the cranberries.

MAKE AHEAD The texture of this cake improves when made several hours ahead.

This beautiful cranberry-studded pie is my take on a homey holiday dessert rooted in the Northeast where I live. My whole grain version is inspired by a recipe by the late Laurie Colwin. I instantly fell in love with Laurie when I first read *Home Cooking*, for her fresh writing and down-to-earth cooking, but especially because of her unabashed admission of being a homebody who is not keen on travel. I felt I finally met my soul mate.

My cake adds significantly less sugar than traditional recipes. A small addition of honey gives this crustless pie dense appeal. Serve with a dollop of crème fraîche or softly whipped cream, ever so slightly sweetened if you like.

Place a rack in the center of the oven and preheat to 350°F. Thoroughly butter an 8 by 2-inch pie pan.

Add the currants and candied orange to a small bowl and drizzle with the liqueur. Set aside, stirring once or twice, while you prep the ingredients. Add the cranberries to a medium bowl and stir in 2 tablespoons of the sugar and 1 teaspoon of the zest. Set aside as well.

Just before mixing the batter, add the dried fruit, including any liquid, to the cranberry mixture and stir to combine. Scrape the fruit mixture into the pie pan and gently spread it to create an even layer.

Add the flour, the remaining ½ cup sugar, and the salt to a large bowl and whisk thoroughly to combine. Make a well in the center. Add the honey, the remaining 1 teaspoon zest, and the vanilla to the melted butter in a small bowl, combine well, and add to the center of the flour mixture. Pour in the eggs. Using a dough whisk (see page 21) or a spatula, gently combine the ingredients, starting from the center, until well blended. The batter should be creamy with a thick pourable consistency. If not, adjust by gently stirring in a bit of heavy cream by the tablespoon.

Scrape the batter, using a spatula, across the fruit mixture, evening out the top and gently spreading it into the corners. A few cranberries might peek out.

Bake until the top has the color of light caramel, the cake's edges turn brown, and a cake tester or toothpick inserted into the center comes out clean, 40 to 45 minutes. Transfer to a wire rack and immediately sprinkle with the 2 teaspoons sugar. Cover with a clean dish cloth and allow to cool completely, at least 2 hours. Cut, using a sharp knife, into 8 pieces and serve at room temperature.

amaranth pudding with amaretto cream

If you don't know if you like an ancient grain, just make dessert with it. Case in point, this easy delightful amaranth pudding. It is creamy and comforting, with a bit of crunch from the tiny seeds, reminiscent of mini tapioca. I have dressed this dessert up for the holidays, with crisp amaretti cookies and a dollop of liqueur-infused cream. Actually, this is how I *always* make this pudding. It's too good! If possible, prepare the dessert a couple of hours ahead to allow the flavors to deepen. ⬛ gluten-free

To make the pudding, add the 2 cups water, the amaranth, zest, and cinnamon stick to a heavy 4-quart saucepan and bring to a boil over medium-high heat, stirring once or twice with a wooden spoon. Decrease the heat to maintain a simmer, cover, and cook for 15 minutes. Stir well, add more water if the grains stick to the bottom of the pan, cover, and simmer for about 5 minutes more, until the grain is tender and translucent. Remove and discard the zest and the cinnamon stick.

Stir in the half-and-half, turbinado sugar, vanilla, and salt and return to a simmer, stirring continuously. Decrease the heat to maintain a gentle bubble. Cook, uncovered and stirring often and vigorously, until the mixture resembles a thick porridge, 3 to 5 minutes more (watch not to burn yourself, as the grain can splatter when it bubbles up!). Stir in the amaretto and ½ teaspoon of the zest. Spoon the pudding into individual small bowls. Allow to cool at room temperature, about 1 hour. Cover with plastic wrap and chill for at least 1 hour (or up to 2 days).

When ready to serve, make the amaretto cream: Whip the cream, confectioners' sugar, and amaretto in a large bowl with an electric mixer at medium speed until soft peaks form. Crush 6 of the cookies between your fingers to get coarse crumbs.

To finish, evenly distribute the crumbs across the top of each pudding (about 1 tablespoon each) and spoon a generous dollop of whipping cream on top. Garnish each bowl with 1 whole cookie and sprinkle with the remaining 1 teaspoon zest.

fine points

Don't rinse amaranth seeds, as you might lose them, even in a fine-mesh sieve.

VARIATION For a little less indulgent everyday pudding, you can replace the half-and-half with 1 cup whole milk.

PUDDING

2 cups water, plus about ¼ cup as needed

1 cup amaranth grains

1 (4-inch) strip lemon zest, white pith removed

½ cinnamon stick (about 1½ inches)

1 cup half-and-half

¼ cup (50 g) turbinado sugar

½ teaspoon vanilla extract

Pinch of fine sea salt

2 teaspoons amaretto liqueur (optional)

1½ teaspoons finely grated lemon zest, preferably organic

AMARETTO CREAM

¾ cup chilled heavy whipping cream

1 tablespoon confectioners' sugar

1 tablespoon amaretto liqueur (optional)

12 amaretti cookies (or almond-flavored gluten-free cookies)

SERVES 6

barley thumbprints with honey and hazelnuts

1¾ cups (200 g) whole toasted hazelnuts

1¾ cups (200 g) whole grain barley flour

½ teaspoon ground cinnamon

½ teaspoon baking soda

½ teaspoon fine sea salt

½ cup extra-virgin olive oil

½ cup honey

4 teaspoons finely grated grapefruit zest (from about 1 fruit, preferably organic)

1 to 2 tablespoons milk, as needed

About ⅓ cup (100 g) apricot jam, preferably reduced in sugar, for the filling, or 32 whole toasted hazelnuts to garnish

MAKES ABOUT 32 TWO-INCH COOKIES

Blogger extraordinaire Tim Mazurek of *Lottie + Doof* introduced me to a barley thumbprint by Gwyneth Paltrow's mom and I couldn't get them out of my mind. I adore the malty-sweet aroma of whole grain barley flour, and the cookies looked beautiful. Never someone to leave a recipe as is, I ended up turning the original upside down: I used hazelnuts instead of almonds, honey replaced the maple syrup, and fruity olive oil, paired with the mellow scent of grapefruit, rooted them firmly in the Mediterranean. Two years of tinkering and seven rounds of tests later, these disappear as fast as they appear on the table.

Add the hazelnuts to the bowl of a food processor, fitted with a metal blade. Pulse until the nuts are finely chopped with most pieces the consistency of pinhead oatmeal and a few slightly larger ones, about ten 1-second pulses. Or chop the hazelnuts by hand.

Add the flour, cinnamon, baking soda, and salt to a large bowl and thoroughly whisk together. Add the chopped nuts and whisk well again, then make a well in the center.

Add the olive oil, honey, and zest to a medium bowl with tall sides and whisk until the mixture is thoroughly blended and turns opaque, about 1 minute. Pour the oil mixture into the center of the flour mixture. Working from the center, combine the wet and dry ingredients with a dough whisk (see page 21) or a wooden spoon. When much of the flour is incorporated, bring the dough together with a few gentle turns—it should be soft and moist. If it is dry, gently knead in a tablespoon or two of milk. Cover the bowl with a plate and set aside for 25 minutes.

Meanwhile, place one rack in the top third of the oven and one in the bottom third and preheat to 325°F. Line two large rimless baking sheets with parchment paper.

Once the dough has rested, divide it in half, working with one half per baking sheet and keeping the remaining dough covered. Using about 1 heaped tablespoon at a time, roll the dough into 1½-inch balls. If the dough cracks, gently press and roll until smooth. Place the balls onto the baking sheets, spacing them about 2 inches apart. Using the thick end of a wooden spoon (about ½ inch) or your thumb or index finger, gently press each ball down to flatten by about a third—don't worry about some cracking—then fill the indentation with about ½ teaspoon jam. If you use hazelnuts, don't make an indentation but press the nut in while gently holding the thumbprint with your other hand.

continued >

Bake until the cookies firm up and are deep golden brown all around but still yield slightly when gently pressed with a finger, rotating the sheets once halfway from front to back and top to bottom, 23 to 25 minutes total. Carefully slide the cookies with the parchment paper onto a wire rack to cool completely. They will firm up as they cool.

fine points

You really want these to brown deeply. Trust me!

A smooth sugar-reduced apricot jam from Trader Joe's is lovely here, but any type will do; strain it through a sieve if it is chunky.

Lemon zest can be used instead of grapefruit. Pair with yuzu or orange marmalade for a treat!

Thumbprints will keep at least 5 days in an airtight container. The jam-filled ones will inevitably soften, in grace, when stored. If you like a crisp thumbprint, fill them with nuts. Thumbprints freeze well for 1 month.

panpepato: chocolate nut domes with spelt flour

Crunchy, chewy mounds of dark chocolate, nuts, and candied fruit, yet not overly sweet—this is the treat I crave during the holidays. These delectable sweets were adapted from a recipe for *panpepato* from the Italian region of Umbria in the magazine *La Cucina Italiana*. Of course, I swapped all-purpose for a traditional ancient wheat flour and shrank them considerably in size to about a third of the original. And, as we do in Greece, I spiked them with a bit of booze (much of which will bake off) to enhance flavor.

Add the candied orange and the raisins to a small bowl and stir in the liqueur. Set aside for about 15 minutes, stirring once or twice.

Meanwhile, add the walnuts, almonds, and hazelnuts to a medium skillet and toast over medium heat until fragrant, shaking the pan a few times, about 5 minutes. Tip onto a wooden cutting board, allow to cool, then coarsely chop (you should have 1 slightly heaped cup).

Add the nuts, chocolate, pepper, cinnamon, nutmeg, and salt to a medium bowl. Drain the macerated fruit, reserving the plumping liquid, and add to the bowl as well.

In a small saucepan over medium heat, bring the honey and 3 tablespoons plumping liquid (add water if you don't have enough) to a simmer. Stir the liquid mixture into the nut mixture, set aside for 1 minute, then stir again until the chocolate is melted. Gradually sprinkle the flour across while gently stirring with a wooden spoon until just combined. Cover (chill on a humid day) and allow to rest at room temperature for 25 minutes for the bran to soften.

Meanwhile, position a rack in the center of the oven and preheat to 350°F. Line a baking sheet with parchment paper.

Use a rounded tablespoon of the chunky dough to create mounds about 1½ inches in diameter. Place on the baking sheet, leaving about 1 inch between pieces; they will not spread. Garnish each mound with a sliver of candied orange.

Bake until the tops appear matte and the mounds have firmed up but still yield a bit when gently pressed with a finger, 10 to 15 minutes. Remove and slide the cookies together with the parchment paper onto a wire rack to cool completely before storing; they will firm up as they cool.

¼ cup (40 g) chopped candied orange or lemon, plus 1 to 2 tablespoons, cut into thin slivers, for garnish

⅓ cup (45 g) golden raisins

3 tablespoons Grand Marnier or brandy

½ cup (50 g) walnut halves and chunks

¼ cup (35 g) whole almonds, skin-on

¼ cup (35 g) whole hazelnuts (filberts)

½ cup (70 g) coarsely chopped dark chocolate (70 percent cocoa)

¾ teaspoon coarsely ground fresh black pepper

¼ teaspoon ground cinnamon

⅛ teaspoon nutmeg, preferably freshly ground

Pinch of fine sea salt

⅓ cup honey

½ cup (60 g) whole grain spelt flour

MAKES ABOUT 22 BITE-SIZE MOUNDS

fine points

White whole wheat flour can be used but brings less character to this sweet.

MAKE AHEAD These are infinitely richer in flavor when made 1 day ahead. They will last for at least a week, stored in an airtight container, layered between sheets of parchment paper.

just fruit holiday cake

⅔ cup (100 g) golden raisins

⅔ cup (100 g) dark raisins

¾ cup (100 g) finely chopped good-quality candied orange

½ cup (75 g) finely chopped dried apricots, preferably Blenheim

½ cup (75 g) finely chopped dried prunes

¾ cup amaretto liqueur, brandy, or apple juice, plus extra for feeding (see sidebar)

1 tablespoon finely grated orange zest (from about 1 orange, preferably organic)

2 teaspoons finely grated lemon zest (from about 1 lemon, preferably organic)

½ cup extra-virgin olive oil or vegetable oil

¼ cup (50 g) turbinado sugar

1 cup (120 g) white whole wheat flour

¾ teaspoon baking powder

¾ teaspoon ground cinnamon

¼ teaspoon cardamom, preferably freshly ground

¼ teaspoon cloves, preferably freshly ground

⅛ teaspoon allspice, preferably freshly ground

¼ teaspoon fine sea salt

¾ cup (100 g) whole skin-on or blanched almonds, plus 11 whole skin-on almonds (optional), for garnish

2 large eggs, lightly beaten and at room temperature

MAKES ONE 8-INCH CAKE, TO SERVE 12

Dried fruits are cherished in many cultures for the sweet bliss they bring to the darker months of the year when fresh fruits were traditionally not available (see "Glorious Dried Fruit," page 210). I created this intensely aromatic cake, packed with a colorful medley of dried fruit, and barely sweetened, in this spirit. Most important, it is dead-easy in an old-fashioned "one-bowl, one-spoon" kind of way—perfect for this time of year where we often feel a little breathless. Once you've chopped the fruits (put on some music and sing), you are practically done.

My impatient self believes this cakes tastes marvelous after a day or two. But, admittedly, if made a few weeks ahead and spiked with more amaretto, it develops an intense complexity with intoxicating hints of marzipan to make it worth your wait. Delicious on a winter day with a good cup of hot tea, or for dessert with vanilla ice cream, or really anytime!

Add all of the dried fruits, the amaretto, and both kinds of zest to a large heavy saucepan, stir to combine, and bring to a boil over medium-high heat. Reduce the heat to maintain a lively simmer, cover, and cook, stirring once or twice, until only a syrupy liquid remains at the bottom, 5 to 7 minutes. Add the olive oil and the sugar and cook, stirring, until the sugar is dissolved, about 1 minute. Remove the saucepan from the heat and allow to cool, uncovered, until lukewarm to the touch, about 20 minutes.

Meanwhile, position a rack in the center of the oven and preheat to 300°F. Lightly grease or spray an 8-inch metal cake pan with olive oil. Cut a piece of parchment the size of the bottom and place it in the pan; lightly grease the paper as well. Dust the pan with flour, tapping out excess. In a medium bowl, whisk together the flour, baking powder, cinnamon, cardamom, cloves, allspice, and salt.

Stir the almonds into the fruit mixture, followed by the eggs. Add the flour mixture in four additions—a ⅓-cup measuring cup helps—stirring until no white streaks remain. Do not overmix. Scrape the dough into the cake pan, evening out the top with the back of the spoon. Decorate the cake by spacing 8 almonds evenly around the outer rim, gently pressing them in, and 3 into the center to resemble flower petals.

Bake until the cake is evenly golden brown and a toothpick inserted into the center comes out clean, 45 to 50 minutes. Transfer to a wire rack and allow to cool in the pan for about 1 hour, then loosen the cake around the edges with a paring knife to unmold it. Return to the rack upside down and allow to cool completely, about 2 hours more. Remove the parchment paper and wrap in plastic wrap for at least 1 day for the flavors to meld. Cut into wedges with a long sharp knife.

fine points

Good-quality dried fruits are a are essential here, especially for the candied orange peel (see "Sources," page 251).

VARIATION Feel free to use other dried fruit such as currants, figs, apples, or cherries. You will need 1 pound (450 g, or a scant 3½ cups finely chopped).

HOW TO FEED YOUR CAKE TO MAKE IT LAST

"Feeding" dried fruitcakes with aromatic spirits, usually brandy, goes back less than two hundred years, explains my colleague and cookbook author Anne Bramley. It is a traditional British way of "enriching the flavor while also extending the life of the cake." After baking, wrap the cake in two layers of plastic wrap and store in an airtight container. About every 2 weeks, unwrap the cake and poke it all over the top with a skewer or a toothpick and brush on about 1 tablespoon amaretto or other liqueur. Allow to seep in, rewrap, and return to the container. Of course, I always cut some to eat at that point and feed only the remaining portion. But in theory, your cake could last for up to 3 months.

candied squash torte with chocolate and hazelnut praline

This festive fall cake is my kind of indulgence, yet it has just a few easy steps that can all be made ahead: a crisp nutty crumb crust with a thin layer of chocolate, topped with maple-infused candied squash and sprinkled with a crunchy hazelnut praline. Most important, it is a soulful dessert yet light and not too sweet, something I appreciate especially during the holidays.

This seasonal dessert was born out of my own need for simplicity as I prepared my very first Thanksgiving turkey in this country, my adopted home. A recipe by food writer extraordinaire Melissa Clark inspired the candied squash filling. I like it so much I now sometimes make it just to spoon onto a bowl of tangy Greek yogurt or on my morning muesli.

First, prepare the hazelnut praline: Place a sheet of parchment paper on a small baking sheet. Sprinkle the sugar evenly across the bottom of an 8-inch heavy saucepan or skillet, preferably stainless steel. Heat over medium heat, gently swirling the pot but without stirring, until the sugar starts to melt and turns amber, 4 to 5 minutes. Add the nuts and stir with a fork to coat them while closely (!) watching the color of the caramel: within 30 to 60 seconds it will turn a deep dark brown, lightly froth at the edges of the pan, and start to smoke. Immediately scrape the nut mixture onto the baking sheet and spread to flatten as best you can. Allow to cool completely, about 30 minutes, then transfer to a cutting board and coarsely chop with a serrated knife. I like to leave a few nuts whole.

While the praline cools, prepare the chocolate crumb crust: Position a rack in the center of the oven and preheat to 325°F. Place a 9½-inch metal tart pan with removable bottom on a rimless baking sheet for easier handling.

Add the crackers, nuts, sugar, and salt to the bowl of a food processor, fitted with a steel blade. Process until finely ground with a few tiny nut pieces still visible, about 15 seconds. Drizzle the butter across and pulse until the mixture resembles wet sand, about five 1-second pulses. Scrape the crumb mixture into the tart pan. Press in firmly and evenly, using your hands or the bottom of a ½-cup measuring cup, creating a 1-inch rim, about ¼ inch thick.

Bake until the crust is fragrant and slightly darkened, about 15 minutes. Remove and carefully slide the tart pan onto a wire rack to cool, about 30 minutes.

HAZELNUT PRALINE

¼ cup (50 g) granulated sugar

½ cup (65 g) toasted whole hazelnuts

CHOCOLATE CRUMB CRUST

16½ (145 g) whole wheat crackers, broken into chunks

Scant ½ cup (55 g) toasted whole hazelnuts

1 tablespoon turbinado sugar (optional)

Pinch of fine sea salt

6 tablespoons (85 g) unsalted butter, melted and cooled, preferably European-style

About ⅔ cup (100 g) coarsely chopped semisweet chocolate (55 to 60 percent cocoa)

CANDIED SQUASH

¼ cup plus 2 tablespoons maple syrup, preferably Grade B

4 cups (500 g) cubed butternut squash (¼- to ½-inch pieces, from about 1¾ pounds)

2 tablespoons limoncello

1 teaspoon freshly squeezed lemon juice

Softly whipped cream or crème fraîche, for serving

SERVES 8

continued >

While the crust is cooling, prepare the candied squash: Have a plate at the ready. Add the maple syrup to a large skillet and bring to a brisk simmer over medium-high heat. Add the squash and spread it into an even layer. Decrease the heat to maintain the brisk simmer, cover, and cook until the pieces are soft when pierced with a knife, 5 to 7 minutes. Uncover, increase the heat to medium, and continue the brisk simmer until the squash darkens and starts to caramelize—the maple syrup will become very foamy and the pan will turn dry in spots, 7 to 9 minutes more (typically less for precut squash). Drizzle with the limoncello and cook until syrupy, about 30 seconds. Immediately transfer the squash to a plate. Drizzle on the lemon juice and allow to cool, about 20 minutes.

Once the crust has cooled, add the chocolate to a microwave-safe bowl and heat on high for 1 minute, stirring once halfway. Repeat, in 20-second intervals and stirring well in between, until melted (or melt over a water bath in a large metal bowl set over a saucepan of barely simmering water, stirring gently; the bottom of the bowl should not touch the water). Spoon the chocolate across the crust and spread it with a pastry brush all around and up the sides as best you can (don't worry if a few crumbs come loose). Set aside until set, about 50 minutes, or chill for 15 to 20 minutes.

To finish, 1 to 2 hours ahead, spoon the candied squash across the crust. Just before serving, sprinkle with the hazelnut praline and cut, using a large sharp knife, into 8 pieces. Serve with a dollop of cream.

fine points

While any graham crackers will work, I suggest you use 100% whole wheat crackers (Carr's brand), as they are the perfect marriage for the squash filling and the nutty praline.

For a more adult version, I use bittersweet chocolate with 70 percent cocoa.

You can replace half the butter in the crust with 3 tablespoons olive oil, but with butter the crust holds up best.

MAKE AHEAD All three parts can be made ahead. The hazelnut praline can be made up to 5 days ahead; store in an airtight container. The crust (with or without the chocolate layer) and the candied squash can be made 1 day ahead. Keep the crust at room temperature under a cake dome or a large turned-over bowl. Chill the squash, covered; bring to room temperature before serving, about 1 hour.

EASY HOMEMADE PRALINE

Making a caramel for praline can be a little intimidating. But once you understand the basic principle, it couldn't be easier. All in all it just takes a few minutes. And you can use pretty much any nuts you fancy. Just be sure to have a parchment paper–lined baking sheet close by.

Caramel tastes most amazing the moment it turns from sweet to bitter, meaning just before it starts to burn. So be attentive after adding the nuts to the melted sugar. As soon as you see foam at the edges of the pan and a bit of smoke, you have to be fast because your caramel can burn in an instant. So watch closely as the color of the caramel turns and immediately remove the pot from the heat and scrape the nuts onto the baking sheet. The first time I made praline again after many years, I noticed the smoke and thought I had gone too far. Then I read a story by cook, baker, and über-blogger David Lebovitz, and he assured me that this was the way it was meant to be. Relief! And the praline was perfect.

ingredients & techniques

aleppo pepper

If you have never tried Aleppo pepper, get ready to get addicted to its entrancing character—from intensely fruity to smoky with just the right kick from heat, more subtle than spicy-hot. This coarse dried chile from Turkey, locally known as *pul biber*, is named after the city of Aleppo in Syria. Ever since I had my first taste years ago, Aleppo pepper is the first spice I reach for almost every day.

almond meal

Almond meal, simply ground almonds, has become widely available. But you can always make your own. Process 1 cup skin-on almonds in a food processor, using the metal blade, until finely ground, about 35 seconds. You want to keep a close eye on them, as the mixture can turn quickly into an oily paste. This yields about 1⅓ cups almond meal.

cardamom sugar

I always have at least one or two flavored sugars on hand to sprinkle onto warm breakfast grains, a bowl of yogurt, or a slice of buttered toast. Sometimes I sweeten my Greek coffee with it, which transforms it into Lebanese coffee.

For best aroma, I recommend making cardamom sugar from the freshly ground seeds of green cardamom pods. As a rule of thumb, you need about 1 tablespoon ground cardamom (from 24 to 30 pods) for 1 cup sugar. You can add the seeds to a clean coffee grinder together with 2 tablespoons of the sugar. Grind until pulverized, then add the flavored sugar to the remaining sugar and combine well. If you don't mind a little upper arm workout, you can grind the seeds with a mortar and pestle. I do this for smaller amounts. Store cardamom sugar in an airtight container at room temperature. Its flavor will last at least 2 months.

coriander sugar

The coriander sugar created by mistake for the Overnight Waffles with Teff, Coriander, and Caramelized Pineapples (page 60) turned out to be a boon in my kitchen. We have become so smitten by its citrus aroma that I suggest you make about double of what you'll need. I like it especially in my afternoon espresso where the coriander adds delicate lemon notes. Or use it to sweeten your bowl of morning oats, sprinkle it on a slice of whole grain toast with butter, or add a splendid perfumed accent to fresh strawberries or bananas.

I suggest you use whole coriander seeds for the best flavor. To make about ½ cup coriander sugar, grind 4 teaspoons whole coriander seeds in a spice grinder or with a mortar and combine well with ½ cup turbinado sugar. Store the coriander sugar in an airtight jar in a cool, dark place.

dried mint

Does your dried mint taste dusty first and minty second? Look for a different source. Dried mint is great to stock in your pantry (see "Sources," page 251), as it can enhance many dishes throughout the year. Add it to yogurt dressings or yogurt sauce, soups, and sautéed vegetables, or use it in a rub for roasted chicken or leg of lamb.

I typically grow and dry my own mint, with spearmint being my first choice for drying. I simply tie a few stems together, rinsed and gently patted dry. Then I hang the bundle upside down anywhere in my kitchen, on a curtain rod or a little-used knob, for about 2 weeks, or until completely dry. The leaves should be brittle when crushed. If you like (I never bother) you can also slip the whole bundle into a roomy paper bag before you hang it up so your herbs don't get dusty. Once the leaves are dry, I cover my work surface with a piece of paper or newspaper and rub the mint leaves off their stems. Label and store the dried mint in a lidded glass jar. It will last in a cool, dark place for about 1 year.

nigella seeds

Pitch-dark nigella seeds, with their strong, pungent aroma, are often sprinkled on pita bread or the Indian flatbread naan (see "Sources," page 251). *Nigella sativa*, also called black cumin, has been valued for centuries for its medicinal properties, especially in the Middle East and Southeast Asia. It is sometimes mistakenly called black sesame or onion seeds.

shell-on shrimp

I'm a huge fan of shell-on shrimp because the shells make for an infinitely more aromatic sauce. In addition, you know this probably intuitively, they also add their flavor to the crustaceans during high-heat searing. I learned this great bit of food science from the smart folks at *Cook's Illustrated*. Leaving the shells on makes it a bit messier to eat, but I am never shy to use my fingers at home.

I prefer to buy frozen shrimp because shrimp on display at the fish counter have often been previously frozen and may have been there longer than you might like.

vermouth

I strongly recommend you use dry vermouth, ideally a freshly opened bottle—not the one you forgot in your liquor cabinet (I'm as guilty as anyone!). The vermouth does not need to be expensive, but its freshness makes a difference. Only when I researched did I learn how crucial this is. Here's why: Vermouth is a fortified wine, made from a combination of sometimes up to 30 different herbs, which gives it a light floral sweetness. Its delicate mix of botanicals shines in simple recipes such as the Saffron-Infused Tomato Sauce with Vermouth (page 172).

But vermouth is also prone to spoilage, especially if you keep it at room temperature in a whiskey cabinet as so many of us do. This is due to its alcohol content, which can be as low as 16% (as in some wines), explains the duo behind the Paupered Chef—Blake Royer and Nick Kindelsperger on the blog *Serious Eats*.

I then understood why my sauce almost jolted me out of my shoes that day: the faint aromas of the freshly opened vermouth worked in tandem with precious saffron, itself a fleeting scent, to create an intoxicating blend. Today, I keep my vermouth in the fridge after opening and don't allow it to linger indefinitely but rather enjoy it while it still exudes its magic.

how to clean leeks

Hauntingly sweet and tender, leeks are revered in France as well as in my native Germany—but if you don't know how to clean them, you might end up eating a bit of dirt that is often hidden between the tightly layered leaves. I used to struggle with this task until a German friend showed me a great technique.

Here is how I do it now: Remove the tough outer leaves of each stalk; cut each stalk lengthwise (but not all the way through to the other side if you want rings!), making sure to also hold it together at the base. Rinse the leek under cold running water, fanning open the leaves and cleaning out any specks of dirt found between the layers. Trim the roots and generously remove any blemished, tough, or dried-out dark green tops. Slice as needed.

dirty dozen

Organic fruits and vegetables can be expensive to shop for if you have a family or are on a budget. When my husband and I were students, we used the Environmental Working Group's Dirty Dozen list to help us make informed decisions. It lists the produce with the most pesticide residue. Because we were on a budget, we would always buy these fruits and vegetables organic. Strawberries and peaches are often on the list, so are apples and potatoes—to this day in my kitchen the produce on this list is always organic.

homemade herbes de provence

I normally don't buy spice rubs or spice mixtures because I enjoy creating new flavors by reaching into my huge selection of dried herbs and spices—with one exception, herbes de Provence. I always keep this enticing mixture from the south of France on hand because it elevates everything without being overpowering—from chicken to roasted vegetables to marinades to soups. I am especially fond of the sweet scent of dried lavender flowers, which can be almost pungent on their own but give the mix a royal twist. Create your own 2 tablespoons by combining 2 teaspoons dried fennel seeds, 2 teaspoons dried thyme, 1¼ teaspoons dried marjoram, and ¾ teaspoon dried lavender blossoms.

pomegranate molasses

No one wants to fill their cupboards with ingredients you will need only once—pomegranate molasses is not one of them. Once you start using it, you will discover endless possibilities to enhance your recipes with its intense tangy-sweet flavor, from salad dressings to rubs and marinades.

I had my first addictive taste of the dark thick syrup as a kid while traveling in Turkey, and I'm forever thankful to Yotam Ottolenghi and Sami Tamimi for making it a household name, together with many other favorite Middle Eastern ingredients. Traditionally used in the cuisines of Iran and Turkey, among others, pomegranate molasses is not a molasses but a concentrated syrup made from boiling down a tangy variety of the leather-skinned ruby-red fruit. Look for good-quality molasses without any additives.

Pomegranate molasses can solidify into one hard block. This once left me completely mystified during busy dinner preparations. My guests were about to ring the doorbell and I couldn't get a drop of syrup out of my bottle. I had no idea why the molasses didn't liquefy after I had removed it from the fridge for what seemed like an eternity. Finally it hit me. Maybe it behaves similar to honey? So I placed the bottle into a small saucepan filled with very hot water. After a few minutes, the thick syrup finally started to melt. Pomegranate molasses will last many months in a cool dark pantry, or store indefinitely in the fridge.

sources

Natural food stores and specialty stores carry most of the whole grains and whole grain flours used in this book. Here, I list online sources in case you can't locate the products locally. Some are mainstream companies with national reach; others are smaller mills and farmers worth exploring. The more familiar you become with whole grains, the more you might also want to check out local flour mills and farms. For a growing list, please visit my blog: www.mariaspeck.com/blog. My selection is subjective and by no means inclusive, but designed as a starting point to pique your interest.

ANSON MILLS

This South Carolina–based milling company is revered by chefs and culinary aficionados alike. In years of dedicated hard work, its visionary founder, Glenn Roberts, succeeded in reviving near extinct heirloom grains from before the Civil War, from corn to rice and wheat. Among them are textured and aromatic grits, cornmeal, farro, and different types of whole grain polenta. The company also sells character-rich stone-ground flours, such as a Colonial-style whole wheat and a coarse graham flour as well as buckwheat and an heirloom rye flour. In 2013, the Chefs Collaborative awarded Roberts the Pathfinder Award for being a "singular leader in the movement to restore heritage grains." www.ansonmills.com

BLUEBIRD GRAIN FARMS

For US-grown whole grain farro, check out this farm in Washington State— their organic "emmer farro" has had food lovers raving for years. The farm also grinds the grain to order into magnificent emmer flour. More recently, they have also started to sell their own einkorn wheat as *einka*. www.bluebirdgrainfarms.com

BOB'S RED MILL

If you don't have a local miller in your area (yet!) and are looking for a reliable source for all your whole grain needs, this is my number one stop. I love the company's unwavering commitment to grinding flour the old-fashioned way, in stone mills. Bob's carries a huge variety of whole grains and flours, most of them also available as organic, and its selection of gluten-free grains and flours is superb. The Oregon-based firm sells about 450 products, from stone-ground whole wheat to pumpernickel flour, from different grinds of cornmeal and polenta to whole grains such as amaranth, buckwheat, barley, millet, and teff, to rolled oats and rye flakes. Their quick-cooking wild rice is a good choice on busy weeknights. www.bobsredmill.com

COMMUNITY GRAINS

This company is fascinating not only for its delicious high-quality products but also for the vision behind it. Founder Bob Klein, owner of Oliveto restaurant in Oakland, California, is spearheading a local grains movement. By closely working with farmers, millers, and bakers, he offers his customers "true whole grains" with 100% of the germ, bran, and endosperm retained. This distinguishes his flour from conventionally milled grains where these components are first separated and then reconstituted when packaged.

Klein also promotes "identity-preserved wheat," a quality standard to trace the grain from the farmer to your product. All grains and products are grown and milled in California. Their products, including whole grain pasta with an intense rich wheatiness, are available through many Whole Foods stores and online: www.markethallfoods.com/brands .php?brand=Community-Grains

KING ARTHUR FLOUR

I have a soft spot for America's oldest flour company, founded in Boston in 1790. The Vermont-based firm is employee owned, and renowned by homemakers and professionals alike for their dedication to quality. I cherish their carefully selected baking tools and their consistent and well-performing flours. The company carries many whole grain and gluten-free flours, including white whole wheat, oat flour, and spelt flour (many of them organic). And the friendly staff at the baking hotline answer any questions you might have about succeeding with scones, muffins, cakes, and more. www.kingarthurflour.com

LENTZ SPELT FARMS

The Lentzes are among the pioneers of ancient wheat growing in North America. The organic farm in Washington State grows spelt, einkorn, and emmer, as well as *Grünkern*, better known as freekeh. Be sure to try their Camelina oil, a nutrient-rich ancient seed oil, which looks like liquid gold and tastes like heaven. www.lentzspelt.com

LOTUS FOODS

The award-winning team behind this company offers some of the best-tasting and sustainable rice varieties in the country. I have been smitten by their Chinese black rice, trademarked as Forbidden Rice, and their flavorful Bhutanese red rice. Or try any of the other varieties, often organic, such as brown jasmine rice or the quick-cooking tiny Kalijira rice, an heirloom variety from the region of Bengal. www.lotusfoods.com

SUNNYLAND MILLS

This organic bulgur wheat producer, founded in 1935, developed a number of quick-cooking products from ancient wheats, including Kamut bulgur and farro bulgur, which they sell on their website: www.sunnylandmills.com. Their delicious new freekeh bulgur is packaged and sold by Village Harvest. www.villageharvestrice.com

SPECIALTY GRAINS

EINKORN This site offers organic whole grain einkorn berries, grown in Idaho, Washington, and Canada. www.einkorn.com

The Heritage Grain Conservancy sells organic whole grain einkorn and einkorn flour, locally grown in Massachusetts by Eli Rogosa and in upstate New York. www.growseed.org

(See also Jovial Foods)

FREEKEH The roasted green wheat is becoming more widely available in stores, or get it online. Freekeh Foods offers US-grown organic freekeh. www.freekeh-foods.com

The grain from the Freekeh-licious brand is imported from Australia. www.freekehlicious.com

(See also Lentz Spelt Farms, and freekeh bulgur from Sunnyland Mills)

HAND-ROLLED MAFTOU Nancy Harmon Jenkins wrote about this delicious toothsome whole grain "bulgur couscous" from Palestine. Made like bulgur from parboiled and cracked organic wheat, it is then rolled into small couscous balls and cooks in just 15 minutes. www.canaanfairtrade.com

QUINOA FLAKES Available in health and natural food stores from the brand Ancient Harvest, or online: www.vitacost.com

WILD RICE The Anishinaabe in northern Minnesota hand-harvest extraordinary real wild rice. www.nativeharvest.com

I've enjoyed the organic variety from the Goose Valley Wild Rice company. www.goosevalley.com

TEFF The US-grown teff from Idaho is available in health food stores or online: www.teffco.com

MILLING

I'm a huge fan of traditional stone grinding of grains. For quality and beauty, the wood-encased tabletop mill of the German company KoMo GmbH can't be beat. You can buy them online: www.pleasanthillgrain.com. The site also sells other grain mills for home use.

The online seller Orb.co also offers a wide range of KoMo mill models as well as grain flakers. www.orb.com

The company KitchenAid sells a milling attachment for their stand mixers. www.kitchenaid.com

ANCIENT GRAINS PASTA

BAIA PASTA Exquisite whole wheat, spelt, and Kamut pasta made with 100% American-grown flour, and using traditional Italian methods. www.baiapasta.com

COMMUNITY GRAINS (see opposite)

EDEN FOODS North America's oldest natural and organic food company sells Kamut spaghetti in health food stores or online: www.edenfoods.com

FELICETTI Delectable farro and Kamut pasta from Italy. Get it online: www.cybercucina.com and www.thefreshmarket.com

GUSTIAMO The Italian food specialist carries amazing rustic buisate pasta from Sicily, made with heirloom Tumminia wheat. www.gustiamo.com

JOVIAL FOODS This company offers delicious einkorn pasta in many shapes, and it carries a very popular gluten-free pasta made from brown rice. In addition, Jovial offers whole einkorn berries and einkorn flour, organically grown in Italy. www.jovialfoods.com

OTHER PRODUCTS

ALEPPO PEPPER World Spice Merchants carries some of the finest Aleppo pepper. www.worldspice.com

CANDIED LEMON AND ORANGE PEEL Good-quality citrus peel is worth seeking out, as supermarket brands often lack flavor. www.magdalenecandies.com www.olivenation.com

DRIED BARBERRIES (Zereshk), ROSE PETALS, and NIGELLA SEEDS are available at the following sites: www.kalustyans.com www.nuts.com

HARISSA This spicy North African pepper paste has become more widely available. I love the one French-born chef Farid Zadi, son of Berber parents, sells online: www.z-kitchen.tumblr.com

PRESERVED LEMON, POMEGRANATE MOLASSES, AND DRIED MINT These products have become widely available in specialty sections of well-stocked markets, or buy them online: www.kalustyans.com

bibliography

Al-Hamad, Sarah. (2008). *Cardamom and Lime: Recipes from the Arabian Gulf*. Northampton, MA: Interlink Books.

Barber, Dan. (2014). *The Third Plate: Field Notes on the Future of Food*. New York: Penguin Press HC.

Bittman, Mark. (2009). *Food Matters: A Guide to Conscious Eating*. New York: Simon & Schuster.

Boyce, Kim. (2010). *Good to the Grain: Baking with Whole-Grain Flours*. New York: Stewart, Tabori and Chang.

Brennan, Georgeanne. (2001). *Olives, Anchovies, and Capers: The Secret Ingredients of the Mediterranean Table*. San Francisco: Chronicle Books.

Brown, Alton. (2004). *I'm Just Here for More Food*. New York: Stewart, Tabori and Chang.

Clark, Melissa. (2011). *Cook This Now: 120 Easy and Delectable Dishes You Can't Wait to Make*. New York: Hyperion.

Cuthbert, Pippa, & Wilson, Lindsay Cameron. (2005). *Ice Cream! Delicious Ice Creams for All Occasions*. Intercourse, PA: Good Books.

Goyoaga, Aran. (2012). *Small Plates and Sweet Treats: My Family's Journey to Gluten-Free Cooking*. New York: Little, Brown and Company.

Henry, Diana. (2005). *Roast Figs Sugar Snow: Winter Food to Warm the Soul*. London: Mitchell Beazley.

Husseini, Suzanne. (2012). *Modern Flavors of Arabia: Recipes and Memories from My Middle Eastern Kitchen*. Toronto, Canada: Appetite.

Jenkins, Nancy Harmon. (2003). *The Essential Mediterranean*. New York: Harper Collins.

Kleinberg, Ann. (2004). *Pomegranates*. Berkeley, CA: Ten Speed Press.

Kochilas, Diane. (2001). *The Glorious Foods of Greece: Traditional Recipes from the Islands, Cities, and Villages*. New York: William Morrow.

Kremezi, Aglaia. (2009). *Mediterranean Hot and Spicy*. New York: Broadway Books.

Laudan, Rachel. (2013). *Cuisine and Empire: Cooking in World History*. Berkeley, CA: University of California Press.

Madison, Deborah. (2013). *Vegetable Literacy*. Berkeley, CA: Ten Speed Press.

Malouf, Greg, & Malouf, Lucy. (2006). *Artichoke to Za'atar*. Berkeley and Los Angeles: University of California Press.

McIntosh, Susan McEwen. (2009). *Glorious Grits*. Birmingham, Alabama: Oxmoor House.

Mehdawy, Magda. (2006). *My Egyptian Grandmother's Kitchen*. Cairo: The American University in Cairo Press.

Moeller Gorman, Rachel. (September/ October 2013). "The Whole-Grain, Reduced-Fat, Zero-Calorie, High-Fiber, Ligthtly Sweetened TRUTH about Food Labels." *Eating Well* magazine.

Morgan, Diane. (2012). *Roots: The Definitive Compendium with More Than 225 Recipes*. San Francisco: Chronicle Books.

Muir, Jenni. (2002). *A Cook's Guide to Grains*. London: Conran Octopus.

Oliver, Jamie. (2014). Jamie Oliver's Food Tube. Retrieved from www.youtube.com/JamieOliver

Oppenheimer, Todd. (September 2012). "Our Daily Bread." *Whole Living* magazine.

Ottolenghi, Yotam, & Tamimi, Sami. (2013). *Ottolenghi: The Cookbook*. Berkeley, CA: Ten Speed Press.

Ottolenghi, Yotam, & Tamimi, Sami. (2012). *Jerusalem: A Cookbook*. Berkeley, CA: Ten Speed Press.

Pollan, Michael. (2013). *Cooked: A Natural History of Transformation*. New York: Penguin Press HC.

Pollan, Michael. (2009). *Food Rules: An Eater's Manual*. New York: Penguin.

Psilakis, Michael. (2009). *How to Roast a Lamb: New Greek Classic Cooking*. New York: Little, Brown and Company.

Psilakis, Nikos & Maria. (undated). *Olive Oil: The Secret of Good Health: Advice on Its Correct Use*. Crete, Greece: Karmanor.

Rowe, Silvena. (2010). *Purple Citrus and Sweet Perfume: Cuisine of the Eastern Mediterranean*. New York: Ecco.

Sass, Lorna. (2006). *Whole Grains Every Day, Every Way*. New York: Clarkson Potter.

Seaver, Barton. (2011). *For Cod and Country: Simple, Delicious, Sustainable Cooking*. New York: Sterling Epicure.

Simmons, Marie. (2004). *Fig Heaven: 70 Recipes for the World's Most Luscious Fruit*. New York: William Morrow.

Smith, Andrew F. (2007). *Oxford Companion to American Food and Drink*. Oxford and New York: Oxford University Press.

Speck, Maria. (2011). *Ancient Grains for Modern Meals: Mediterranean Whole Grain Recipes for Barley, Farro, Kamut, Polenta, Wheat Berries, & More*. Berkeley, CA: Ten Speed Press.

Swanson, Heidi. (2011). *Super Natural Every Day*. Berkeley, CA: Ten Speed Press.

Tanis, David. (2013). *One Good Dish: The Pleasures of a Simple Meal*. New York: Artisan.

Warinner, Christina. (2013). Debunking the Paleo Diet. *TEDxOU*. Retrieved from www.youtube.com/watch?v=BMOjVYgYaG8

Weiss, Luisa. (2012). *My Berlin Kitchen: A Love Story, with Recipes*. New York: Viking.

Wolfert, Paula. (2011). *The Food of Morocco*. New York: Ecco.

index

Published in the United States by Ten Speed Press, an imprint
of the Crown Publishing Group, a division of Random House LLC,
a Penguin Random House Company, New York.
www.crownpublishing.com
www.tenspeed.com

Ten Speed Press and the Ten Speed Press colophon are registered trademarks
of Random House LLC.

Library of Congress Cataloging-in-Publication Data
Speck, Maria.
  Simply ancient grains : fresh and flavorful whole grain recipes for living
  well / by Maria Speck. — First edition.
      pages cm
  Includes bibliographical references and index.
  1. Cooking (Cereals) 2. Grain. 3. Heirloom varieties (Plants) I. Title.
  TX808.S6653 2015
  641.6'31—dc23

                              2014036879

Hardcover ISBN: 978-1-60774-588-4
eBook ISBN: 978-1-60774-589-1

Printed in China

Design by Ashley Lima
Food Styling by Valerie Aikman-Smith and George Dolese

10 9 8 7 6 5 4 3 2 1

First Edition

Measurement Conversion Charts

VOLUME

U.S.	IMPERIAL	METRIC
1 tablespoon	½ fl oz	15 ml
2 tablespoons	1 fl oz	30 ml
¼ cup	2 fl oz	60 ml
⅓ cup	3 fl oz	90 ml
½ cup	4 fl oz	120 ml
⅔ cup	5 fl oz (¼ pint)	150 ml
¾ cup	6 fl oz	180 ml
1 cup	8 fl oz (⅓ pint)	240 ml
1¼ cups	10 fl oz (½ pint)	300 ml
2 cups (1 pint)	16 fl oz (⅔ pint)	480 ml
2½ cups	20 fl oz (1 pint)	600 ml
1 quart	32 fl oz (1⅔ pints)	1 l

TEMPERATURE

FAHRENHEIT	CELSIUS/GAS MARK
250°F	120°C/gas mark ½
275°F	135°C/gas mark 1
300°F	150°C/gas mark 2
325°F	160°C/gas mark 3
350°F	180 or 175°C/gas mark 4
375°F	190°C/gas mark 5
400°F	200°C/gas mark 6
425°F	220°C/gas mark 7
450°F	230°C/gas mark 8
475°F	245°C/gas mark 9
500°F	260°C

LENGTH

INCH	METRIC
¼ inch	6 mm
½ inch	1.25 cm
¾ inch	2 cm
1 inch	2.5 cm
6 inches (½ foot)	15 cm
12 inches (1 foot)	30 cm

WEIGHT

U.S./IMPERIAL	METRIC
½ oz	15 g
1 oz	30 g
2 oz	60 g
¼ lb	115 g
⅓ lb	150 g
½ lb	225 g
¾ lb	350 g
1 lb	450 g